writing
to
be
read

HAYDEN ENGLISH LANGUAGE SERIES

Robert W. Boynton — Consulting Editor

*Former Principal, Senior High School
and Chairman, English Department
Germantown Friends School*

GRAMMAR BASICS: A Reading/Writing Approach (Second Ed.)
Jean Malmstrom

LANGUAGE IN SOCIETY (Second Ed.)
Jean Malmstrom

**WORDS, WORDS, WORDS
Vocabularies and Dictionaries (Second Ed.)**
Richard R. Lodwig and Eugene F. Barrett

WRITING TO BE READ (Second Ed.)
Ken Macrorie

TELLING WRITING (Second Ed.)
Ken Macrorie

ENGLISH I and II: A Contemporary Approach
R. W. Boynton, Ruby K. Johnson, and Ruth E. Reeves

EXERCISES IN READING AND WRITING
Alexandra Davis and O. B. Davis

COMPOSING: Writing as a Self-Creating Process
William E. Coles, Jr.

THE IMPACT OF MASS MEDIA
Pearl G. Aldrich

RHETORIC and COMPOSITION: A Sourcebook for Teachers
Richard L. Graves

FORMING/THINKING/WRITING: The Composing Imagination
Ann E. Berthoff

**CONFRONT, CONSTRUCT, COMPLETE: A Comprehensive Approach to Writing,
Books 1 and 2**
Jack Easterling and Jack Pasanen

Other HAYDEN books by Ken Macrorie:

**UPTAUGHT
A VULNERABLE TEACHER**

KEN MACRORIE

Professor of English
Western Michigan University

writing

to

be

read

revised
second edition

HAYDEN BOOK COMPANY, INC.
Rochelle Park, New Jersey

The author would like to thank the proprietors for permission to quote from copyrighted works, as follows:

RAY BRADBURY: from "Seeds of Three Stories," written for *On Writing, By Writers*, William W. West, Editor; copyright 1966 by Ginn and Company. Reprinted by permission of the publisher.

ANATOLE BROYARD: "The Obstetrics of the Soul," a review of *Death As a Fact of Life.* © 1973 by The New York Times Company. Reprinted by permission.

SAMUEL BUTLER: from *The Complete Works of Samuel Butler* and *The Notebooks of Samuel Butler*, published by Jonathan Cape Ltd. Reprinted by permission of the Executors of the Samuel Butler Estate.

TRUMAN CAPOTE: from *Writers at Work, The Paris Review Interviews*, edited by Malcolm Cowley. Copyright © 1957, 1958, by The Paris Review, Inc. Reprinted by permission of The Viking Press, Inc.

STUART CHASE: from "Writing Nonfiction," written for *On Writing, By Writers*, William W. West, Editor; copyright 1966 by Ginn and Company. Reprinted by permission of the publisher.

JOHN CIARDI: from "Work Habits of Writers," written for *On Writing, By Writers*, William W. West, Editor; copyright 1966 by Ginn and Company. Reprinted by permission of the publisher.

W. H. COHEN: translations of two Haiku poems by Issa and Oemaru from *To Walk in Seasons*, compiled and edited by W. H. Cohen, published by Charles E. Tuttle Publishing Co., Inc., Tokyo. Reprinted by permission.

SIDNEY COX: from *Indirections for Those Who Want to Write.* Reprinted with permission of the publisher. Published by Alfred A. Knopf, Inc. Copyright © 1947 by Alfred A. Knopf, Inc.

T. S. ELIOT: from *Writers at Work, The Paris Review Interviews*, Second Series, Copyright © 1963 by The Paris Re-

Library of Congress Cataloging in Publication Data

Macrorie, Ken
  Writing to be read.

  (Hayden English language series)
  Bibliography: p.
  Includes index.
  SUMMARY: A writing textbook stressing readability.
  1. English language — Composition and exercises. [1. English language — Composition and exercises. 2. Creative writing] I. Title.
PE1408.M3326 1976   808'.042   74-34039
ISBN 0-8104-5980-9
ISBN 0-8104-5979-5 pbk.

Printed in the United States of America

6 7 8 9 PRINTING

81 82 83   YEAR

acknowledgments

Most of the examples of good writing cited in this book are the work of students who have followed part of the program it embodies. Some wrote in my classes; many wrote in the classes of John Bennett of Central High School, Kalamazoo, Michigan, who for six years has been publishing with me a broadsheet of our students' writing.

Here I wish to thank all teachers around the country who have sent me writing by their students—so much that I have occasionally lost the source of a writing used in this book. Luckily none was copyrighted, so I have committed no low crimes or misdemeanors; but I apologize to anyone not properly thanked.

I will not repeat my thanks to all those named in the first edition of this book, but simply speak my gratefulness this time to Sister Marie Tucker of St. Teresa's Academy (Kansas City, Missouri); James Gardner of Manchester Community College (Connecticut); Mary Ann Gates of Hickman High School (Columbia, Missouri); James Giachino, formerly of Berkshire Community College (Pittsfield, Massachusetts); Marjorie Donker of Western Washington State College; Will Brenner of East Grand Rapids High School (Michigan); Mindy Stiles, practice teaching at South Junior High School (Kalamazoo, Michigan); Patrick Morey, whose address I cannot locate; and Robert Boynton, my consulting editor.

The notion of free writing, so fundamental to the program presented here, comes from a suggestion to persons who want to become professional writers made by Dorothea Brande in *Becoming a Writer* (Harcourt, Brace, 1934).

K.M.

preface

Most of the student writings
in this book are alive.

They tell truths that are
surprising and memorable.

I can't think of two more shocking statements to be made in a textbook on writing. Out of hundreds of texts I've examined in the last twenty-five years, I've seen no others which present a solid body of good writing done by persons who followed the program in the books.

Yet all such books are supposed to improve the writing of their users. Improve it! Most of the phony, pretentious, dead sentences "composed" in "English" courses do not need improvement, but embalming.

Since writing the first edition of this book I have talked with hundreds of teachers around the country who are ashamed that American taxpayers pay money to support the teaching of writing which no one wants to read. The publication of *Writing To Be Read* was one of several indications that these individuals were not alone in their feeling. Conversations and correspondence with them have shown me that fundamental in the making of writers is not a knowledge of this or that grammatical point, a strategy of style, or a strong desire to write, but fully carrying out the act of writing to be read by real persons who respond.

New material in this second edition helps put that act into process for students and teachers: Chapter 10, "The Helping Circle," Chapter 15, "Your Subject Choosing You," and the final section, "Suggestions for Teachers."

For the many who have used this book in *creative writing* as well as *composition* courses, I have added the chapter "Writing Poems." It is designed for the beginner who approaches that adventure feeling ignorant and shaky.

The passages printed in boldface type are the work of students who wrote through programs similar to that presented here. They are answers to the only valid test of any writing course: does it bring forth from students writing that is alive and valuable?

K.M.

contents

chapter 1

the language in you

THOUSANDS of persons in the United States believe they don't know how to write well. But look at what children do. A third-grade girl writes:

> **When mother fride my egg this morning it limbered out like corn surp. Then it got buggles. They went up, then went down, like breethen heavy.**

The writer surprised the reader with an original use of the verb *limber,* meaning to become supple or flexible. She compared the movement of the egg to the slow spreading of corn syrup in a pan. She invented her own term, *buggles* (playing on *bubbles*), and showed she knew what she was talking about. She compactly described the movement of a frying egg. This passage is not only fresh and surprising but precise and true. It puts the reader there, watching the egg and feeling its action through his own experience, "like breethen heavy."

1

At times every young child makes memorable statements in writing or speaking. But as he advances in school, his language turns ever duller and emptier. By the time he becomes a senior in high school, he is often submitting papers to his teacher which sound like this:

> I consider experience to be an important part in the process of learning. For example, in the case of an athlete, experience plays an important role. After each game, he tends to acquire more knowledge and proficiency, thereby making him a better athlete. An athlete could also gain more knowledge by studying up on the sport, but it is doubtful if he could participate for the first time in sport with study alone and without experience and still do an adequate job.

The writer says nothing new—athletes learn by experience. And he does not put the reader there, watching a player bunt foul or tackle a half-back. A five-year-old boy at breakfast says, "The Rice Krispies are doing the dead man's float." He doesn't tell the reader anything new either, but he speaks originally. With the metaphor he puts the reader in the milk.

A second-grader told to quiet her feet in class said, "They're too Saturday to listen." She expected the listener to make the jump necessary to understand her metaphor. The boy writing about athletes expected nothing of his reader.

A sixth-grader wrote a letter to the custodian of a state park who had showed his class around:

> Dear Mr. Lemmien,
> I liked the trailer ride and the dips got my stomach. Thank you for everything.
>
> > Your Friend,
> > David Booth

David communicated a significant moment in five short words: "the dips got my stomach." The word *dips* gives the passage authority. The sentence is believable, unforgettable. None of the sentences in the writing about athletes carries as much meaning.

Young children do not always talk and write with such point and liveliness, but they do so often enough that their parents repeat their sayings and writings to other persons with delight. When these children grow up and become high school and college students, they seldom turn in writing that is memorable. Yet outside class, they often use language with power. A student poster for a dance reads:

35¢ Stag. 50¢ Drag.

Metaphor. Rhyme. Economy in words.

Entering the school cafeteria, a girl says that she can't see a clear table. Her friend answers:

> I don't see one either. It's like looking for your best friend at the Rose Bowl on T.V.

At times you have spoken and written skillfully. You can rediscover your tongue—if you've lost it—and bring your writing to life. One way is to take the pressure off for a while. In schoolrooms where students have been asked to write freely, they have written like this:

> I like to go fishing. But I don't like to touch the soft, elongated, repulsive nightcrawlers. They wiggle and contract themselves. Then I can't grab the one I want. Of all the other things in this world I can't stand, baiting the hook is the worst. It's like giving a shot. Sometimes the hook won't go through the worm's wrinkled, slimy body. Then I have to wiggle and force it. That's like stepping on a cockroach and hearing the bones crack, or piercing a stubborn earlobe.

> GERTIE BAX

> The wooden bars on the chair look like prison bars as they reflect on the floor from the light. I was in trouble once and getting into trouble makes a person feel bad that it happened and that it never should have happened but it did and there is no way around. I had to sit in a room for three hours waiting, hoping that my brother would be all right and hoping the other boy was too, although from those minutes on, I knew I hated him. Only a chair, a desk, and a man saying, "I'll be back in about a half hour," which really became three. I had to sweat it out walking back and forth in the room with nothing to look at but four lousy walls, I wanted to get out. I wanted them to come and get me out of there. Thoughts passed through my mind as I sat there in the only chair. Chairs can be made to look like different things when their shadow is lying on the floor. The chair over there in the corner looks like part of a ladder. The chair in the police station was uncomfortable and I couldn't sit in it. It was a cheap looking chair in a cheap looking room meant for people who are wrong.

> (NAME WITHHELD)

A girl once told her teacher that she couldn't write any kind of paper because she had been raised in a Polish-speaking home and couldn't compose sentences in idiomatic English. Encouraged to write freely of what she cared about, she wrote this of her father:

> **The only difference between him and a lion is that a lion does not laugh. Upon meeting up with him, one most naturally will see the strict lines on his face and his mouth set just so. He may appear tough, but he also has the devil in him. His appearance is stirring. He looks like a foreign foreigner. His voice is low and scary. It really frightens my friends, even male ones. Sometime when I call to say I may be home later, he answers the phone with a deep, husky, and broken "Haaallooo" and I feel I should apologize for calling.**
>
> (NAME WITHHELD)

Outside of class, and in the years of childhood, you and every other person have at times expressed yourself forcefully, with art. It is nonsense to say you cannot do that again when you want to.

> *Man's maturity: to have regained the seriousness that he had as a child at play.*
>
> FRIEDRICH NIETZSCHE

COLLECTING ONE: Listen for what children say and look for what they write. Use a tape recorder if available. Write down five statements you think are memorable. Include the age of the child if possible and the situation in which he spoke or wrote. Ask your parents if they remember a phrase you spoke when you were young. Perhaps they preserved a bit of your writing. Record children's statements that are remarkable because they reveal freshness, accuracy, and invention in language. Do not record statements that are humorous only because the child speaks out of ignorance of the world or of language.

COLLECTING TWO: The language in that pretentious paragraph beginning "I consider experience" was once dubbed *Engfish* by a student. You see it in school work and government publications and business letters. "The area of disagreement which led to the outbreak of hostilities could be characterized as involving territorial questions relating to the possession and utilization of waterways." What the writer meant to say was "The war broke out over the ownership of the Suez Canal." Look for examples of Engfish. Collect three or more and bring them to class.

On a huge hill,
Cragged and steep, Truth stands, and he
that will
Reach her, about must, and about must
go . . .

JOHN DONNE

chapter 2

writing freely

TELLING TRUTHS

ALL GOOD writers speak in honest voices and tell the truth. For example, here is Eudora Welty in her novel *Delta Wedding* writing about India, a girl of nine, watching her Uncle George make up with his wife after a quarrel:

> Just now they kissed, with India coming up close on her toes to see if she could tell yet what there was about a kiss.

Asked what makes students write badly, Eudora Welty once said:

> The trouble with bad student writing is the trouble with all bad writing. It is not serious, and it does not tell the truth.

This is the first requirement for good writing: truth; not *the* truth (whoever knows surely what that is?), but some kind of truth—a connection between the things written about, the words used in the writing, and the author's real experience in the world he knows well —whether in fact or dream or imagination.

Part of growing up is learning to tell lies, big and little, sophisticated and crude, conscious and unconscious. The good writer differs from the bad one in that he constantly tries to shake the habit. He holds himself to the highest standard of truth telling. Often he

5

emulates children, who tell the truth so easily, partly because they
do not sense how truth will shock their elders.

A seventh-grade boy once wrote:

> **I'd like to be a car. You get to go all over and get to go
> through mud puddles without getting yelled at . . . that's
> what I'd like to be.**

The style of this passage is not distinguished. *Get* is here not a key
word and yet it is employed three times. The writer switches confusingly from *I* to *you*. The language of the passage is not exciting.
No memorable pictures are projected. Yet the statement strikes with
force because the boy speaks truly: his shoes and the tires of the car
do become muddy. He gets yelled at by his parents and the car does
not. The comparison surprises. Its candor draws a smile from the
reader.

> *I never think I have hit it hard unless
> it rebounds.*
>
> SAMUEL JOHNSON

Any person trying to write honestly and accurately soon finds
he has already learned a hundred ways of writing falsely. As a child
he spoke and wrote honestly most of the time, but when he reaches
fifteen, honesty and truth come harder. The pressures on his ego
are greater. He reaches for impressive language; often it is pretentious
and phony. He imitates the style of adults, who are often bad writers
themselves. They ask questions. So he asks questions in his writing:
"Did you ever think what might have happened to South Africa if
the Boer War had not been fought?" A false question. The writer
knows most—if not all—of his readers have not thought of this
possibility. However well meant—a false question. In class this person
is anxious to impress the teacher, so he begins his paper by saying:

> **The automobile is a mechanism fascinating to everyone
> in all its diverse manifestations and in every conceivable
> kind of situation or circumstance.**

His first remark is simply untrue. Cars do not fascinate everyone.

In this paper the writer has placed his vocabulary on exhibit
(*mechanism, diverse, manifestations, conceivable, situation, circumstance*) rather than put it to work. An honest writer makes every word
pull its weight. In this writer's opening sentence, the words *kind of*
are not working at all. They could be dropped with no loss. What
does he mean by "all the diverse manifestations" of a car? Cars don't

occur in manifestations but in models. If the cars he is referring to are custom-made and not strictly speaking "models," then he should say he is writing about hybrid cars. At the opening of his paper, his reader has no inkling that he is talking about home-made cars. And nothing could be more untrue than the thought conveyed by the last phrase—that everyone finds cars fascinating "in every conceivable kind of situation or circumstance." When the valves need regrinding at 17,000 miles at a cost of $125.00, even the car lover finds his loved one repulsive.

Compare this writer's pretentious and untrue statement about cars with this account:

> Thundering down a Northern Michigan highway at night I am separated from the rest of the world. The windows of the car are all rolled down and the wind makes a deep rumbling as the car rises and falls with the dips in the pavement. The white center lines come out of the darkness ahead into the beams of the headlights only to disappear again under the front edge of the hood. The lights also pick up trees, fenceposts, and an occasional deer or raccoon standing by the roadside, but like the white lines they come into view only for a few seconds and then are lost in the blackness behind me. The only signs I have that any world exists outside the range of the headlights are the continuous cheerping and buzzing of the crickets and the smells from farms and sulphur pits I pass. But the rushing wind soon clears out these odors, leaving me by myself again to listen to the quickly passing crickets I will never see. The faint green lights and the red bar on the dashboard tell me I'm plunging ahead at 90 m.p.h.; I put more pressure on the pedal under my foot; the bar moves up to 100 . . . 110. The lines flash by faster and the roar of the wind drowns out the noise of the crickets and the night. I am flying through. I can feel the vibrations of the road through the steering wheel. I turn the wheel slightly for the gradual curve ahead and then back again for the long straightaway. I press the pedal to the floor and at the same time reach down to touch the buttons on my left that will roll up the windows for more speed; the bar reads 115 . . . 120, buried. With the windows up, the only sound is the high-pitched moan from the engine as it labors to keep the rest of the machine hurtling blindly ahead like a runaway express

train. Only I have the power to control it. I flick on the
brights to advance my scope of vision and the white lines
come out of the black further up ahead, yet because of the
speed, they're out of sight even faster than before. I am
detached from the rest of the world as it blurs past. I am
alone.

HENRY HALL JAMES

This boy may have been driving at an immorally high speed--even
for a relatively uninhabited region—but he was writing morally,
because he was staying true to the feel of his experience. Writing this
way requires a quick jump in the car and a zooming away before one
remembers all the driving habits he has picked up watching bad
older drivers. Try writing for truth.

Never say that you feel a thing unless
you feel it distinctly; and if you do not
feel it distinctly, say at once that you do
not as yet quite know your own mind.

SAMUEL BUTLER

WRITING FREELY WITHOUT FOCUS

WRITING ONE: Write for ten minutes as fast as you can, never
stopping to ponder a thought or consider spelling, punctuation, or
grammar. Put down whatever comes to your mind. If nothing comes,
write, "Nothing comes to my mind" until you get started. Or look
in front of you or out the window and begin describing whatever you
see. Let yourself wander to any subject, feeling, or idea, but keep
writing. When ten minutes is up, you should have filled a large note-
book-sized page. Remember you are hitting practice shots. If what
you write is bad or dull, no one will object.

Save all the writing which you produce while reading this book.
Keep it in a manila filing folder so you can go back to it to revise
it or look for paragraphs or pages that may be combined or expanded
into stronger work. As time passes, you will see your words differently
and sometimes learn from them without doing further work.

Here's what one student wrote in ten minutes:

I still haven't gotten used to the dull routine of school. I
still feel like I should sleep in the morning until I wake
up—naturally. Usually the only things that get me up, even
naturally, are an empty stomach and a full bladder. I
haven't seen half the new TV shows yet. Those that I have

seen don't look too horribly bad. It's funny how the weekends always have the worst TV and the weekdays the best.
My aunt's been in the hospital lately, so all my cousins
are over. It's funny how all these "little kids" are now all
grown up and almost ready for high school. I can still
remember when I, as the "big cousin," always directed the
tricycle rides up the street, always got to carry the money
out to the popsicle man, and always got to go to the Santa
Claus parade and stand on Grandma's shoulders while the
rest groveled underneath.

That free writing probably kept your attention because it was honest,
but it is not memorable. You will probably remember the following
free writing longer. In the third sentence the writer says, "this time"
and with that phrase begins to tell a story. Most good writing, fiction
or nonfiction, depends a great deal on stories—a long story, or maybe
a number of little stories used as examples. Professional writers know
The Secret of Once. It opens a writer and gets him going, telling of
this real object and that uttered word, and soon he has created a
world which compels his reader to enter it. For example:

My Grandma and Grandpa had always lived on a farm in
Alabama. I used to love to go there when I was young. I
loved the cows and chickens and the smell of grass. But this
time things were different; I didn't smell the grass, or see
the cows, or hear the chickens. Everything was still. The
funeral was held the day after we arrived. I couldn't understand why one bunch of ladies sat around the body
until I heard them talking. They talked about who cried
the longest and who cried the least. I hear the same bunch
gets around to all the funerals.

That statement impresses but does not let the reader touch a cow
or hear one chicken's feet scraping the doorsill of a particular chicken
coop. And it doesn't tell who died.

A good part of the time he is writing, a writer must sense his
reader out there. The poet William Stafford said, "When you write,
simply tell me something." Vague advice, but valid. In a sense a
writer becomes his own reader while he writes. He talks to his reader
and hears that talk himself. When you acquire that knack, other
persons will come along with you. Easy as this habit is to learn, many
persons never learn it. They are like those who try to turn a piece
of pottery on the wheel and never create a cup which holds coffee.

The following free writing forgets the reader out there, talks big, but does not tell the reader enough. It does not employ The Secret of Once.

> I don't want to grow up yet! I'm too young to be burdened with all the responsibilities of adulthood. Someday I'll get married and have a home and children of my own, but for now, I'm going to enjoy every moment of my youth in freedom.
>
> I want to be an unique individual. I spent much of my junior high years trying to act mature, seldom allowing my real self to emerge for fear of non acceptance. I only succeeded in mimicking others. Life is so brief. When I think of all the time I've already wasted conforming, it makes me sad.

Mr. Stafford would say, "Tell me something you did." This writing lacks an authentic voice. No individual person seems to be speaking, but rather a recording of excerpts from textbooks and magazine articles about contemporary youth. In contrast, here is a real girl speaking:

> Everyone around here is having an awful time getting along with me. I'm being positively intolerable. Mom is trying really hard not to say anything in the wrong tone of voice, so that I feel kind of—what's that old-fashioned word, *ashamed* of myself. One day I'm in a great mood, and you could yell at me all you wanted without making me mad or hurt. The next day (or the next hour for that matter) you could say "Good morning," then yawn, and I'd burst into tears. I suppose that is not awfully abnormal (at least that's what Mom says—in her psychological tone, "It's just a phase. You'll grow out of it.") By the way, that makes me mad, too. I don't like to have my life summed up in a series of phases. It seems like she's saying, "You can't help acting like an idiot. It comes natural at this age. But don't worry, you'll outgrow it. It'll pass."

The writer of the next statement used The Secret of Once and puts the reader in the situation.

> He swore at me. It was the first time he ever had. I deserved it but that didn't lessen the shock any. I had gone out on him, then lied to him about it. It was always easy

for me to bring on tears when I was hurt by his actions, but this time I'd hurt him. I couldn't feel sorry for myself. My eyes burned. My fingers picked at my knee. I kept twisting my ring around my finger while he repeatedly and very calmly asked me to please get out. The quiet summer night and full moon seemed to mock my every word. Ironic. I wanted to explain but I couldn't. I wanted him to hold me but he seemed repulsed at my touch. I couldn't leave. Earlier, I could have tossed my head, laughed it off, maybe saved face. But I confessed. Playing on his mercy. He wasn't being merciful. Disgusted, as his elbow brushed my knee, he leaned over and shoved open the door. When I look at the black scar in the street, I can always hear the screaming tires and feel the force of his arm.

Most of these ten-minute free writings keep the reader awake. At times disconnected and perhaps meaningless for a reader, they are full of surprise, as so much writing is not. Some of their surprises came because the writers were not trying hard, but riding with the waves, letting strange and exciting things drift up from the bottom. Most are not finished pieces of writing to be published for an audience, but they come alive.

WRITING TWO: Write three or more of these absolutely free writings. Choose times when no one will disturb you, before breakfast or late at night perhaps. Go beyond ten minutes if the river keeps flowing. But don't expect anything. You're just warming up. Maybe none of your ten-minute writings will produce an interesting sentence. Don't worry. Write. And don't think about punctuation or grammar or style. Put down one word as a sentence if you wish. Maybe your writing will be completely uninteresting to others. As long as you are trying to write honestly and you are writing fast and steadily to fill up a page or two without stopping, you are practicing.

WRITING FREELY WITH FOCUS

Free writing is practice. It involves no pressure on the practicer. It never requires perfection. If the practicer goofs, he has not lost the game or produced a work disgraceful in the public eye. He can forget the bad shots. They do not penalize him. If a writer produces a good passage, he can show it to other persons because he has it down on paper. He is luckier than the golfer, who cannot take a shot off the practice tee home to show his family.

After a game of golf, an amateur spends hours complaining that he missed three short putts. Before a game of golf, a professional spends hours in putting practice. If he hits bad putts, he tries a different stroke, and when he finds one that produces good putts, he grooves it.

WRITING THREE: Now try free writing with more purpose. Stay on one subject as the writer did when she said that everyone thought she was being positively intolerable. But if you find that subject takes your mind off to another related subject, let yourself go to that. The one necessity in such practice is that you keep writing freely and quickly.

> *Thought is an infection. In the case of certain thoughts it becomes an epidemic.*
>
> WALLACE STEVENS

Here is a free focused writing:

> The building was old and dingy. We opened the doors and an even older odor hit us; it smelled of must. I followed the group closely. I was afraid of this quiet solitary place. I walked through the halls peeking around every corner cautiously. I might bump into one of them. Through every open door I saw their faces and bodies. In beds. Sitting looking out windows. Holding dolls, silently humming. I couldn't understand. Would I end up here some day? I'd rather die. Being old was a torture, not the pleasure I'd thought it to be.
>
> After a slight tour of the building, we stopped to eat our sack-lunches. The food didn't taste very good. It was dried-up and molded—I couldn't erase the feeling. Even the bathrooms provided were old like the people using them. Oh God, I prayed, why do they have to live on?
>
> The clocks seemed to never move. Suddenly, walking through a sun-deck, I found her grabbing at me. Her bony little fingers clutched my arm. I was afraid. I imagined her bones cutting into my flesh. I wanted to jerk away. I looked in her face for a long time; she just stared. Her eyes were the first young things I'd seen. They reflected my friends and me. I saw it coming. I understood. That one big tear made everything clear. How much I loved her. She tried to

rise. Her clumsy bars wouldn't let her. It was like she knew she'd die there. She touched my hair. "Angel-hair," she said. All I could hear as I walked away were sobs.

JANE LENARDSON

This passage speaks with authority. The writer passed on to her reader enough of what made her respond so that he could respond also. She found surprising realities and communicated them: old ladies holding dolls, young eyes in an aged head.

Free writing is random rehearsal. Don't let it become dress rehearsal or first night. If you insist that you speak in an honest, not phony, voice, and you write freely and fast, you will write foolishly at times, and at other times with astonishing wisdom.

Here is another focused free writing:

I keep slugging that yellow rubber ball harder and harder. It's tattooed by the skin off my knuckles and comes back for another mark. My hands sting. The kids behind the net can't return those hard balls. Sweating. I gulp down a cold Coke and go over to the trampoline. This web is huge and the air belching from the pressure of bouncing bodies cools me off. It's my turn to show off. As I jump, my sweatshirt parachutes and my jeans come unsnapped. Enough of that. I charge Mike just as he throws a long pass at the rim of the basket. He misses. I run after it and bounce it in. Mike grabs it and I'm right behind him trying to steal it. I sink it from the middle of the floor. Stop it! Girls aren't supposed to do that.

If you have had your attention directed to the novelties in thought in your own lifetime, you will have observed that almost all really new ideas have a certain aspect of foolishness when they are first produced, and almost any idea which jogs you out of your current abstractions may be better than nothing.

ALFRED NORTH WHITEHEAD

As you dash off these writings, don't plan ahead. Write. Spill out whatever comes to mind and eye. Put down honestly what you feel and see. A day after you have finished them, read them over aloud and underline those sentences which you think say something alive for a reader. If you find no such sentences, don't despair. Keep writing. If you find a great many consecutively lively lines, mark a vertical pencil stroke next to them in the margin. Soon you will be writing more and more good lines.

> ... what is always provocative in a work of art: roughness of surface. While ... [these writings] pass under our eyes they are full of dents and grooves and lumps and spikes which draw from us little cries of approval and disapproval.
>
> E. M. FORSTER

Here is a young hunter's free focused writing. It speaks with terrifying truthfulness.

> I had always wanted a BB gun, but I never had one until now. We were going out to a friend's farm near Paw Paw and my dad bought me one to take along. At first I took it home to practice. I thought it was a big thing to hit an empty Joy bottle from twenty feet.
>
> After I got to the farm, the owner asked me to shoot some blackbirds for him. For a long time no blackbirds came around. At last one landed in a walnut tree in the yard. I walked under it quietly so I wouldn't scare it. The stupid thing just sat there begging to be shot. I fired my first shot. I saw the little gold BB fly past his head. Dumb bird. It still didn't move. I shot again and the bird's face reacted with pain. It fell over, hanging upside down by one foot from its branch. I shot again. It still hung there. I could see blood on its feathers even from where I stood. With the fourth shot it fell, its black feathers red.

Here is one more free focused statement by a beginning writer. In this book "beginning writer" refers to one who has not been frequently published. He may be talented but not yet know his worth because he has not received responses to his work from a number of persons. Most professional writers are often writing freely. When producing by steady daily effort, they frequently break a log jam in the river of their associations and find their thoughts and words flowing rapidly downstream. Making anything well is a combination of conscious and unconscious production.

He doesn't have legs. Not ones that feel or move. It's been that way almost four years now. Wheels. I was scared to talk at first, felt like a kid asking what it is that everyone's talking about. But we did. We used to goof around and tell dirty jokes. I always felt a little fake. Dan and I took him to the bathroom every day. Had to be done in a special way. Were there once. Dan asked a question. I don't remember. I answered, "What do you think I am, a cripple?" That's what I said. I didn't look at anyone, just the wall. For about half an hour, I felt very whole, but my stomach was tin foil. They were quiet, both of them. Quiet as being alone. I wished someone would cut off my arms.

> . . . I sometimes begin a drawing with no preconceived problem to solve, with only the desire to use pencil on paper and make lines, tones and shapes with no conscious aim; but as my mind takes in what is so produced a point arrives where some idea becomes conscious and crystallizes, and then a control and ordering begins to take place.
>
> HENRY MOORE, SCULPTOR

WRITING FOUR: Write freely for twenty or thirty minutes about something or somebody you stumbled upon once. Let yourself record the lumps and grooves, the dents and spikes.

chapter 3
what
is
good
writing?

HERE is a poem written by a high school
girl.

hitchhikers
dive up
thumbs leaping
pleading narrowed eyes
against the rain
please dad
please stop
my hands curl
my voice muffles a drum in my throat
you speed up
against the wind
in the guilt-swish pass
every hopeful outstretched arm
little smile—

". . . our car's too small
for hitchhikers, and it's
against the law."
your eyes uncomfortable skirt around mine
sliding away from my gaze
like two slippery stones
another sorry thumber
vanishes into gray behind scape
with the shiny tire tracks
down the rain road

ROBIN RENSEVER

This is good writing. It puts the reader with the hitchhikers (their eyes narrow in the rain) and the girl in the car (her hands curl in frustration). The event happens for the reader as it happened for the writer ("the guilt-swish pass"). A few of the crucial words from father, not all the talk that probably took place in the car. Daughter hates father, but recognizes he feels "uncomfortable." So much said in so few words.

There is no wing like meaning.

WALLACE STEVENS

Any kind of writing improves as it approaches the skills with which Ms. Rensever wrote "Rain Road." For example, economy. The man who writes directions for opening and storing a jar of peanut butter improves as a writer as he learns to say more with fewer words. The writer for the Sears Roebuck catalog improves as he learns to dramatize more fully the product in use—to put the reader there, seeing and feeling what he will buy. Here is a good piece of writing from the *Sears Spring Through Summer Catalog,* 1966:

Dropped in mid-summer from a helicopter when loaded with 25 pounds of sand . . . also dropped when frozen at 20° below zero . . . IT BOUNCED. But Sears new exclusive Trash Can simply wouldn't break! (and because it's all heavy-weight plastic, there was *no noisy metallic clang*).
Sears Best . . . because of these important reasons:
Because Handy Bottom Grips plus side handles and lid handle for easy portability. No hand-cutting bail handle here.
Because friction-fit Top stays on without twisting, fits snugly without getting stuck.

> Because No Seams. Holds water, won't leak. The utility
> area stays cleaner . . . won't be as likely to attract pests.
> Because Stands Boiling Water, "boiling" hot sun . . .
> "boiling" hot concrete. Made to withstand the weather.
> Treated with SANI-GARD to retard odor and bacteria
> . . . Won't "pick up" odors . . . resists the growth of fungi,
> mildew and bacteria that cause them.

In some senses, Robin Rensever's "Rain Road" cannot be compared with an advertisement for a trash can; its intention is different, its achievement greater. But the Sears writer comes closer to creating good literature than many admen. He does not shoot off a roman candle of unsupported adjectives—Magnificent! Unheard-of! Stupendous! Instead he tells clearly how the can was tested for durability. Like Robin Rensever he makes the reader believe, because the details he presents suggest that he knows what he is talking about.

Writing a sports report, "Orioles' 16 Hits Rout Yanks, 9-4," for *The New York Times,* August 11, 1966, Joseph Durso shows that like a poet he knows how to make his words speak to each other as well as to the reader:

> The barrage consisted of these consecutive elements: a
> triple to left by Russ Snyder (leading the Yankees to draw
> their infield in), a single past the infield by Frank Robin-
> son, a single past the infield by Brooks Robinson and a
> home run past everybody by Powell.

Repetition and rhythm. Robin Rensever wrote "sliding . . . slippery . . . sorry . . . scape . . . shiny . . . down the rain road."

Steve Smith begins his column "Sport" in *Car and Driver,* September, 1966, with this paragraph:

> After completing our six-car comparison road test (else-
> where in this issue), we started back to the city on the
> Long Island Expressway, known variously as the L.I. Dis-
> tressway, and the world's longest parking lot. It was a quiet
> Tuesday afternoon, so we weren't expecting much traffic.
> Soon, however, the three westbound lanes reached the
> saturation point, slowed to a crawl and then to a stop.
> Temperatures and tempers rose. Some of the traffic bled off
> onto the two-lane parallel service road, allowing about
> half-a-mile of progress before clotting. Somebody had the
> bright idea of trying three abreast, and traffic telescoped

another few hundred yards. In desperation, drivers veered off the roadway onto the center mall and the outside verge, becoming trapped by cars that had pulled off to let radiators cool. Finally, those that were able inched north and south the width of the island, then turned east. Within three hours, every major artery into the city was hopelessly snarled. Nothing moved. The System had broken down once again.

Mr. Smith cites two humorous names for the Long Island Expressway, employs sound beautifully in ending his sentence "slowed to a crawl and then to a stop" and makes the words *bled* and *clot* speak to each other in a metaphor. Like Robin he seldom uses dull and empty verbs like *have, make, is,* and *come.* Instead he says *telescoped, veered, trapped, pulled off, inched, snarled,* and *broken down.*

In *The Field Book of Ponds and Streams* (G. P. Putnam's Sons, 1930), Anne Haven Morgan writes:

> Mayfly nymphs are of many shapes and sizes; some have flattened heads and bodies and their sprawling legs are held akimbo as in *Heptagenia.* Active runners, like *Calliboetis,* are set high on spindling legs, while the little creeper, *Leptophlebia,* almost drags its low slung body.

Like Robin, Dr. Morgan employs adjectives that are not vague and inert, but precise and active: *flattened, sprawling, spindling, low slung.*

Guidebooks are usually crammed with fact but written without flavor. *The New York Guidebook* edited by John A. Kouwenhoven (Dell Publishing Company, 1964), includes a chapter by Jean Shepherd, a disc jockey, who writes:

> After midnight you can fuel up for your stroll at Riker's Corner House on the northeast corner of Sixth and 57th. By day it is filled with quick-lunch office types, but after midnight (it's an all-night, seven-day-a-week operation) there's as motley a crew as you can find this side of an average painting by Hieronymus Bosch. Good guys and bad guys, reverends and chicks, all assembled for a plate of scrambled eggs with onions, or a slab of chocolate cream pie. There are no tables, only a horseshoe-shaped counter, which is served from somewhere in the kitchen by an endless belt on a high podium in the center. At Christmastime the podium is covered with elves, brownies, and a tiny

electric train that I once saw derail and crash into seven banana splits. The applause was deafening. In the spring, this same treadmill is decorated with plastic daffodils and rubber tulips, and so each succeeding season is celebrated amid the hamburgers. It's the only way some of the customers can tell what time of year it is. Many of them have not seen the sun since they were kids.

Before you start east on 57th, look up Sixth Avenue. Two blocks north you will see the dark mass of Central Park, unfortunately an excellent place to stay out of after dark. There are romantics who will disagree with this. But there are equally large numbers of experienced patrolmen and unfortunates who have been mugged, who will tell you the truth.

Like all good writers Mr. Shepherd chooses from his experience what surprises him and will surprise his reader, and he delivers it in sentences that hammer the surprise: ". . . a tiny electric train that I once saw derail and crash into seven banana splits." He knows the strategy of using unexpected words together: "each succeeding season is celebrated amid the hamburgers." And he is not willing to gloss over truth in order to make Central Park at night seem romantic to tourists.

Writing is good not because of who writes it or where it appears. Shakespeare and William Faulkner have written badly at times, and good publishers have marketed bad work. Writing is good because of what it says, how it opens up a world of ideas or fact for readers. And how accurately and memorably it speaks, a voice issuing from a human being who is fascinating, surprising, illuminating. But still a person and a writer who does not always strike sparks.

> . . . failure . . . is the poet's only real business. The one hope is for a better and better failure . . .
>
> JOHN CIARDI

Most good writing is clear, vigorous, honest, alive, sensuous, appropriate, unsentimental, rhythmic, without pretension, fresh, metaphorical, evocative in sound, economical, authoritative, surprising, memorable and light. If you set out to collect examples of good writing you will be surprised to find how many writers you admire are humorous or light. *Hamlet*, a story of decadence and tragedy, is at the same time one of the lightest plays ever written. Mark Van Doren, a professor at Columbia University who encouraged many young persons in America to keep writing until they became successful authors, used to say in his literature classes that a great work of art possesses a quality of lightness. It is never like a ponderous public building that looks as if it is going to sink into the ground. Lightness can be achieved in many ways—by varying style; by continually lifting the reader with genuine, rather than trick, surprises; by not taking oneself too seriously for the circumstances. For example, directions for cooking need not be boring and deadly: Irma S. Rombauer and Marion Rombauer Becker take space in *The Joy of Cooking* to put some joy into their opening discussion of salads:

> I remember the final scene of a medieval Maeterlinck play. The stage is strewed with those dead or dying. The sweet young heroine whimpers, "I am not happy here." Then the head of the house, or what remains of it, an ancient noble, asks quaveringly, "Will there be a salad for supper?"

This in a cookbook. Here is a college teacher's dittoed instructions for her students:

> Trippers will meet at 7:15 (Kalamazoo time) in front of the Union. The bus will leave promptly at 7:30 a.m. There will be no watering stops between Kalamazoo and Chicago, so I strongly recommend that you all eat something vaguely resembling breakfast before we start—something substantial and comforting like a Hershey bar.
>
> At 11:15 (Chicago time) we will go en masse to the Berghoff for lunch. The Berghoff is a marvelous old German place where the food is good and the prices are low. I think that the $1.50 lunch will make you all feel genial and broad-minded about Chicago, the museum, and modern art.
>
> After lunch everyone is on his own in the museum. Museum fatigue is a very real phenomenon and I caution you to use some restraint in your viewing, taking the 20th century first and whatever else you can manage after that.

The teacher who wrote these directions did not strain to be funny; she simply let her own voice take over instead of the voice of doom we often take on when we feel ourselves in a position of authority.

We can all find an honest voice (yet different voices for different circumstances) in which we can speak with life and vigor. Alan Levy, Bernard Krisher, James Cox, and Richard Flaste, the writers of the

Signet paperback book *Draftee's Confidential Guide* (1966), succeeded in conveying wittily their honest feelings about life in the army. On the first page they said:

> This book is not an exposé; it won't tell you the Army is rotten. The Army isn't rotten. It varies from post to post, but in each place it's the product of our country's needs and of the people who are in the Army—including you. This book will give you quite a few hints, however, that may keep your own Army life from being rotten.

Later in the book they present excerpts from diaries they kept. The passages are dramatic. Persons speak and create tension between each other. Some of these excerpts show army life to be cruel and sadistic, but the last one ends with a note of tolerance that proves the writers were honest when they said earlier they believed the army isn't rotten.

> At formation this morning Sergeant B———— made us hold our rifles above our heads for 10 minutes. Then we had to lift them up with one hand and hold them for another five minutes. It seemed like hours. He looked at us and said: "I know what you're thinking of me. You're calling me all sorts of names. I'm not running a popularity contest, so I don't give a damn what you think. And whatever you're thinking—'gentlemen'—the same to you." . . .
>
> We always have our share of surprises waiting when we return to the barracks after a weary day at the range. Sometimes the inspecting officer turns our beds upside down. Tonight we found all our spit-shined boots muddied.
>
> We began bayonet training yesterday. Whenever we practice with the weapon we have to shout, "Kill . . . Kill . . . Kill." The instructor said anyone who didn't want to say "Kill" could say "Lollypop." No one did.
>
> The cadre and officers are puzzled that we haven't griped as much as we're supposed to—according to Army regulations, I guess. They're not too happy about our strange, passive attitude and consequently we haven't had a night off in a week. One officer said he didn't believe we were capable of showing any emotion. He said it was unhealthy not to let off steam. He directed us to growl for five minutes. We complied, but he wasn't satisfied. It wasn't sincere enough, he said, but he finally gave up.

The worst thing about basic is not the KP, or the lack of sleep, or the harassment, but the fear of the unknown. Everyone was afraid of the gas indoctrination chamber, the infiltration course, and the first day at the rifle range. But hardly anyone would hesitate to go through them now. Much of the griping in basic (and the diarrhea) is the result of anxiety. If we had known beforehand that everything had been planned down to the minutest detail in Washington, that hundreds of thousands of men had gone through the same thing before and were none the worse for it, and that every safety precaution is taken, I think many of our fears would have been considerably calmed.

Part of the power in this writing comes from the lively words the authors have quoted.

If you feel you can never write as well as John Steinbeck, Charles Dickens, or the writers quoted in this chapter, you may be right. But you can write as well as you spoke at your brilliant best when you were five years old, and you can write as well as some of the catalog or guide book writers presented in this chapter—if you find a voice that rings true to you and you learn to record the surprises of the world faithfully. The free writing by beginning writers quoted in the preceding chapters displays many of the characteristics of good writing discussed here; for example:

Surprise: I sink it from the middle of the floor. Stop it! Girls aren't supposed to do that.

The author speaking in an authentic voice: I hear the same bunch gets around to all the funerals.

Economical use of words: The next day (or the next hour for that matter) you could say "Good morning," then yawn, and I'd burst into tears.

Words that put the reader there: My eyes burned. My fingers picked at my knee. I kept twisting my ring around my finger while he repeatedly and very calmly asked me to please get out.

Strong metaphor: I felt very whole, but my stomach was tin foil.

Words that speak to each other: . . . an *empty* stomach and a *full* bladder.

A record of the authentic voice of another person: "It's just a phase. You'll grow out of it."

Strong adjective: Her eyes were the first *young* things I'd seen.

Strong, full verb: The stupid thing just sat there *begging* to be shot.

Strong repetition: It fell over, *hanging* upside down by one foot from its branch. I shot again. It still *hung* there.

Powerful rhythms: I knew I hated him. Only a chair, a desk, and a
man saying, "I'll be back in about a half hour," which really
became three.

The persons who produced these free writings are on their way. They
may need to master additional skills, but they have already produced
many sentences that ring true and stay in the reader's ear.

> *The best writing, both prose and poetry,*
> *as Shakespeare pre-eminently shows,*
> *makes use, with condensation and selec-*
> *tion, of playful, impassioned, imagina-*
> *tive talk.*
>
> SIDNEY COX

You may wonder how I can be so sure what good writing is. Not
everyone likes the same authors or reporters. Readers will always
disagree. When you sit in the circle of writers and responders discussed in the Preface and Chapter 10 of this book, you will devise
your own standards. They will differ somewhat from those of others
in your circle and in other circles, but probably not on certain fundamentals. Those who have worked in the circle have studied the reactions of the members as they listened to writings being read aloud.
From the expressions on faces, grunts of approval, sighs, actions
signifying boredom, and spoken comments, they slowly came to believe that most good writings gain their power in these ways:

1. They do not waste words.
2. They speak in an authentic voice.
3. They put the reader there, make him believe.
4. They cause things to happen for him as they happened for the
   writer (or narrator).
5. They create oppositions which pay off in surprise.
6. They build.
7. They ask something of the reader.
8. They reward him with meaning.

*I hate anything that occupies more space
than it is worth. I hate to see a load of
band-boxes go along the street, and I
hate to see a parcel of big words without
anything in them.*

WILLIAM HAZLITT

chapter 4

tightening

GOOD WRITERS meet their readers only at their best. If you should read the sentences in their wastebaskets, you would find them full of bad starts and complete misses. When you write, you can discard your bad tries and forget them.

Benjamin Franklin, who helped Thomas Jefferson write the Declaration of Independence—a skillfully revised document—once told this anecdote to Mr. Jefferson:

> When I was a journeyman printer, one of my companions, an apprentice Hatter, having served out his time, was about to open a shop for himself. His first concern was to have a handsome signboard, with a proper inscription. He composed it in these words: "John Thompson, Hatter, makes and sells hats for ready money." with a figure of a hat subjoined. But he thought he would submit it to his friends for their amendments. The first he shewed it to thought the word "hatter" tautologous, because followed by the words "makes hats" which shew he was a hatter. It was struck out. The next observed that the word "makes" might as well be omitted, because his customers would not care who made the hats. If good and to their mind, they would buy, by whomsoever made. He struck it out. A third said he thought the words "for ready money" were useless as it was not the custom of the place to sell on credit. Every one who purchased expected to pay. They were parted with, and the inscription now stood "John Thompson sells hats." "*Sells*

hats" says his next friend? Why nobody will expect you to
give them away. What then is the use of that word? It was
stricken out and "hats" followed it, the rather, as there was
one painted on the board. So his inscription was reduced
ultimately to "John Thompson" with the figure of a hat
subjoined.

You can cut out the unnecessary words in your writing in this
way. The principle is simple: don't repeat words or ideas unless they
strengthen what you want to say. "Hatter . . . makes hats" repeats *hat*
to no avail. Don't tell your writer that "Mr. Smith is a man who—."
The words *Mr. Smith* reveal that Smith is a man. Don't say "Lincoln
School is a *school* that I really like." Look at what happens when a
writer cuts out weak repetitions:

Original. He looked at Mike. Mike was his brother.

Tightened. He looked at his brother Mike.

Original. The beginning of the play shows Richard as a confident and
strong man while the end shows him as a desolate and weak man.

Tightened. The beginning of the play shows Richard confident and
strong; the end shows him desolate and weak.

Before you get carried away with cutting out weak repetition,
remember that strong repetition is the heart of all good writing, in
fact the heart of all good music making, hurdle racing, hammering,
walking, or courting. Repetitions set up pattern. Only with pattern
can you achieve emphasis and variety. Da-da-da, da-da-da, da-da-dum.
That *dum* is smart because it comes after all those *da's*. It picks up
its power as you wait through all those *da's* for something to happen.
Repeat and vary. That is the secret of achieving significant form in
all art and communication.

This book will demonstrate how the repeat-and-vary pattern
strengthens writing in many ways, but for the present, consider only
how to omit those repetitions in your writing which are not working
powerfully, which get in the readers' way rather than drive them
down your road. If you can learn to say in a few words all you want
to say, with precision and fullness, you will delight yourself and your
reader. We all love a man who says a great deal in a few words. Most
of us feel that life will be too short; so we praise the man who can
hammer the nail with only three blows. We don't want to hear:

> In order that the ruling organization of a country that is
> committed to a democratic organization organized to give

the people a voice in its procedures, and thinks of their well-being, shall not become disorganized and come to an end in these times . . .

And we don't want to hear:

That government of the people and government by the people and government for the people shall not perish from the earth.

That's so much government that we can't hear the people. We want to hear

. . . that government of the people, by the people, for the people, shall not perish from the earth.

That statement repeats *people,* not *government*. The man who wrote those words respected people and knew his *repeat-and-vary* principle. Further examples of how to repeat words powerfully will be presented in Chapter 9.

REVISING ONE: In your WRITING ONE and WRITING TWO papers, lightly circle all repeated words. Then consider each one. Do you want to retain it? If you want to omit it, draw brackets in pencil around it so that after you show the revision to others and give it time to cool off, you can restore an omitted word easily if you choose. Thomas Jefferson used brackets to recommend omissions to others, and most editors today follow him.

> *Life is the elimination of what is dead.*
> WALLACE STEVENS

The words *which, who,* and *that* often clutter up sentences. Good writers remove excessive Whooery, Whichery, or Thatery.

1. Mr. Rendew, Alice's father, [was a man who] actually liked to have his lawnmower go wrong so he could tinker with its motor.
2. George [is the type of man who] always shines his shoes before going downtown.
3. [The people that] I would like to tell you about [are] Father and Mother.

Other words, for example *all* and *what,* often fail to add meaning to a sentence and need cutting.

1. [All] I wish [is that] he would admit that passion has a respectable place in our lives.

2. [What I mean to say is that] no child should eat his grandmother.

The careless use of the word *thing* is more serious and damaging.

Original. The thing that enrages me is mosquitoes inside my open shirt collar.

Revision. Mosquitoes inside my open shirt collar enrage me.

3. [The] first [thing] I'd like to say [is] . . .

Original. Of all the things in the world I can't stand, boiled hot dogs are the worst.

Revision. I can't stand boiled hot dogs.

Why do schools turn out students so masterly in word wastery? Simple. Knowledge consists to some extent in naming and ordering things. So schools teach categorizing—how to place things in classes, species, etc. (Note that the word *things* is used twice in the two preceding sentences, but meaningfully, not emptily. These two uses of *things* are necessary and justifiable.)

Thus educated persons become addicted to such categorizing words as:

| type | situation | phase | factor |
| kind | area | aspect | one |

Often the words are not pulling their weight in a sentence.

Original. The first level of the poem gives the situation of a dull sergeant speaking to a group of new recruits.

Revision. The first level of the poem presents a dull sergeant speaking to a group of recruits.

1. The Queen realized that her life was not [a] carefree and spotless [one].
2. He was a typical [type of] fraternity man.

When a writer must categorize and generalize, these words are valuable, but often they are abominations.

Namery, another sickness, is the habit of naming things which do not need naming. Consider this passage:

Juliet and Rosalind are women who fall in love. This is one of the few similarities between these two characters. They are different in age, with Juliet being an impetuous adolescent and Rosalind being a mature adult. This difference is illustrated by the manner in which each character falls

> in love. Juliet rushes into romance and gets married as
> quickly as possible while Rosalind makes sure of her love
> for Orlando—a much more rational and logical choice than
> Juliet's.

This paragraph is devastated by Namery. The author says that Juliet
and Rosalind fall in love and then unnecessarily says these acts are
similar. He says the two are different in age and then later says one
is an adolescent and the other an adult. He wastes completely the
sentence:

> This difference is illustrated by the manner in which each
> character falls in love.

because the next sentence shows the difference specifically. The paragraph could be cut in half without losing essential meaning:

> One of the few similarities between Juliet and Rosalind
> is that they both fall in love; but Juliet rushes into
> romance while Rosalind makes sure of her love for Orlando.
> Juliet is an impetuous adolescent, Rosalind a mature adult.

Essentially Namery is a failure to recognize that one's audience
may possess brains. The writer says:

> George came in with a new idea. It was a thought that had
> never struck his boss.

The reader doesn't need to be told that an idea is a thought. All he
needs is

> George came in with an idea that had never struck his boss.

In schools, Namery usually involves a special vocabulary.

> The causes of the basic difficulties in the area of mathe-
> matics are manifold. Fractions present the student with an
> entirely new set of assumptions.

The introductory sentence stupefies the reader with its dull buzzing.
The writer should have said:

> Fractions are hard to learn because they present students
> with new assumptions.

Too often writers introduce everything to their audience: "Now we
are going to look at large cities and then we are going to compare
them with small towns," they say, when all they mean to do is compare Chicago, Illinois, with Bad Axe, Michigan.

REVISING TWO: Take one of your free writings you like best and tighten it by removing all Whooery, Whichery, Thatery, and Namery.

When you examine your own writing for weak repetition, you may not be able to see it. You need a way of looking for it. Ask yourself where you have said something twice without meaning to. The following passage from a student paper shows weak repetition of both words and ideas. Try cutting it in about half.

> **Hands, did you ever notice how many different kinds of men's hands there are? I first began to notice hands when I found that all men's hands were not as large as my Dad's hands. They were large, strong, and forceful, yet always gentle like the man. His hand encompasses mine even now when he takes it gently yet firmly, as though providing it with a cover of protection against the outside world. But he has always been like that, strong and protective, yet gentle. When those hands hold a baby, the baby stops crying and is quiet as though calmed by their strength and gentleness. When those hands take a pencil and draw an idea, the lines are firm and confident. Other men seem to respond when they shake his hand to the friendliness and strength behind the handshake.**

The assertions in that passage are simple and unsurprising. They do not need a lot of repetition to be clear to the reader.

REVISING THREE: Look over two of your past writings for meanings unnecessarily repeated. For example:

Valerie scrutinized my face [carefully].

The word *scrutinize* means to examine carefully.

Original. Richard has a consistently bad habit of not listening to what people are saying to him unless he is sure it will please him.

Revision. Richard consistently fails to listen to people unless he is sure they will please him.

The word *habit* means a consistent or frequent action. Because *consistently* is used, *habit* can be eliminated.

The ground felt [peculiar. It was] soft as clouds.

If the ground was soft as clouds, it must have felt peculiar, and the writer need not make the opening comment. In the revision he hits the reader with his surprise. He does not waste a word telling him a surprise is coming. Note how the following verbose statement is brought alive by simple tightening:

Original. I see a man whose face is hidden by shadow except where the sun reveals it.

Revision. I see the sun-lit half of a man's face.

You may properly think of wasting words as a form of dishonesty. No one means to do it; but when he does, he risks losing both the reader's attention and trust.

> *A young author is tempted to leave any-thing he has written through fear of not having enough to say if he goes cutting out too freely. But it is easier to be long than short.*
>
> SAMUEL BUTLER

*Start out with the conviction that abso-
lute truth is hard to reach in matters
relating to our fellow creatures, healthy
or diseased, that slips in observation are
inevitable even with the best trained
faculties, that errors in judgment must
occur in the practice of an art which
consists largely in balancing probabili-
ties—start, I say, with this attitude of
mind, and mistakes will be acknowl-
edged and regretted; but instead of a
slow process of self-deception, with ever-
increasing inability to recognize the
truth, you will draw from your errors
the very lessons which may enable you
to avoid their repetition.*

SIR WILLIAM OSLER

chapter 5
deceiving oneself

SOMETIMES writers set out to deceive
their readers, as Roget's *Thesaurus* puts the words, to hornswoggle
or bamboozle them, to throw dust into their eyes; to engage in window dressing, hanky-panky, chicanery, pettifogging, flam, bam, flim-
flam, or cajolery; to speak mealy-mouthed buncombe, to beat about
the bush, to quibble, counterfeit, fake; to write two-faced, bare-faced,
or smooth-faced; to tell taradiddles and whoppers, to gild the pill.

But more often they set out to tell the truth and speak seriously,
as Eudora Welty advises them, and still they gild the pill and throw
dust into their own eyes as well as the reader's. No writer knows how
often he deceives himself and his reader until he becomes a professional and listens to the complaints of editors and readers. Then he
often sees that he has unconsciously

(1) not written about what really motivated him to put pen to paper, or

(2) not spoken truly when he thought he was being faithful to the world he experienced, or

(3) told only a small part of the truth, or

(4) forgotten to tell the reader the facts that make convincing what he insists the reader must be overwhelmed by, or

(5) grandly asked questions that everyone knows the answer to, or

(6) apologized for not being an expert on what he writes pages and pages about, or

(7) used awkward and phony language that does not belong to him, or

(8) used six words where his reader needed only two.

The best writers commit these sins. You cannot rid your writing of them, but you can reduce them if you learn the identifying marks of the snakes and where they are likely to slither into your paragraphs.

Any writer, beginner or professional, feels pressed to imitate successful writers. Often the beginner echoes an idea he has heard before without remembering how the thought was imbedded in a fact of his life. He generalizes on his knowledge instead of putting his reader through the experience that led to the generalization. He presents a conclusion but does not tell the story that led him to it. Here, for example, is a poem published in a high school newspaper:

PLAY TODAY

Yes, my child, use this time for play,
Tomorrow will be too late.

Play with your soldiers, cannons and guns,
Use them while they are a toy.

Be happy that the world is not yours.
Tomorrow it will be, but today it is mine.

Let him live today as a time of freedom and play!
Tomorrow he will work and he will have no time to play.

This is a time for pleasure and a time so short,
So be a child of joy and of troubles forgotten.

Tomorrow is too late my child.
Tomorrow, you are a man.

The writer may have seen her small brother playing with soldiers and then her father came home from work too tired to do more than eat, read the paper, and go to bed. The thought she wishes to convey, that a child should enjoy his life of play while he can, is old and moldy. No reader wants to encounter it unless it is brought alive with power and originality. If the writer had revealed her brother and father in the uniqueness of their experience, she might have produced a good poem. In the following writing, note how a mother showed her child at play and opened the lid on a mystery. She did not deceive herself about what story she wanted to tell.

MY SORCERESS

My daughter is a spare-toothed, seven-year old sorceress. Her brown hair is too short for a ponytail, too long for anything else. Yet if her hair were cut, some of her magic power would disappear. Her sparkle and infectious laugh assure control of her victim. When her thirteen-year old brother says, "I hate your guts," she dances around him and chants, "I love you, I love you." Then she breaks a vial of laughter in the room and he is in her power. Although his words do not change, he has taken up her chant.

CAROLINE BOWMAN

Often an author generalizes on his experience but does not relate it: double mistake. One experience usually makes an unconvincing base for a generalization. Without the personal story, the writer may not be able to keep his reader awake. A writer must learn that his authority resides in his knowledge, not in an attempt to sound like someone else. What led a writer to begin writing often can tell him where his subject hides. The young man who began a paper with this paragraph (part of which was quoted in Chapter 1) probably didn't realize that he was faking his way through every sentence:

I consider experience to be an important part in the process of learning. For example, in the case of an athlete, experience plays an important role. After each game, he tends to acquire more knowledge and proficiency, thereby making him a better athlete. An athlete could also gain more knowledge by studying up on the sport, but it is doubtful if he could participate for the first time in a sport with study alone and without experience and still do an adequate job. I think that this is the very important point which Thoreau is trying to show. He is not opposed to education, but thinks that we can be educated many times better with ex-

perience. I have the impression that he feels that it is better
for most people to gain experiences and not waste so much
time on unrelated things that will be of little value to them
in gaining their goals more quickly in life.

What spurred this boy to spend so many words telling the obvious
fact that an athlete gains from experience? Who doesn't? Probably
he was thinking of a football game in which he made three mistakes:
missed a tackle because he hit too high, threw an interception because
he couldn't see over the red-dogger's hands, and failed to make a
clear signal for a fair catch. If he had put the reader dramatically
through these experiences, he might have written a memorable paper.
But he didn't. He wrote as if he were a philosopher instead of a
football player, and his philosophy was old and dully stated.

> . . . *creativity is continual surprise, and
> only because it is surprise can it be truth.
> When we grow self-conscious we hide,
> we cloak, we disguise, we lie. So the true
> writer artist always hopes, through work-
> ing swiftly with his emotions to spring
> forth the delights and terrors, to trap
> them before they escape.*
>
> RAY BRADBURY

Another way writers deceive themselves is to speak only to themselves and yet expect the public to be fascinated. This act might be
called private writing. For example, a girl publishes a poem in a high
school paper:

SORROW
MY TRUE STORY

Now, I want to tell you people
My true story and it's sad
I will shout it from the hill tops
How I really had it bad

How I cried each night just for him.
How I missed him when he left.
I believed the lies he told me.

Then his heart grew tired and restless
And he soon stopped loving me.
He would flirt behind my back
And he thought I didn't see.

Now, I know he was unfaithful
But my hurt just wouldn't show
For I loved him, too much even
To ever let him go.

I wonder as I look back if
I did right, or was I wrong?
To let him think he deceived me
When I knew it all along.

He finally asked for his freedom
So, I had to let him go
Now my friends say to forget him

But they don't even know
That when I hear his name or see him
All the memories creep inside
Then my heart is filled with
Sadness and the tears are hard to hide.

I'm sure you recognize my story
For it happened to you too.
That's why I'm shouting from this hill top
How did it end with You???

The person who speaks in this poem cried, she missed her boy friend; he told her lies, he stopped loving her, he flirted behind her back. A pattern of experience that almost every girl has known, yet the writer tells not one convincing detail—what was the boy like? how did he treat her? Blatant or devious lies? Finally, she says, she let him go. Was she in a position to let him go? He had already gone in the sense of being unfaithful. She asks what might be a penetrating question:

I wonder as I look back if
I did right, or was I wrong?
To let him think he deceived me
When I knew it all along.

Does she really wonder? She accuses him of deceiving her and then admits deceiving him. If she had faced this question squarely and probed the reasons both deceived each other, she might have found truth valuable to herself and her readers. She says she felt such sorrow that she is now shouting from this hill top "How did it end with You???" What does this question mean? It may be false, covering up some other question or attitude. Is she really interested in knowing how other students' loves worked out? Or does she mean only to suggest her superior knowledge—that love turned sour for her and will for others? In the next to the last stanza she says:

> But they don't even know
> That when I hear his name or see him
> All the memories creep inside.
> Then my heart is filled with
> Sadness and the tears are hard to hide.

Unless her friends are inhuman, they would expect that when she heard his name or saw him she would remember moments with him— whether she had despised him or loved him. But what memories? She never tells anything about this boy that convinces the reader she loved him or even knew him as a person.

> *"If the artist does manage to be ruthless with himself," said the voice, "must we not think of him as the luckiest of men? How many men can afford the luxury of being ruthless with themselves in their dreams of doing a perfect thing?"*
>
> JOHN CIARDI

Often a writer deceives the reader and himself by attempting a trick ending or beginning, holding back the identity of someone or something when such holding back does not heighten meaning. The materials of a story or experiment should determine whether the writer is justified in reversing the natural order of events or holding back information that normally would be communicated at once. The reader is always out there. The best writers forget him at times but finally remember that writing is to be read. Life is full of ambiguity. A writer is justified in building mystery into his work. But to pump false suspense into writing is to cheat the reader. The beginning writer often destroys the excitement in an experience by insisting to the reader that he is about to be amazed. For example:

> **I began wading across the river on the sandbar. Deeper and deeper I went into the water. Up to my waist, then chest, then shoulders. The sandbar was narrow here—only about a foot wide. One misstep and off I would go. I was just about midway when IT HAPPENED.**

The IT forgets the reader. He wasn't there. What actually happened may have been exciting, but the writer must give the reader a chance

to determine how exciting the happening was. Note how the story
goes without the false suspense signal.

> . . . I was just about midway when I tripped. I fell, went
> under the water, and the sandbar disappeared beneath me.
> I was carried downstream.

Holding back is justified when the significance of a series of events
or progression of ideas is enhanced by the mystery. For example, the
following passage opens with a sentence that puzzles the reader:

> Grandma, Dad's stepmother, welcomed us warmly, but gave
> us whole wheat biscuits with our meals.

What is the point of whole wheat biscuits? A mystery. The next sentence reveals the answer:

> Many times we watched from another room as she served
> her own grandchildren the preferred biscuits made from
> white flour.

This is the way the experience came to the writer, as a mystery
revealed later when she saw the white biscuits. She makes the reader
wait for understanding, but the wait is rewarding. A writer should
expect intelligent reading from his audience, but the line between
writing privately and publicly is difficult to draw. Suspense is a
common ingredient of life, but in writing it should not be artificially
introduced. It should exist in the materials the writer has discovered.

And so with questions. They should belong to the writer and
his body of materials or he should not ask them. "Did you ever
fall down a basement stairway while eavesdropping and land in your
sister's boy friend's lap?" The answer is easy. "No, I never did."
Not only does this question give away what might be a smash ending
to a humorous story, but it is not really meant. Ask questions when
you mean them, when you have really wondered about what they ask.
Avoid them when you know your readers know the answers. "Are
children wiser than grown-ups?" The reader knows the writer is
going to say next: "Yes, sometimes." But the writer deceives himself
about his job. He should not be running a question and answer show.
He probably wanted to tell his reader about a time when he saw a
child act wisely. He should forget the hanky-panky and get on with
the story. A writer who frequently asks lame questions ultimately
becomes as irritating as a six-year-old child who prefaces every assertion with the words, "Mom, you know what?"

Closely related to false questions are apologies and irrelevant introductions. Any editor will tell you that most manuscripts he sees wind up three times before they deliver the ball. Begin the paper. Wind up once and throw the pitch. The difficulty with beginnings comes from that sticky old relationship with the reader. Will he believe me? Will he like me? How can I impress him with my wisdom or honesty? One sure way to depress the reader is to apologize before starting a long article.

> I may not know much about politics, but I'm sure of one
> thing.

A reader may be tempted to say, "If you don't know much about politics, why are you writing this long article about it?" Modesty is one thing and false modesty another. To pretend he knows almost nothing of a large subject he is writing about is inexcusable in a writer, but to admit that he does not know this or that bit of information, or that he is not sure of his understanding on one point, is proper and even persuasive to the reader. For example, Stephen Spender, poet and critic, writing about another man's poem, says:

> The idea—if I understand it—is that the poet, through
> allowing his isolated self to die, enters into that life . . .

Mr. Spender admits that the poem is hard to understand; he does not deceive himself or his reader.

Naturally beginnings are difficult for a writer because they establish or fail to establish a strong relationship with the reader. Often the writer doesn't know all the persons who will read his work. And even when he does, he cannot be sure how each reader will comprehend his sentences. When a person is uneasy about how others will understand him, he often acts pompous, speaking words that he has not really made his own. And so he does not find his own voice. Everything becomes strained and artificial rather than easy and sure and winning. The urge to impress readers at the outset is so powerful that in their first drafts of a piece of writing writers feel obliged to make sweeping statements about mankind when they actually have a much smaller story to tell. For example, here is a professional writer beginning an article in a magazine about high-performance boating:

> Time has a way of perpetuating events, situations and
> people. As one event dies another is born. As one situation
> dissolves, another is conceived. As one person disappears,

another appears. The cycles of life's activity renew themselves constantly.

In the unlimited circle a few years ago sports reporters
bemoaned privately the loss of colorful figures. Lee
Schoenith had mellowed from blustering "bad guy" of the
pits to Chairman of the Unlimited Commission. Bill
Muncey, Peppery Willard Rhodes and their *Thriftway*
retired, and with them went the possibility of fiery hassles
and pungent statements. Col. Russ Schleeh of plumber's
helper fame left the sport (and Air Force) for staid duties
behind a desk of industry. And so it went. "Story material,"
said one tired writer, "is lacking—and that's an understate-
ment."

Into this void strode big, bouncing, boisterous Bernie
Little and his beautiful buoyant, bewitching four-seater,
Tempo.

The opening paragraph of this article is highly pretentious. Everyone knows persons die and are born, and men rise to fame and retire.
The writer speaks these obvious truths in a voice that should belong
to a prophet. All she is trying to do is introduce the story of Bernie
Little, an attractive racing boat driver who appealed to her for his
humor and manliness.

Nothing helps a writer more than immediately finding a voice
in which to speak—one natural and right for him and fitting for
his material and audience. This writer didn't find it here. After
beginning in prophetic voice, she shifts in the third paragraph to
corny repetition of "b" sounds that would sound right only in the
mouth of a carnival barker on the Midway who knows he is kidding
himself and his audience as he says, "A bevy of buxom beautiful
Bunnies."

But she wrote well in other parts of her article. In the opening
she experienced a common difficulty of all writers—finding words that
speak honestly and validly.

A writer must test every word for its pitch: does it hit the note
he was aiming for? Does it say what he meant it to say? The simplest
word can be falsely used. *And* looks innocent, but often gets writers
into trouble.

She came by our house swinging her ever-present black
parasol *and* Dad was trying to fix the fertilizer distributor
so he could get the potatoes planted faster.

And is the wrong word there. Ordinarily it joins like or equal things. The woman swinging the parasol and Dad fixing the fertilizer distributor are not equal or related until the writer brings them together. He should drop the *and*, make two sentences, or replace *and* with a word like *while*.

Frequently writers employ the loose, imprecise language of casual conversation which will not stand scrutiny as it must if it is to be writing that tells the truth and speaks seriously. A writer says:

> I saw the victim lying beside the car, his left leg separated from his body and blood all over the highway. I was rather shaken . . .

Rather is here a false word and should be omitted. In this use it belongs in the family of expressions like *not exactly* and *not too nice,* permissible in informal conversation but often sloppy and inexcusable in writing.

> Again and again he had lied to his daughter about what her fiancé had said about her. As a father I guess he wasn't exactly nice.

No, not exactly.

Phony language like this creeps into the best writers' work. They must be ever on guard against it. They like the sound of their sentences and don't listen closely enough to hear that they have said:

> Johnny was hanging suspended from the highest branch.

or

> The talk has a tranquilizing effect on him.

when they could have made the same point in fewer words:

> Johnny was hanging from the highest branch.

and

> The talk tranquilizes him.

The ways of deceiving oneself about what he is saying are too numerous to illustrate completely here. One more conversational habit that may lead writers into trouble:

> I *did* have to disarm one student last year.
> Something interesting *did* happen when the sisters came to that camp.

Sometimes, but rarely, this use of *did* to emphasize a verb signals the reader that what is being told now is unexpected. Something said earlier implied otherwise. But usually the writer will save words and lose no meaning by saying:

> I had to disarm one student last year.
>
> Something interesting happened when the sisters came to that camp.

"Something interesting did happen" sounds dull. Make it happen. If it was so interesting, tell it so the reader will be fascinated. Hit him with the surprises you have collected. Don't weaken them with excessive *did's.*

I hope you did like this chapter on Deceiving Oneself and that it did teach you many valuable and important things that you did find interesting.

But to have a full kit of auditory patterns curved to real emotions we do need to listen. We need to listen, with inside matching on our own part, to those whose phrases fit their inner state. We are lucky if we listen less to lecturers and experts, more to farmers, mechanics, truck drivers . . . laundresses, and children out of school.

SIDNEY COX

chapter 6

people talking

"You WANT to go or don't you?"

"Where?"

"Where? What difference does it make? We're going with the guys."

"Well—"

Nothing much gets accomplished in that dialogue but it probably made you want to know what was going to be said next. Conversation is so much our lives: waiting for sentences to clear, asking when they don't, and then waiting for the answer to our asking. Two people talking together create constant tension. Will these words do? Will those words help?

Conversation is responsive, like hitting a ball back and forth over the net quickly. Even when one speaker does not answer the other's questions, as in the dialogue above, his refusal is still a response. That's one of the reasons conversation makes writing more intense: it builds suspense. Another reason is that it gives the sound of life.

On paper you can put down all kinds of conversations. For example, listen to your mother—or any mother—talking to her eight-year-old son when he rushes in from school at 3:00 P.M.:

"Hi, Mom. Guess what."

"Hi, Bobby. You hungry?"

43

"Ya. Hey, guess what. Next Monday all the guys are
bringing their S.S.P.'s and racing um in the hall. You gotta
get me a new S.S.P. Sidewinder cuz mine's broke. Will ya?"

"No! Christmas was only four weeks ago and I'm not
buying any toys now."

"Aw Mom, you gotta. I'll be the only guy without a
racer."

"Now Bobby, how many times must I tell you, your being
the only one without an S.S.P. is not a good reason for
getting one. It sets a pattern of the need to conform to
what is important for someone else. It robs your character
of individualism. I know you probably don't understand
all of what I'm trying to say right now but someday you'll
see I'm right."

"Mom?"

"What, honey?"

"Your nose wiggles funny when you talk."

RUTH FENTON

That conversation will speak to many parents—help them see how
pompous they get at times. It shows the delightful candor of children,
who haven't learned well enough yet how to be diplomatic and dull.
Maybe that's the age—about eight—for here's another such boy, this
time aged seven. The writer is the mother:

"Hi, David, how are you?"

"OK, I guess. Didn't have a good day at school, though."

"Oh? What happened?"

"Nobody likes me. John wouldn't let me play on his football team at recess."

"Um, wonder why. You always have before. Did you say
or do something to make him mad?"

"Nope. He just said, 'Brown, you can't play today.' "

"Didn't you ask why?"

"If I had, he would have said, ' 'Cause you're too stupid.'
Nobody likes me."

"David, you know that isn't true."

"Yes it is. Mrs. Strand wouldn't ask me a question either."

"Well David, I know everyone in the class can't be asked
a question every day. There just isn't enough time."

"Mom, there are thirty-two kids in my class. Everyone
else was asked a question."

"Oh good grief, David, *everyone*?"

"Well almost. She doesn't like me, either. You don't even like me, do you, Mom? You just yelled at me."

"David, why don't you go in your room and play awhile?"

(He gives a big grin.)

"OK, Mom."

Those are conversations. Two persons exchanging words, listening to each other, responding. Like most good writers the authors wrote out of close knowledge. If they had been writing of someone they hadn't known, for example, diplomats in Washington, they might have distorted the dialogues because they couldn't use their ears as they wrote.

You can quickly tell when a written conversation is phony, delivered in Engfish. The supermarket cashier is saying, "Oh, it's been delightful to have you as our customer today, Miss Watkins." Or the bank manager is saying, "O.K., Watkins, you write the check properly, we give you the bread."

When you write conversation, try for truth to the feeling and ideas expressed by persons in real situations. Try also for the true sound of each speaker's language—his languages. Every person speaks the native language of his country. He also speaks several dialects, which belong to a part of his country or the social groups he associates with at school or work or play—the gang from 14th Street or the guys at the Aerospace Company. And he speaks an idiolect, or personal language, which is his alone. It has a distinctive sound; it is spiced by a word or two he made up himself, or an original grammatical construction he fell into at age four and never climbed out of. Here's another real conversation:

John: You're so crazy I love you.

Carol: That's three times you've said that.

John: You are crazy, you know that?

Carol: That's not what I mean—think about it.

John: Oh, I know what you mean.

Carol: Those words don't come easy for you, I can tell.

John: No, they don't.

Carol: It almost scares you while you're saying it.

John: You're crazy, Carrie, for the fourth time.

There is a great deal of *love* in those lines but the word is mentioned only once.

I notice particularly the cadence of their voices, the sort of phrases they'll use, and that's what I'm all the time try-

*ing to hear in my head, how people
word things—because everybody speaks
an entirely different language . . .*

FRANK O'CONNOR

The above dialogue was presented in dramatic form, like a play, with nothing but the spoken words and the names of the speakers given, and therefore it did not need quotation marks. But in most writing conversation must be marked off clearly. And so must the speakers. If you run together the spoken words and the narrative, you may confuse your reader. Example:

> We got into the elevator and I stood as far away as possible. His eyes felt my body. He came toward me, slowly, arms extended, fingers stretching, stiffened, ready to grab me. What's the matter? You afraid I'll rape you? He laughed. Uh, no—uh, I'm shy. We left the elevator and entered a dimly lit hall. I wondered where he was taking me. What are you studying here, Doug? Tool and Die. Oh, how long you been going here? Eight months. Aren't you going to hold my hand? Um, uh—remember? I told you I was shy.

With no indication of who is speaking, that passage becomes hard to follow. To prevent this confusion, conventional ways of punctuating and paragraphing conversation have been established. In the following story, which contains conversation along with narrative, you can see how the above passage is unconfused by the indention of a line every time a person begins speaking. And quotation marks indicate which words belong to that person, to differentiate them from the author's narrative words.

FOR A WALK?

> The bus pulled up in front of the State Technical Institute and Rehabilitation Center. I said to myself I don't want to go in there and talk to those boys but I knew I did or I wouldn't have come. What would I say? I didn't know how to talk to strangers, especially boys.
>
> The sixteen members of my group walked into a lobby filled with young men anxious to see the faces and bodies of some young women.
>
> At first, for moral support I stayed with some of the girls I came with. After about an hour I ventured off by myself to find the restroom. I was approached by a tall, thin boy

wearing bell-bottoms that were too short and a baggy green shirt. His hair nearly covered his face.

"Wanna go for a walk?" he asked.

"Uh, ok. Your name is Doug, isn't it? I met you earlier."

"Yea. I don't remember your name."

"Kathy."

We got into the elevator and I stood as far away as possible. His eyes felt my body. He came toward me, slowly, arms extended, fingers stretched, stiffened, ready to grab me.

"What's the matter? You afraid I'll rape you?" He laughed.

"Uh, no—uh, I'm shy."

We left the elevator and entered a dimly lit hall. I wondered where he was taking me.

"What are you studying here, Doug?"

"Tool and Die."

"Oh. How long you been going here?"

"Eight months. Aren't you going to hold my hand?"

"Um, uh—remember? I told you I was shy."

"Oh yea, I forgot. You're shy."

We walked into a well-lighted lobby where there were two other people and a grotesque statue that I raved about until he could tell I was insincere. I resigned myself to walking another dark hallway. We reached a dead end in conversation and space. I stood on my tiptoes to look into the window of an auto shop. When I lowered myself from the window and turned around, his lips brushed the back of my head.

I began slowly walking away. "I have this industrial arts class for elementary school teachers and we're gonna get to work with wood and metal and electricity and—"

"You don't like me, do you?"

"I don't even know you. You're a nice boy, and very friendly, but like I already told you, I'm shy and don't know what to say."

As we continued walking, I could feel a nervous headache beginning to grow above my eyes. I felt selfish and inexperienced. I was wounding his ego and all I could think of was what a bad time I was having.

"You going to hold my hand now?"

"No I—"

"I know. You're still shy. Well, I don't believe you."

We were approaching the familiar crowded lobby. I suggested we sit down. Immediately we were joined by Doug's friend Gary, who was confined to a wheelchair. After the "What are you studying's" and the "Where are you from's" our conversation died. Gary suggested that somebody say something. After he said it a second time, I knew I was a failure. I thought it was just Doug I couldn't talk to. Gary was much more pleasant, but I couldn't talk to him either. I decided I was a shallow person and had lived a sheltered life. The ache in my head became a pounding, and even though I'd had a three-hour nap that afternoon, I was exhausted. I kept watching the clock because I wanted to get out of there and never come back. I still had thirty minutes.

We went downstairs to shoot pool, but there wasn't an empty table. We just stood there.

"What's wrong?" Doug asked.

"Nothing, I just have a headache."

"You don't like it here, do you?"

"No. No. It's not that. I just have a headache and I'm tired."

"I have to go call my mother. Wanna come to my room?"

"Well, uh—it's almost time to leave. I'd better go find Judy."

He walked away, wheeling Gary with him. I could hear them talk and laugh. They were laughing at me.

Two other points about writing conversation: professionals identify a speaker with phrases like *said John* only when necessary, and they do not keep nudging the reader with Insistery ("Go to hell, said John *angrily*"). If John says "Go to hell," he is probably angry. If he is not, the writer has to do more than simply say, "said John gently." He must establish by the context of the whole conversation and the character of the relationship between the speakers that "Go to hell" in this instance is a gentle, comradely comment rather than an angry dismissal.

The spoken words in the following lines were taken from the above story "For a Walk?" They appear right after the first three paragraphs. Here below they are handled amateurishly, with unnecessary explanations and identifications beyond the spoken words. In the story they were handled expertly—the reader given no more than he needed.

"Wanna go for a walk?" Doug asked questioningly.

"Uh, OK. Your name is Doug, isn't it?" said Kathy obligingly. "I met you earlier."

"Yea," he said matter of factly. Then he added, "I don't remember your name."

"Kathy," she said shortly.

If you check this passage in the original, you will see that there the author did not employ these words in her version: *Doug, questioningly, said Kathy obligingly, he said matter of factly, Then he added, she said shortly.* If there are only two persons in a conversation, seldom do they need to be identified. If three or more, the reader is more likely to become confused at times; but the fundamental remains—do not insult your reader by giving him more than he needs.

WRITING FIVE: Write two dialogues that carry truth that counts for you and voices that speak truly and individually.

It's helpful for a beginner to write his first conversations in dramatic form, with the names of speakers preceding each spoken line. Then he will not be encouraged to clutter his writing with explanations and comments like "he said disgustedly."

Here's another sample of a dialogue that in every way asks a lot of the reader; two college roommates are talking.

MOVE

"You're going to move tonight?"

"Yes, I might as well get it out of the way before classes get started."

"Are you sure it wasn't anything that I said or did?"

"I've explained that to you so many times! It's not you. It's your people."

"OK, OK. Is there something I can do for you?"

"Yes, you can close up my record player."

"All right. Did you say you were going to room with Darleen?"

"Yes."

"Is she militant?"

"That's not really a good term, but she is. Yes. Your tact is terrific."

"Do you agree with her?"

"In some ways. Jan, she's one of my people."

"I'm not blind. Here's your record player."

"Thanks. Have you seen my James Brown album?"

"I think Darleen borrowed it."

"That's right. You know it has to be this way, don't you?"

"I can't say that, but I'm trying to understand."

"Well, look at Barbara Jean. How many Blacks have you seen talking to her lately?"

"I haven't really noticed."

"You've got to notice, Jan! There is no middle of the road, or at least there won't be."

"Have they been giving you any static about living with a White?"

"This is my own decision."

"Now you're not noticing!"

"Well, I guess I'm ready."

"Maybe I'll see you around, huh? You don't have to tell anyone that you lived with a Honky."

"To be shoor, Miss Jan, ah wunt do dat!"

"Bye."

"Good-bye."

People talking. They say so much more than their words say.

Shams and delusions are esteemed for soundest truth, while reality is fabulous. If men would steadily observe realities only, and not allow themselves to be deluded, life, to compare it with such things as we know, would be like a fairy tale and the Arabian Nights' Entertainments.

HENRY THOREAU

chapter 7
fabulous
realities

MOST OF US go through each day looking for what we saw yesterday and we find it, to our half-realized disappointment. But the man who daily expects to encounter fabulous realities runs smack into them again and again. He keeps his mind open for his eyes.

Asked to expect surprise, a number of students explored their nearby worlds for fabulous realities. Here are some they found:

1. I was speeding along the highway when I saw a small yellow sign.

SLOW
MEN
WORKING

It was followed by a larger one in black and white, reading

YOUR HIGHWAY DOLLARS
AT WORK

2. At a football game yesterday at Waldo Stadium a blind man sat next to me listening to his radio.
3. I stood in the checkout lane behind a boy who looked about sixteen. He waited for the clerk to begin ringing up his package

of Pall Malls, then reached out and added five packs of bubble gum.

4. Ever since Rennie found out that Jane, his co-worker, doesn't like him, he tries to upset her when they are together. I asked him why he did this. He said, "I hate intolerant people."

5. At the Allegan County Fair I approached the cotton candy stand and told the girl I wanted pink. After she gave it to me she turned to get my change and I noticed a piece of cotton in her ear.

6. Today I found a dead bird in the gutter with its mangled wing held in place by "Magic Transparent Tape."

7. A drunk teenager trying to cross West Main at Michigan assisted by a little old lady.

8. I excitedly opened my only two valentines from males. They were just alike.

9. A girl with a deep V in her blouse holding her books over it.

10. A man returned to his parked car to find its hood and fenders gashed and crumpled. On the dashboard he found a piece of folded paper. Written in a neat feminine hand, the note said: "I have just run into your car. There are people watching me. They think I am writing down my name and address. They are wrong."

11. A small boy, obviously lost, walked up to a security guard at Hudson's department store, and asked, "Did you see a lady walk by here without me?"

12. A pregnant woman carrying a globe of the world in front of her up a steep sidewalk in the city.

13. In the middle of a heated argument with me, my wife goes to the refrigerator, gets a bottle of ginger ale, fills two glasses, gives me one, and continues the argument.

Each statement surprises. It is not fairly surprising, but absolutely surprising, because it is unique. A robin sitting in the April snow in Illinois or Massachusetts would not qualify as a fabulous reality. In those states a late short snow often occurs after robins have arrived.

Tension is necessary to make a fabulous reality. Two things that do not belong together touch in some way. And their touching creates waves of further suggestion that are not stated. In the middle of the young man's argument, his wife interrupts him, but not to put him down, rather to make him more comfortable. The argument is heated; she gives him a cold drink.

When I went to those great cities I saw
wonders I had never seen in Ireland. But
when I came back to Ireland I found all

the wonders there waiting for me. You
see they had been there all the time;
but my eyes had never been opened to
them. I did not know what my own
house was like, because I had never been
outside it.

BERNARD SHAW [*Keegan speaking*]

COLLECTING THREE: This weekend keep a piece of paper or notebook in your pocket or pocketbook and jot down five fabulous realities you see. When you have a chance, write them in sentences. Keep revising them until you have built up to the surprise rather than given it away weakly. Note that most of the above fabulous realities (1) place the happening in a particular setting, (2) put the reader there through telling details, (3) make the action happen for the reader as it happened for the writer, (4) do not waste words, (5) do not explain, but present facts and force the reader to find the surprise, (6) put the kicker at the end.

Note how the facts in this fabulous reality do all the telling by themselves.

A pimply-faced, dirty, barefooted, greasy, string-haired girl smoking a cigarette and eating a peanut butter and jelly sandwich riding a crowded elevator at the University of Michigan while reading *How to Win Friends and Influence People*.

COLLECTING FOUR: Collect five or more additional fabulous realities. Do not be easily satisfied. Tension. Punch at the end. Uniqueness. Implications or suggestions that spread beyond the statement.

The looking and discovering involved in producing fabulous realities is not a trick and not an exercise. It is the way good writers see. Because their eyes are not tired, their readers turn their pages with surprise. In *People of the Abyss,* a book about the city of London, Jack London wrote:

From the slimy spittle-drenched sidewalk, they were picking up bits of orange peel, apple skin, and grape stems, and they were eating them. The pits of green gage plums they cracked between their teeth for the kernels inside. They picked up stray crumbs of bread the size of peas, apple cores so black and dirty one would not take them to be apple cores, and these things these two men took into their mouths, and chewed them, and swallowed them; and this, between six and seven o'clock in the evening of August 20, year of our Lord 1902, in the heart of the greatest, wealthiest, and most powerful empire the world has ever seen.

Note that Jack London is here not just telling an unusual incident but is writing toward an idea—that the great English capital city did not save its citizens from degrading poverty. Surprising realities suffuse good essays and articles as they do good stories. One of the reasons students in schools seldom write powerful themes or essays is that they mistakenly think good nonfiction writing is abstract and dull. Actually, the best writers of nonfiction (articles, essays, autobiography, history, etc.) continually surprise their readers with fabulous realities.

When you read accounts others have written of surprising realities, like Jack London's, you may feel they were lucky but you were never blessed. But reality is often fabulous for the man who remains awake.

> He [Thoreau] knew how to sit immovable, a part of the rock he rested on, until the bird, the reptile, the fish, which had retired from him, should come back and resume its habits, nay, moved by curiosity, should come to him and watch him.
>
> RALPH WALDO EMERSON

The unfamiliar frequently appears amazing, as does the familiar when it is scrutinized more closely than usual.

WRITING SIX: Write a fabulous reality that is a page or more in length. You may already have found one that you can expand. Or you may have done a free writing that you can work up into a fabulous reality.

Here is such a free writing done by a high school student:

THE REPORTER

The news last night was about the dam breaking. A reporter was talking to a boy who was about ten or eleven

years old. The boy said, "My mom told me to get out of the
house because a flood was coming. As soon as the water
hit the house, it collapsed." He stopped; he was trying so
hard to keep from crying that he couldn't go on. The reporter said, "Then what happened?" The boy said, "Then,
then my mother, my two sisters and brother, were drowned."
It made me sick when that reporter made him tell what
happened. Couldn't he see that it was about to kill the kid
by talking about his family? I don't like reporters; they
always have to probe into people's lives.

This piece of writing would gain if it employed point 4 of the
requirements for a fabulous reality: making the reader work to find
the significance of the event on his own. Suppose the last three
sentences were dropped so that the tale ended with the kicker. But
without the last three sentences a reader might miss the point. Maybe
if the phrase "The reporter said" were replaced with "The reporter
kept pressing," the reader would be cued sufficiently to see how the
writer felt about what was happening.

While the writer is sharpening this tale so that it becomes a fabulous reality, he might use conversation paragraphing to make more
apparent the change of speakers. And he might think about cutting
one of the *about's* in the first two sentences. That kind of repetition is
common in speech and writing: we say a word like *about* and use it
again because it has printed itself on our language machine. Sometimes the second printing is powerful; here it is not. As so often happens, the move to delete a wasted or weakly repeated word leads to
an improvement in other phrases. In this account the writer says
"a boy who was about ten or eleven years old." He doesn't know
how old the boy was. One year's difference will not count with the
reader, so the writer might as well say "a ten-year-old boy." Here is a
tightened version of the story:

THE REPORTER *(Revised)*

The news last night was about the dam breaking. A reporter was talking to a ten-year-old boy who said, "My
mom told me to get out of the house because a flood was
coming. As soon as the water hit the house it collapsed."
He was trying so hard to keep from crying that he couldn't
go on.

The reporter kept pressing. "Then what happened?"

"Then, then my mother, my two sisters and brother were
drowned."

Now the passage requires the reader to see that the reporter's question should not have been delivered at that time. It infringed upon the boy's privacy agonizingly. Surprising that anyone could be that cruel? But true. A fabulous reality.

Here's another longer free writing that is not pointedly a fabulous reality, but behind its lines lies the irony that in this setting, where a patient is supposed to feel one way, she feels another.

PATIENCE

I've always gotten along pretty well with doctors, until last Friday, anyway. I swung open the door and was immediately confronted by six pairs of eyes—a young guy on crutches, an old woman with her daughter, a lady in her twenties, and another lady with her baby. Everyone seemed to look me over as if I were a cow for sale. The receptionist greeted me with a large toothy smile, and I said hi. I proceeded to give her my name, address, telephone number, have you ever had thises and have you ever had thats, stopping every now and then to repeat myself.

I then took a seat and picked up a copy of *Sports Illustrated* and began to wait, and wait, and wait. I waited for an hour and ten minutes. I must have read the magazine twenty times.

Finally a plump little nurse came out and said in a witchy tone of voice, "Casarri, please." She escorted me to a room and said, "Strip down to your underwear and put this on." She handed me a hospital gown and left.

I did what she told me but then made a mistake—I sat in the aluminum chair. Oh! was that cold. Again I waited, but this time for only ten minutes. Those gowns are so starchy if I moved I cut myself. The doctor did show up but not for long. He did a few quick taps here and a pull there, then off to the X-ray room. Again I waited and again I sat in a cold aluminum chair. After X-rays I went back to the room and waited. That's all I seemed to do. Wait.

Some young guy brought the X-rays back, but alas no doctor. So he made some wise-ass remark as he slapped a picture on the viewer, like, "Bet you've never seen your back before." I had to chuckle to make him feel good and to get him out of there. I don't think I could have taken any more of those intern jokes. When the doctor finally came back, I had gone through the X-rays and could have told him what was wrong with me. He looked at them this way and that and then wrote down a prescription while mumbling some witchcraft incantation like "Oooo, EEEE, ah ah ah welllll, maybeee." Then he wrote something in some foreign tongue and handed it to me. I looked at the piece of paper, then I looked at him. I couldn't read it but I didn't want him to know that. He then left me standing there—half-naked, with a piece of ancient hieroglyphics in my hand, wondering what was going on.

That is an unusual story. It is beautifully quick and humorous at times and overwritten at other times. Behind the lines lies the irony that in this medical setting, where a patient is supposed to feel secure because she is in the land of scientific techniques, she feels the opposite. The waiting becomes ludicrous, the aluminum chairs cold, and the impression grows that she is in the hands of a witch doctor. A first step in cutting would be to drop the phrase "proceeded to" in the fifth sentence and simply say "I gave her . . ." You might consider other ways to tighten this writing. It is worth working on, for it makes a large point about how patients feel with doctors.

Here's another passage which takes on the power of a fabulous reality:

KISS

I first kissed a girl in the fifth grade, during basketball season. I decided it had to be this cold November night. With the north wind blowing, it had to be done in a car or on the south side of the gym. I got to the basketball game late. We held hands until half time, and that was when I decided it would have to be now. We went out to my parents' car with my best friend and his girl friend. Rita and I just stared straight ahead. I was shaking so badly with fear that I couldn't get any words out. She broke the silence finally by saying, "We better go in or our parents will be looking for us." So I made a deal with her. We could go in as soon as we went on the other side of the gym. The first thing I remember her saying was, "Well, we are on the other side of the gym." I tried to kiss her but missed. So I led her over to a foot high rock. I climbed up so I could reach her, and I finally kissed her for a second but then it felt like a long time.

Another giveaway opening, but with the first five words cut and a new title supplied, this would be a fine fabulous reality. It puts the reader in the action with short, building statements. The last statement of the passage, "but then it felt like a long time," is more an explanation and less an action than the endings of most successful fabulous realities, but here the words create a sufficient surprise to make the story work.

Life is routine more than it is fabulous. Without the steadiness of the expected, newness is impossible or chaotic. But most of us would gain from confronting and recognizing a great deal more newness than we do.

If you stand right fronting and face to face to a fact, you will see the sun glimmer on both its surfaces, as if it were a cimeter [scimitar], and feel its sweet edge dividing you through the heart and marrow . . .

HENRY THOREAU

Sit down before fact as a little child . . .

THOMAS HENRY HUXLEY

chapter 8

writing case-histories

Fog is beautiful from above or outside —rolling, wispy. But once your car enters it, your journey becomes nightmare. Where you are, how fast you are going, what direction, or what other vehicle will loom up, you do not know. You cannot drive at a reasonable speed and you may very well slide into a ditch or river before you know it. There is simply too much unknown.

This is what happens often to students in school. The beginning writer should take his journeys on the back of his hand or in his own yard. And simply tell us what he knows. A case-history of how he carried his papers on the route one morning, of how he prepares for school in a family of seven in a house with one bathroom, of how he got ready to play his first game of varsity basketball. A day, a week, an hour—some interval of his life through which he takes us as he carries out one connected action or watches someone else or something else go through a process. No fog should be involved.

A person does not have to be a professional writer to tell a case-history with authority and power. He has only to know his

59

journey intimately and carry some attitude toward it which enables him to select details that keep the history alive and significant— something more than a bad list of names and dates. Michihiko Hachiya, a medical doctor in Japan, was wounded on August 6, 1945, by the first nuclear explosion directed against human beings. The next morning he awoke to groans of patients and a new Hiroshima. He told the story of his experiences, a simple case-history of what happened to him then.

> Dr. Katsube looked me over and after feeling my pulse, said: "You received many wounds, but they all missed vital spots."
>
> He then described them and told me how they had been treated. I was surprised to learn that my shoulder had been severely cut but relieved at his optimism for my recovery.
>
> "How many patients are in the hospital?" I asked Dr. Koyama.
>
> "About a hundred and fifty," he replied. "Quite a few have died, but there are still so many that there is no place to put one's foot down. They are packed in everywhere, even the toilets."
>
> •   •   •
>
> Downstairs, I ran into Mr. Hirohata sitting on a bench and sat down beside him. Mr. Hirohata had been employed in the Telephone Bureau and was at work in the building when the explosion occurred. Despite the fact that he was less than four hundred meters from the hypocenter, Mr. Hirohata escaped injury.
>
> "How did you avoid injury when nearly everyone around you was killed or hurt?" I asked.
>
> "The thick concrete wall of the building protected me," answered Mr. Hirohata, "but people standing near the windows were killed instantly or died later from burns or cuts. The night shift was just leaving and the day shift coming on when the explosion occurred. Forty or more were killed near the entrance. About fifteen employees in the construction department, stripped to the waist, were outside taking gymnastics. They died instantly.
>
> "Doctor, a human being who has been roasted becomes quite small, doesn't he? Those people all looked like little boys after the explosion. Is there any reason why my hair should be falling out and I feel so weak? I'm worried, doctor, because I have been told that I would die and this

has already happened to some people I know who didn't seem to be hurt at all by the *pika*."

"Mr. Hirohata, I don't believe you need worry about yourself," I answered, trying to be reassuring. "Like so many others, you've been through a dreadful experience, and on top of that have tried to work night and day here at the Bureau. What else could one expect? You must go home, stay absolutely quiet in bed, and get all the good nourishing food you can."

This excerpt from a 233-page book shows that Dr. Hachiya wrote down his experience in incidents and conversations as they came to him. He called the book *Hiroshima Diary: The Journal of a Japanese Physician, August 6—September 30, 1945.* He told what he did, what others did, whom he saw, what they said to each other. The writer of a case-history tries to put the reader there, right in the process, the place, the action. If he sees a man riding a bicycle with a broken red reflector on its rear bumper, he does not write: "I saw a man riding a damaged bicycle," but "I saw a man riding a bicycle with a broken red reflector on its rear bumper."

If you record the details of a process or experience and then write them into a case-history, in one sense you are an authority. You may not know more about that process or experience than some others, but your written record commands respect by its truth to particular fact. Here is a case-history written by a student:

THE BIRTH OF A LAMB

As my father and I fed our ewes at night, I could easily pick out which ones had serious thoughts for the long night ahead. Their ears would be streamlined like the wings of a jet. Their sides would be concave from their backbones like the sides of the pup tent. After we finished chores, I would climb into the straw mow where I would be the king looking down on a command performance. Tonight I would watch a miracle people never have the opportunity to see —watching the coming of a new life.

I couldn't tell how long the birth would take. If it were hard, it might take three or four hours—only an hour if it were easy. First came the water bag. I was surprised to see it because in my excitement I was looking for the lamb. My anticipation bounces me over many surprises because I remember only the end.

The bag was pliable like a transparent sack made of rubber bands. It held nearly a pint of antifreeze colored liquid. As the birth progressed, the water bag bounced lower and lower like a spider coming down his web. When the bag touched the dirty straw in the pen, it acted like an anchor as it pulled the rest of its container from the ewe. This accomplished, it opened, spilling its deep purple antifreeze onto the straw like a fallen handkerchief full of BB's that has been held by the corners. The new element sponging through the dirt-freckled straw united the freckles into a solid dirty brown.

A gummy material followed the water bag, threatening the worn straw again. It was thick and sticky; it looked and felt like petroleum jelly with gum added. The work was coming heavier to the ewe as a pair of tar black hoofs covered by a slimy plastic bag emerged. The ewe pushes from her front shoulders down. I can follow the strain down to her rear shoulders, then up again as she relaxes. She holds her breath and pushes so hard that her lips curl outward, sometimes emitting a little "ma-at"—not a "blat" like most people think.

The nose and eyes are out, but the hardest part remains. The straining eases now. The anxious ewe thinks her labor is over. She gets up expecting to find the lamb behind her, but finds nothing. She licks the spot where his head has touched and lies down to try again. Once the lamb is out past his shoulders, the rest is easy. Now I sigh and realize that I've pushed and strained with the ewe for the last hour.

The lamb doesn't need me, but I rush down from my throne, stumbling because my eyes see only him. He lies coughing to clear the phlegm from his throat. I reach into his plastic puddle and force my finger into his throat, clearing it.

The mother communicates with me. A recognizable smile unites me with her feelings. I could have had the birth and she could have been the king.

She doesn't have a doctor to hand her the baby, so she forces herself up to lick off his sticky coating. Our union of feeling ends; she's a sheep and I'm a curious little boy. I can't understand how the slimy plastic sack tastes. Too many people can't understand.

MAX SLISHER

Writing a case-history will point you in the opposite direction from which this high school student went when he wrote the following comment for his school newspaper:

DAYS GONE BY DON'T RETURN

> Everyone has heard the expression from their parents, "Well when I was young . . ." What parents need to realize is that life is different now; the problems of teenagers are still present, but the problems are new and different.
>
> Today's teenagers are pressured more than any other generation has been before. A constant threat to this age is one of worrying about college and being "in" a crowd at school.
>
> These problems existed when parents of today were younger, but not to the extreme that they do now. A job today requires a college education; before, this was not necessary.
>
> Teenagers are more socially conscious now than in past generations. Fads must be met, the new places must be visited, the group must be followed in order to be considered "in."
>
> Times change; with them come joys and problems. Life for the teenager seems easy to most parents but it is difficult. New problems arise before old ones are solved. It is a never-ending battle of pressures and difficulties.

Maybe a good point, but never made convincing. Had this writer presented a short case-history of a student learning to observe a fad, or visiting one of the "new places that must be visited," or going through the actions necessary to become "in" with a group, he probably would have produced a valuable piece of writing.

> *The momentum of the mind is all toward abstraction.*
>
> WALLACE STEVENS

WRITING SEVEN: Write a case-history of some job, process, action —what happened through a period of time. An hour working at the telephone switchboard, a day in the body shop, one swimming lesson you gave a five-year-old, one vacation day when you did "nothing" for eight hours. If possible, take notes as you go through the experience, or right after the act, and record details you can remember.

Choose an action that is fun or misery for you, exciting or boring. Speak factually most of the time, as did Dr. Hachiya and the author of "The Birth of a Lamb." Make your reader respect you as an authority on this action by the way you reveal its intimate workings, but remember not to lose him in meaningless technical terms.

Pack in the detail but make it add up to reveal the essence of the job, or your feeling toward it. A case-history should be useful and fascinating. You can make it alive by remembering to keep asking "So what?" as you assemble materials and write. When the reader finishes your history, he should go away with one or two major impressions in mind, and possibly feelings, as well as a memory of close details.

Note how the following case-history of a few minutes at a music festival reveals the feelings of a performer and a judge. Like all good writing, it does not oversimplify. It centers on the embarrassment of one person and goes deeply into its complex causes. And so humorously.

REED

Maybe I could faint again. I did at the Solo-Ensemble Festival. Almost, anyway. That's where instrumentalists memorize a solo and go play it for a rating from some judge who knows all about whatever instrument it is and spends all his Saturdays listening to the same solos over and over. But I was playing along on mine and hoping I'd remember the next note because I'd only memorized the piece the night before and I kept getting short of breath and gulping. Pretty soon I felt faint but I thought I better keep going instead of being one of those whimpering fainting females. I began wondering what would happen if I did faint right there.

It would wreck the reed for sure. The reed is what makes the noise. No reed, no sound, and the hellmost torture for a clarinetist is wrecking a reed because the good ones cost forty-five cents apiece and only come in boxes of ten and only two or three of these will work with luck, and two or three won't work at all and the rest will just kind of thud a lot.

So when I thought of falling over on my good reed, I decided I better stop, so I asked the judge if I could stop for a while, except I said, "Sir, I feel faint." The judge was a heavy man who looked like he should have been bald, but he wasn't. Anyway, my accompanist hadn't heard me and it was at the end of a rest and I was supposed to come in again, so she kept playing my cue over and over. I walked over to the judge's desk and said I felt faint and wanted to sit down. He wore black glasses and looked at me over them like what was I doing stopping in the middle of a piece like that? I was supposed to just play and not interrupt his judging routine with sudden stops. He took my elbow and my clarinet, which he put on his desk after checking the make of instrument and mouthpiece I had because he was a devoted clarinetist and probably hated fainting whimpering females. I hoped then that I was using a fifteen dollar Kaspar mouthpiece some character sits around making by hand in Ann Arbor, except he's retired now. This is like my mother telling me to always wear pretty underwear in case I get hit by a car and have to go to the hospital. Maybe she said that because once she fell down the stairs and broke her leg and was embarrassed to tears at having to ride all the way to the hospital in an ambulance with ugly underwear.

The judge kept my elbow and showed me to a chair. He told me to "take a whole bunch of deep breaths." While I was doing that, a group of people came into the room because they thought I was through playing. It was supposed to be a science classroom regularly except that Saturday when clarinetists performed in it and people were only allowed to come in between performances. When I got up and started in the middle of the solo it puzzled them a little, but when I was through they clapped anyway and the judge told them they hadn't heard very much, but the rest was just as good. That's one of those devious, double-sided comments people say and leave a person wondering exactly what they meant for some time afterward. I volunteered to play the whole thing again but the judge kind of shoved me out to the hall and collapsed in a chair.

LOUISE FREYBURGER

If you prefer, you may write a history of someone else's actions. Choose what you can observe first-hand, clearly and completely— an incident or event you can sit and watch like a cat. Take notes. Ask questions if necessary. Get the facts right.

You might sit in the library and write down what you see for an hour. Sit opposite the circulation desk, close by, where you can hear and record what the clerk does and says in a half hour.

Think of what your finished writing will look like. Choose a process or event small enough in time and limited enough in scope that you can cover it with satisfactory thoroughness. Don't write a case-history of your high school career or a year's performance by the basketball captain. Each would require volumes. Aim at a paper of two to six pages, double-spaced if typewritten, a little more if in longhand.

REVISING FOUR: When you have finished your first draft of the case-history, put it aside for a day. Then read it aloud to see whether any leading idea or feeling emerges. If you find one stirring a little, consider cutting out those parts that do not touch this idea or feeling, and adding more details that strengthen it.

If you care about what you write, and know or observe it closely, you will reveal to your reader things he doesn't know. Stay awake when you observe. If you or other human beings are in action, the chances are high that you will be recording some fabulous realities.

One professional caution: Change any real names in your case-history to fictional names. What if your work becomes published, or passed around locally? What you consider an unbiased report of how Mrs. Smithweather, the science teacher, swore at John Saunders in lab may not strike Mrs. Smithweather in that way. If you had money, she might properly sue you for libel. Some real names you must keep in your writing or its point may be lost, but inspect all names and weigh the need to change them. Samuel Butler wrote a long book which became the classical English story of a sensitive son and a tyrannical, self-righteous father. Butler's real father was a sadist to him, but he refused to publish this book until after his father had died. And then it came out as a novel, with Butler's father carrying a fictional name. Butler himself died before *The Way of All Flesh* was published and he never knew that he had written one of the finest novels in the English language. The least you can do is protect Mrs. Smithweather and yourself by changing names.

> *It is much easier to sit at a desk and read plans for a billion gallons of water a day, and look at maps and photographs; but you will write a better article if you heave yourself out of a comfortable chair and go down in tunnel 3 and get soaked.*
>
> **STUART CHASE**

Repeat: *to double, re-double, renew, parallel, echo, match, mirror, reproduce, regenerate, reincarnate, multiply, revive, reaffirm, reassert, accentuate, emphasize, build, hammer, slap, thump, beat, bang, punch, jab, convince, charm, lull, caress.*

chapter 9
repeating

WEAK AND
STRONG REPETITION

IF SOMEONE you love keeps saying he loves you, the repetition is beautiful. But if someone you dislike keeps saying he loves you, the repetition is unbearable. And there are places and moments where you don't want to be told you are loved. Even the heartbeat, with its repetitious but slightly irregular liveliness, can become monotonous—for example, if recorded day after day in a laboratory.

Repetition can comfort or bore, clarify or confuse, astound or outrage. Consider these repetitions:

> I think Ethel was rebelling when she refused to follow my suggestion. She was rebelling against her ability to recover, her ability to heal, her ability to retain her youth. She had lost her youth, yet she was still fighting. Fighting for a lost cause.

They clog the passage rather than emphasize what needs to be emphasized.

The professional writer reads his work aloud to himself and to others. He hears repetitions his eyes did not see. The beginner and the professional need to find ways of getting inside their writing and hearing it objectively. One way is to listen for repetitions, which are easily detected. Those that the writer is surprised to find are usually weak: he didn't intend them. They may become valuable to him as flags indicating other failures or surrenders. If he didn't notice them before, he probably missed other weaknesses. Read the following passage aloud and you will find weak repetition. It will help you spot other weaknesses.

> One of the specific aspects of the speech was the question and answer period. I feel that the panel during the question and answering period was very biased in their questions to Governor Barnett of the state of Mississippi. In so much as the questions directed toward Governor Barnett were mostly concerned with segregation in general.

The passage needs massive cutting. Here is a possible revision:

> In the question and answer period, the panel was biased toward Governor Barnett of Mississippi. Most of the questions concerned segregation.

In another part of his column, this writer ran into a snag with the word *fact*.

> Governor Barnett has said that the North is just as segregated as the South. This is of course an overstatement of fact, but it still does contain a certain amount of fact. There are no signs forbidding Negroes from using a drinking fountain or from buying a bottle of Coke from a vending machine, but I have experienced prejudice in the North and even helped the cause of segregation in Lansing, Michigan.

The second sentence might be revised in this way:

> This is an overstatement but still contains a certain amount of fact.

Note that in both excerpts from this column, the writer employed weak repetition when he was generalizing, not when he was giving particular evidence. His last sentence in the second excerpt ("There are no signs . . .") is well written. In it he has found his voice and speaks with his natural powers.

Often weak repetition blooms when a writer tries to impress his reader, as in this passage:

> When one sits before an open hearth and can see the flames shooting from the burning wood, hear the crackling of the fire as it engulfs its source of fuel, and feel the

> warmth given off, one enters another "world," a "world"
> which is quiet and peaceful . . . You may ask why we
> spend so much time by the fire, and that should be a diffi-
> cult question to answer. But I believe it is the "mystery" of
> the fire that intrigues us. This "mystery" of the fire has a
> way of captivating your thoughts and putting you in a
> trance-like atmosphere.

Here again words appear close to each other in ineffectual repetition.
To show how unprofessional he is, the writer also puts quotation
marks around *world* and *mystery*—which he uses in the commonest
way—and insults his reader. Instead of saying the crackling fire
"engulfs its *wood*," he says "engulfs its *source of fuel*." He so feared
repetition that he went to ridiculous lengths to find a synonym. Wood
is fuel, but here the general subject of fuel is not being discussed.
If the writer cannot stand to hear the word *wood* repeated, he should
remove its first use, not its second. Then the passage would read:

> When one sits before an open hearth and watches the
> shooting flames, hears the crackling as the fire engulfs the
> wood, and feels the warmth given off . . .

Avoidance of repetition sometimes leads writers to silly substitutions
for a key word in a passage. If the principal subject of your writing
is *cats,* use the word *cats* frequently. Don't say *cats,* then *felines,
furry friends,* and *four-legged bundles of fur.* Sports writers often sin
with this "elegant variation." For example, a good sportswriter in a
student newspaper began his article with *The Rich track team.* Then
he calls them by their name *The Olympians.* Next he says, "Then
the squad began to show." Up to that point his variation in naming
is inoffensive, but next he says:

> Still improving, the Central cindermen then overran T. F.
> South and Lockport West, finishing the season in grand
> style. The Olympians captured nine firsts . . .

By that point the paper's regular readers are probably fatigued by
the writer's attempt to avoid repetition, and an outsider is probably
lost, wondering whether *the Central cindermen* still refers to *the Rich
track team* or to one of their opponents.

The writer who has found a voice that belongs to him repeats
words with power, not with weakness. If he wants to hit a word
hard, he repeats it. Dr. Seuss does:

Then Horton the elephant smiled. "Now that's that . . ."
And he sat
    and he sat
        and he sat
           and he sat . . .
And he sat all that day
And he kept the egg warm . . .
And he sat all that night
Through a *terrible* storm.

Thomas Paine, the pamphleteer who helped persuade colonists to join George Washington's army, wrote:

> I call not upon a few, but upon all: not on this state or that state, but on every state: up and help us; lay your shoulders to the wheel; better have too much force than too little when so great an object is at stake.

These repetitions helped create the United States.

In Shakespeare's *Macbeth,* Macduff speaks to Malcolm, reminding him of the sad state to which Scotland has fallen under the rule of the murdering King Macbeth:

>   Each new morn
> New widows howl, new orphans cry, new sorrows
> Strike heaven on the face, that it resounds
> As if it felt with Scotland and yelled out
> Like syllable of dolor.

Here the word *new* murders husbands, fathers, happiness, and creates widows, orphans, sorrows. It is not at all like the *new* which appears on so many packages of detergent, toothpaste, and shampoo in the supermarket. The manufacturer thinks the word will sell his product and he changes the product ever so slightly once a year, or changes it not at all, and stamps *new* on the package. Too many *new's* on packages have killed the force of them all.

Professional writers usually avoid starting a sentence with the same word that ends the preceding sentence:

> I found out his name was John. John was an engineer.
>
> The last topic on the program was rehabilitation. Rehabilitation is an urgent matter in Michigan because prisons are overcrowded.

In his second or third draft, the professional writer looks for repetitions of this sort—he knows they will be there—and expunges them. But frequently he achieves his best repetition unconsciously. An idea, or a fact, often epitomized in a key word, dominates his mind. He repeats it when he writes.

A good way to utilize repetition without being dull is to shift the form of the repeated word, or play with it in some way. Here a writer makes the word *uncivilized* speak to the word *civilized*:

> **I don't like picnics. That's against the great American tradition, I guess. I don't like to combine the civilized way of eating with uncivilized surroundings.**

When you write out a first draft hurriedly, you may find one key word appearing again and again. Before you eliminate the repetitions of it, think twice. Some of the repetitions may give strength to your writing and let the reader know what objects or ideas dominate your thought. Here is a memory of childhood that needs cutting. It contains too much good writing to be allowed to remain in this state marred by weak repetitions. But some of its repetitions are essential; for example, of the word *outside,* which is central to the writer's point. (Some of the major repetitions are indicated here in italics.)

> **Summer seems more fun during childhood. I remember those *screen-door days.* The back *door* to my house was covered with two sections of *screen* that bulged from being pushed by an endless chain of small hands. I doubt that the *door* was ever shut without a *bang*; in fact it seemed to be there for the sole purpose of shutting with a *bang.* To butt out that *door* without hearing the familiar b-r-r-zing *BANG!* would have been as unnatural to me as giving my sister some of my candy—well almost. I was always in a great hurry to get *outside.* Summer is an *outside* time. I had an outside mind. I could only think in *outside.* Sometimes in my haste to join my mind *outside,* I would fly at the *door* only to discover, too late, that a security-conscious grandmother or some such menace of childhood had locked it. I would come to a tire-tearing halt, like a cartoon car stopping on a dime. I had to peel my face off the *screen* like a waffle, and looking very much like one only with much smaller squares. I would *cuss* at whoever locked the *door.* If I did not know who the culprit was I would *cuss* at**

everyone just to be on the safe side. However my anger was silent, or mutterings at best. My mother's children left much to be desired where brains are concerned, but she did not rear any of us to be *stupid,* at least not so *stupid* as to be caught *swearing.* My father was a great strong *swearer.* He could invoke deities and conjure up demons that made my bottom sore before the *belt* was even off his waist. I was always puzzled by the fact that I could say *"god-darn"* this and *"god-darn"* that depending on whatever I wanted *God* to mend, and yet *"goddamn"* always removed the belt from my father's waist. The sin was in the "damn" not in the "God." I always wondered what God thought about it and how big a belt he had.

MICHAEL MANUEL

In this reflection on childhood, the notion of *outside* is crucial to the story because it is the urge to get outside quickly that led the boy to swear and to confront his father and think upon the effects and causes of profanity. But too much emphasis on *outside* and the screen door makes the ending discussion of profanity seem like an afterthought rather than the major subject the writing builds toward.

Here is a revision of the story with a number of the repetitions cut out:

> The back *door* to my house was covered with two sections of *screen* that bulged from being pushed by an endless chain of small hands. That *door* seemed to be there for the sole purpose of being slammed. To butt out it without hearing the familiar b-r-r-zing BANG! would have been as unnatural to me as giving my sister some of my candy.
>
> I could only think in *outside.* Sometimes in my haste to join my mind *outside,* I would fly at the *door* only to discover too late that a security-conscious grandmother had locked it. I would come to a halt like a cartoon car stopping on a dime and would peel my face off the *screen* like a waffle. Then I would cuss—at everyone, just to be on the safe side—but silently, mutteringly. Mother did not rear us to be so stupid as to be caught *swearing.*
>
> Father was a great strong *swearer.* He could invoke deities and conjure up demons that made my bottom sore before the *belt* was off his waist. I was always puzzled because I could say *"god-darn"* this and *"god-darn"* that,

depending on whatever I wanted *God* to mend, and yet
"god-damn" always removed the belt from Father's waist.
The sin was in the *"damn"* not in the *"God."* I always
wondered what *God* thought about it and how big a *belt*
he wore.

Repetitions remain but they are necessary, therefore not tedious
but powerful. To gain their full effect, some words should not be
repeated at all. The writer should save them strategically for one
best moment. In the above story if the word *bang* is to sound loud,
it should be heard only once.

Rhyme is a form of repetition, of sound, not word. It can be
used in prose if the writer remembers that its effect there is customarily humorous. Lilian Moore wrote a book she called *A Pickle
for a Nickel* in which she had Mr. Bumble say truly, "Boys like noise."

REVISING FIVE: Examine your story about childhood. Omit the
weak repetitions and consider adding strong repetitions. Use penciled
brackets so that you may restore words or phrases should you later
change your mind.

WRITING EIGHT: Dash off two 10- to 15-minute free writings in
which you play frequently with repetition. Repeat words in as many
different patterns as you can. Repeat a word three times in a row,
then repeat it as the key word in three phrases: "He was a bumbling
carpenter, a bumbling father, a bumbling fisherman." Then separate
the repeated words even more from each other. Try repeating all kinds
of words—verbs, adverbs, prepositions, adjectives, nouns, etc. Use a
word once with one meaning and then with another meaning. If you
feel stalled, study advertisements in magazines and commercials on
television to find still other ways to repeat. Study poems; almost all
good ones repeat words skillfully. In all your practice in repeating,
do not make up nonsense phrases or sentences that are lists of words
unrepresentative of thoughts or feelings in you. Try always to say
something you mean but play while you do that. Play around—seriously.

PARALLEL CONSTRUCTION

One of the fundamental beats in all good writing is parallel construction, which is based on repetition. No competent writer's ear is
deaf to it. Take this statement:

**George liked Jean and often walked beside her on the way
to school. Jean was also sometimes accompanied to school by**

Ronald, who also liked her, but who often could be seen walking behind her.

Here is a shorter version:

George liked Jean and often walked beside her on the way to school. Jean was also accompanied by Ronald, who walked behind her.

But it is still awkward. Seeing that the sentences compare George's and Ronald's walking with Jean, the professional writer would cast each part of the comparison in parallel form:

George liked Jean and walked beside her to school. Ronald liked Jean and walked behind her to school.

Tightened and paralleled in this fashion, the sentences now emphasize that Ronald was bashful. They could be paralleled in another way:

The boys liked Jean. George walked beside her to school and Ronald behind her.

At the same time that most parallel patterning throws into simple and dramatic comparison two or more ideas or persons or things, it shortens a statement so severely that it requires work from the reader. This is an ideal combination of qualities: challenge and delight.

The writer who wonders how his words will strike his reader need only ask how they strike him as he patterns them. If he finds himself unchallenged or bored, he should know he is not writing well. His words should speak to him as well as to his audience—and to each other. Parallel patterning helps give them voice. Here is a beginning writer making words speak to each other:

I like to bounce when I get into bed, and pick up my pillow and throw it down, then pick up my head and drop it into the pillow, like someone picking up a little kitten and dropping it in some out of the way place so that it won't get *under* foot. Good thing I've got the upper bunk . . . I couldn't be any more *out* from *under* foot.

Train your ear so you hear a word when you write it, and then ask whether it needs an answer from another word soon. Here is a beginning writer who was listening as he wrote:

Why not be natural, free, untimed, unlimited?

Here is a professional advertising writer listening as he wrote:

> You ought to watch Longchamps meat experts buying
> beef for your dinner. They stride through the refrigerators,
> sniffing and poking each rib on the rack. They know what's
> what. So butchers give them their best. Well marbled steaks,
> tender as butter. Naturally aged meat, with a rich, beefy
> taste. Longchamps experts are tough. That's why Long-
> champs steaks are tender . . .

All writers who want to hammer an idea employ repetition and
parallel construction. A high school girl gets out her hammer in the
following article from the Lakeview High School *Crystal* of Battle
Creek, Michigan (May 6, 1966):

> NASTY NAZI SYMBOL OR HARMLESS FAD?
>
> **Most teenage fads are inoffensive and short-lived. A current
> fad in Battle Creek is far from inoffensive and should be
> stopped at once.**
>
> **Teenagers are adorning themselves with symbols of Ger-
> man militarism such as German army helmets. Some are
> wearing an Iron Cross on a chain around their neck. Else-
> where, the Nazi swastika is in style.**
>
> **These symbols recall the death of 291,000 Americans and
> the slaughter of six million Jews.**
>
> **They recall an upheaval during and after the war, started
> by a man who used the swastika as the symbol of an evil
> philosophy.**
>
> **Human memories are short, but not so short that they
> blot out this devastating period of history.**
>
> **These military symbols are probably just an expression
> of rebellion. Some kinds of rebellion are healthy. This kind
> is sick.**
>
> JANICE NEMRAVA

Here are some parallel patterns in the writing of professionals. Read
them aloud to yourself and put them into your reservoir of sounds.
Later when you are writing, you may hear echoes.

1. Every day, the sun; and, after sunset, Night and her stars.
   Ever the winds blow; ever the grass grows. Every day, men and
   women, conversing—beholding and beholden.

   RALPH WALDO EMERSON

2. We have rates by the hour, day, week, month, or by the job.

DICK'S KALAMAZOO JANITOR SERVICE,
YELLOW-PAGES ADVERTISEMENT.

3. Other people cannot see what I see whenever I look into your father's face, for behind your father's face as it is today are all those other faces which were his. Let him laugh and I see a cellar your father does not remember and a house he does not remember and I hear in his present laughter his laughter as a child.

JAMES BALDWIN

4. Cut flowers at proper stage of development. Dahlias when fully open; gladioli when first floret is open; peonies when petals are unfolding; roses before buds open. In general, cut while in bud.

The Pocket Household Encyclopedia

5. Remember that young uncooked spinach makes a good salad; that cooked buttered spinach and grapefruit salad are an ideal reducer's luncheon; and that cooked spinach greens are superb with Hollandaise Sauce . . .

IRMA S. ROMBAUER AND MARION ROMBAUER BECKER

WRITING NINE: Write two 10-minute free writings comparing two objects, acts, or persons. Let yourself drift frequently into parallel patterns. Do not try to make every sentence parallel, but seize upon whatever opportunities present themselves.

Before you start writing, read this passage by a student playing with the ideas in this chapter:

I get the feeling that I repeat myself. I get the feeling that I repeat other people. I get the feeling that other people repeat me. I get the feeling that other people repeat things about me. I get the feeling that I get a lot of feelings.

*. . . the mere act of reading aloud put
his work before him in a new light and,
by constraining his attention to every
line, made him judge it more rigorously.
I always intend to read, and generally
do read, what I write aloud to some one;
any one almost will do, but he should
not be so clever that I am afraid of him.
I feel weak places at once when I read
aloud where I thought, as long as I read
to myself only, that the passage was all
right.*

SAMUEL BUTLER

chapter 10
the
helping
circle

ALMOST EVERY GOOD WRITER has learned
to write in circles. First, he writes for himself and then reads aloud
his writing and listens. It sounds different, as if it had made a circle
and become someone else's writing. He can judge it better.

Second, he reads it to a friend or member of the family. Now it
sounds different than it did when he read it to himself. He begins to
sense how the writing may come across to another person who didn't
share the experiences and feelings he wrote about. The listener doesn't
have to say anything, but simply be there—and the writing becomes
an object apart from the writer. He's getting objective about it.

The writer can ask the listener to tell how he felt when the writing
was being read to him. But that presses the listener, for he is the
only one responding. What if he wasn't moved by it? or couldn't follow it? He hates to say anything that may hurt. That's why—especially

in the beginning—a student is lucky to be in a large circle of responders. For they feel less strain in speaking frankly of the writing. They
know there will be others who will agree with them, and some who
will not. The differing opinions make the comments easier for the
writer to take. He can carry them home with him, and later decide
which he will use or ignore.

So the circle—at times it will frighten every writer—is the writer's
third best resource. The first is his own experience (including his
thoughts, feelings, and knowledge picked up from others). Second
is his skills as a writer. And third is the help the circle can give him
to hone those skills.

In the beginning of a course, the writer is unsure. He should
be given only encouragement. So the group agrees to comment on
what they like in initial free writings. If they don't like a piece of
writing they hear, they say nothing. That's not a lie. It's a helpful
decision not to talk. If they like anything about the writing—a word,
phrase, ending, idea—they say so. Perhaps the writing puts them in
an event fully enough to call up a similar feeling they thought no
one else had experienced. After three or four meetings, when enough
free writing has been done that everyone or almost everyone has heard
praise of his writing from the circle, the prohibition against negative
comments may be dropped.

> *Think of and look at your work as
> though it were done by your enemy.
> If you look at it to admire it you are
> lost . . . If we look at it to see where
> it is wrong, we shall see this and make
> it righter. If we look at it to see where
> it is right, we shall see this and shall not
> make it righter. We cannot see it both
> wrong and right at the same time.*
>
> SAMUEL BUTLER

Now imagine yourself in the circle. The following piece of writing
by one of the members has just been read aloud.

IT'S SUNDAY

**It's Sunday, and I'm in church. The Mass has just started,
and it's particularly warm and crowded. The lady on my
left is wearing great amounts of a stifling dime-store perfume, and the little old Italian woman on my right smells
strongly of garlic mingled with whiskey. One of the women**

in front of me (I think she's wearing last year's hat with new plastic flowers) just pointed out to the other that Madge Russell sewed the rip in her black coat with brown thread. Oh, and the good mother in the last pew hasn't stopped slapping her six children once to participate in the service.

Lucy Dowden, the first one in line for communion, has been seeing her husband's best friend for the past two weeks—or so they say. And look at that lady in the third pew, the elderly one in shocking pink. She forgot to zip up her dress all the way. The kids in back of her are showing no mercy. They're carrying on so loudly that everyone's noticed her now. Sally and Deb are up there talking—probably about poor Mr. Cronson's ulcers. They think he has them because his daughter had to get married.

The two women in front of me are gossiping so intently that they have huge perspiration rings under their arms. I wonder who they're talking about now. Maybe if I kneel up straighter I can hear. Why, they're talking about me! The nerve of them! Why don't they just take part in the Mass instead of looking around and minding everyone else's business? Some of the biggest hypocrites go to church on Sundays, don't they?

In the circle no one calls on you. You speak up if you have strong feelings. Truthfully. The moment you or anyone else in the circle makes a phony comment to please the writer or teacher, or to show off his own knowledge, the power of the circle is diminished. It may not be killed, but it is weakened; and such wounds will continue to disable it unless energy is restored.

As you are listening to the story being read aloud, try to read your reactions. And when the end comes, check in on your feelings, as if you were connecting the jack plug for the earphone to your transistor radio. Then you can simply report your feelings. You don't have to say something you think the teacher wants to hear, something profound. You don't have to use literary terms. The writer doesn't care about them. He wants to know whether he has scored with you, made you believe, moved you enough that you may remember his writing tomorrow or next week or month. If you don't know why you liked or disliked it, he still wants to know that it moved you. He doesn't have to know the reasons. He'd like to know them, but he'll take the general reaction if that's all he can get. If you say you liked the piece, and don't know why, perhaps another in the circle will help you see why. And thus you will both help the writer.

Here's an honest response to "It's Sunday" from the author of this book:

"I liked it. I was led along by all the unfriendly remarks about the people in church—and I believed them, maybe because of details like 'huge perspiration rings under the arms'—and it all began to get pretty ugly for me. Then I was surprised at the turn at the ending: 'They're talking about me!' I didn't know it was going to go that way and I'm glad it did. I believed so much in the people in church, and I despised them along with the author. So when she (or he) showed that she was herself being talked about while she was calling the others hypocrites, I not only knew she was a hypocrite but that I have been one like that myself."

At that point, I would stop talking. That's enough. Give someone else a chance.

In the circle, Lisa says—thinking about how much tightening has helped her own writing—"I think you could do without the word *particularly* before *warm* and the word *strongly* before *of garlic*. When your nose meets garlic and whiskey together, the smell must have been strong."

Carol says, "I like it. It makes me laugh. It's so real." And the writer feels wonderful. She wants to go home and write another story.

Ted says, "The little things—forgot to zip up that shocking pink dress all the way, and the daughter had to get married—I liked them. It's very short, but it gets a lot said." And the writer feels like writing more stories.

Francis says, "I'd like to see the last three sentences dropped altogether. I already got the idea that if the other people in church are hypocrites because they are looking around and minding everyone else's business, then the writer was also hypocritical. Because that's what she was doing, too."

Mike says, "Well, yeah, you and I may be smart enough to get that, but maybe some reader wouldn't be. I'd like to see it end the way it does, just to make sure."

Carol says, "Don't be so sure other people are going to be that dumb. I'd like to see the story end with 'Why, they're talking about me!' That makes a great ending—wham!"

Gerald says, "I think it's a fine piece of writing. I agree that the details are terrific—like 'kneeling up straighter' so she can listen. But I'll have to say, and I hate to say it, that the whole thing doesn't grab me as much as it did some of the rest of you. I'm tired of writings making fun of people in church."

If left there, the discussion may now have turned for the writer. We are all sensitive. At that point the writer might have gone home thinking that the initial praise for her writing was not representative. She may have remembered the comments about the words *particularly* and *strong,* the two assertions that her ending was weak, and the last comment about picking on churchgoers. And she may have been discouraged from working further on this writing or giving her full effort on subsequent papers.

But the fact may be that everyone in the circle except the last speaker, Gerald, liked the story a great deal. Those who made small suggestions were only trying to help make what they thought a fine story perfect. So it is helpful for the members of the circle to try to sense how full a response the writer is getting. Just the comment "I thought it was great" or "I really liked it" from half or more of the group will ensure that the writer's confidence is not destroyed. And the danger on the other side must be considered also: if most persons were not moved by the writing, the writer should be told. No need to insult her, a great need to help her keep going as a beginning writer—but still truth from the circle.

As the course progresses, the members of the circle will become more and more adept at helping. At any given moment they will perceive who needs encouragement, who needs facing up to his weaknesses. A supposedly helpful comment this week may be damaging, although two weeks from now it may be helpful. You can wait until a writer can use this suggestion or that.

> *He [Ezra Pound] was a marvelous critic because he didn't try to turn you into an imitation of himself. He tried to see what you were trying to do.*
>
> T. S. ELIOT

Not all writings that come before the circle will be as short and clear as "It's Sunday." The following story, for example, strikes me as exciting. But it does not satisfy me, and I do not know what to suggest to the author about it.

OLE EDNA

Good ole Edna Mulloney. When I try to picture her all I see is knees. She used to sit at the table on the platform in

study hall, her knees, top of her hose, and garters showing
under a skirt that was too short. And her toeless shoes with
the little bows. Next I see her sagging bust in a tight
sweater. She always wore suits with a sweater and there
was always a wrinkle across the front of her skirt. It was
either too tight or just wrinkled from sitting. She had
fuzzy, wild grey hair and an automatic or mechanical pencil—anyway the kind you put lead in. Not a wood one.
That pencil. It was so much a part of her as an arm or
leg. While she talked and gestured, it clicked. It flew across
the room the day she slapped Red Tompkins across the
face. She seemed flustered because she'd lost control. I
don't think anybody made a sound for the rest of the
period. There was quite a buzz around school about it but
nothing ever happened. That was 7th or 8th grade. And
she used to send me up to the Ag Room when she caught
me chewing gum in class. The Ag Room—tiny, and it had
a skylight. It was in a condemned part of the building on
the top floor. Mr. Cannon, the principal, would be there
teaching the Ag Class—about 10 or 15 junior and senior
boys. I just knocked on the door, said Mrs. Mulloney sent
me, and sat down, hoping he wouldn't say much. And he
didn't. He just went on teaching class. I can't remember
that he ever asked me why I was there and I was there
pretty often. Eventually she stopped sending me up to the
Ag class. I know I didn't stop chewing gum. I think I just
became better at concealing it. The walls were really ugly,
tan on the bottom, cream on the top, the colors chosen by
the same person who chooses the colors for prisons. Big
ugly windows with dirty tan or green shades except once in
a while when I'd look out and the sun was shining and
the trees and the grass were so green.

Mrs. Mulloney lived in East Linden and raised cocker
spaniels. I don't think she had any children. She taught
Latin and had studied in Rome. I remember my mother
telling me she was a very fine, well educated teacher. She
had studied abroad. That doesn't necessarily make her a
good teacher. I liked her Latin class but I can't remember
much about her English class except that we had to write
our autobiography and try to begin it some other way than
I was born in so and so on such and such a date. That
autobiography was really dull. Engfish. All it had was dates

and places and not what I felt, which would have made it the story of *my* life. Anyone can make a list of dates and addresses. I knew it was uninteresting but I couldn't figure out why. In school nobody cared what I thought. All they were interested in was what they thought I should learn.

In the circle, after others had had a chance to comment, I might say this: "That opening picture of Edna is marvelous. 'All I see is knees'—that's great. And the big fuss about chewing gum is good. It tells so much about school. But I think the story needs rearranging. It doesn't build for me. It's got little pieces that are wonderful—the walls like prison, the great statement about nobody in school caring what she thought. And the last sentence—I think it's one of the best indictments of school I've ever read. But altogether, the story doesn't connect. You go from Edna to Mr. Cannon, to walls like prison, back to Edna and cocker spaniels, on to writing autobiography, and then the general statement about school. It's probably a first draft and simply needs some reviewing. I'm sorry I can't say now how it might be reordered."

At that moment someone else in the circle might suggest a solution. If not, the writer must find one when she has time to read the piece over several times and think about it. Maybe more could be added, maybe something dropped. The persons in the circle can make suggestions, but they shouldn't feel responsible for the final rewriting of any work presented to them.

> *A writer is unfair to himself when he is unable to be hard on himself.*
>
> MARIANNE MOORE

As a member of the circle, you are party to a contract. Others will help you. You must speak up and help them. If only a few members respond and the others remain silent, there is no circle. If one person dominates, soon others will not listen to him, no matter how wise his comments. This group can become literally a circle of energy. You have probably seldom experienced a relationship like this in which a group of people are praising your work and helping you make it better—or saying it's weak and helping you make it better. Over the weeks and months that helping spirit builds. It can give you the confidence to do what you've never done before, if you will take part in the circle. When everyone is responding to others' writing, then the writing and the responding improve.

If you don't keep up in your writing, but continue to comment on others' work, they will eventually resent your remarks. They will think: "You are not pulling your weight here. What right have you to tell me what's wrong with my writing?" If you write powerfully and consistently and receive praise from the circle but refuse to help others, they will resent you for two reasons: You are not being fair, and as a powerful writer you are especially qualified to help the rest of them.

The most surprising outcome of working in the circle is that your remarks about the other person's writing will help your own writing. When you comment on how a writing might end better or why its metaphors are strong, you are printing that thought about writing on your brain more sharply than when you simply have the thought. Speaking it under the pressure of the group makes it yours, perhaps forever. One day writing a metaphor or an ending, you will think of what you once said in the circle, and your help to another person will become help to you.

SOME REMINDERS TO CIRCLERS:

1. Avoid beginning comments about a writing with small points. First, let the writer know your large reaction, especially if it is positive. Then later in the discussion bring up the small suggestion; for example, to cut a word or change a phrase.

2. If you are the leader in the circle, don't let an argument drag on about a point that has been discussed fully. You can say, "Well, John has now been given several alternatives. He can take them home and decide which one he wants to use in re-writing his work, or he can turn down all of them." The circle is not a debating society but a gathering of helpers.

3. If you find yourself talking too much or too little, remember that the most helpful responder presents his best thought—the one most apt to surprise and be useful. He resists the impulse to make obvious comments.

4. If you feel reluctant to talk, think of your responsibility to others. Responsibility—ability to respond. There is no other you in the world. No other person with the same set of past experiences. Only you can say what you feel and think, what *your* response to a writing was. That is what every serious writer is looking for: the effect of his writing upon individuals. You can't say anything wrong to him if you truthfully report your response to his work. And you may help him a lot.

5. Occasionally close your eyes while listening to a writing being read. But only in a circle whose members already know that listeners are apt to do that on purpose, not because they are bored.

6. As a responder you can sometimes draw out another responder who is reluctant to speak fully his feelings. "You said the story was too cute. Can you say more about why you felt that way?"

7. As a writer listening to comments on your own work, you may turn off the help if you start defending your writing too quickly or vigorously. "Well, I didn't mean by that ending to suggest I knew it all." Or "Maybe you're just too dumb to understand that passage. You know one of the eight fundamentals of writing is to make the reader work." That sort of response may generate attacks rather than help. Wise and strong writers look everywhere for help. They want to make their writing as powerful as it can be. At times, they encourage a responder to tell them more and more. To a hostile or highly critical remark they may say, "Yeah, O.K.," or "Thanks." They should be thankful for any comments. They cannot expect that every comment will be helpful. They know that at times they have been hurt and irritated when their work is being discussed and then later at home, with time to simmer down, they have found that some of the suggestions they resented are valuable, and they use them.

8. Here's a trap to watch out for. If you hear a writing read in the circle about a grandmother, you may begin thinking about your own grandmother and then say, "I liked your story because my grandmother's like that, too." That's a human reaction and touches one of the reasons we write: to show each other we have had similar experiences. But by itself it's no proof that the writing was strong. When a paper read in the circle turns you to your own experience, check it out carefully. Did it put you in the writer's experience powerfully? Did his grandmother—or whatever—come alive, or was she merely a trigger for your memory?

9. When there is too much writing to be read and helped in the circle, break the circle into smaller circles. If a paper is read in one of the smaller groups that demands hearing by the whole group, make sure it gets a later hearing, or publishing on the bulletin board or in a handout for everyone.

10. When you are the writer taking comments from the circle, remember that you are the final authority about your own work. No one can insist that you follow the advice you get. You are to weigh everything you hear and use what you think will help your writing. But weigh—don't throw it back before you put it on the scale.

COLLECTING FIVE: Lest this chapter should remain too general, here is a specific matter that every responder and writer should ponder [Good echo of sound—*responder, ponder*? No. And now that I look

at that sentence closely, I see that the command "every responder
and writer should ponder" is insulting to my readers. Sounds like
Mother dressing the kids for church. And I don't need the comment
about the chapter perhaps remaining too general. Just give the facts,
Macrorie, without the lecture. So I'll start again]:

You can help people in the circle find worn-out expressions in
their writing. You do not need to pounce on them gleefully and
scornfully. You can simply say calmly, "And I found several clichés—
Line 5, 'in the final analysis'; last paragraph, 'with tender loving
care.'" And the writer can remove them later if she sees fit.

Copy in your journal a dozen or more clichés you find in print
and in the writing of your classmates. Here are some examples, along
with fresh expressions which possess their own unique truth. Some of
the latter were written by junior-high students:

CLICHÉS	FRESH EXPRESSIONS
1. out of the clear blue sky	1. That man is hairless as a window.
2. cold shivers up my back	
3. eyes glued	2. If this kid was a dog, he looks like he's been chasing parked cars and punched his nose in.
4. down in the dumps	
5. racked our brains	
6. broke my heart	3. Her mouth looks like she has been eating red candy and got it all over.
7. lump in my throat	
8. safe and sound	
9. well aware	4. His eyes look like you picked them up from a kids' marble game, big and brown.
10. one and only	
11. last but not least	
12. not a care in the world	5. It was quiet in the woods and smelled of hot pine trees.
13. heavy as a rock	
14. light as a feather	6. His wooden leg was lying on the bedroom floor by the side of his bed, on the rug, like a faithful dog.
	7. I watched her trace the path of the blood [on a medical chart] and felt my heart pumping.
	8. All the colors outside are muted as if someone forgot to dust off the trees and grass.
	9. I turned my head to the side, resting it on his shoulder and could feel his warm Listerine breath on the back of my neck.

There was a Boy ...
                                        many a time
At evening, when the earliest stars began
To move along the edges of the hills,
Rising or setting, would he stand alone
Beneath the trees or by the glimmering
            lake,
And there, with fingers interwoven, both
            hands
Pressed closely palm to palm, and to his
            mouth
Uplifted, he, as through an instrument,
Blew mimic hootings to the silent
            owls ...

                    WILLIAM WORDSWORTH

chapter 11

remember-
ing
childhood

ACHIEVING DISTANCE

REMEMBERING CHILDHOOD is not childish, but wise and sweet and necessary. We go back because we loved those years of play. We go back because remembering moves us closer to the children around us today. We go back because in writing through these years we gain a second life.

The best writers take this journey. Mark Twain wrote *Huckleberry Finn*, a novel about a boy with a gifted tongue, who once said:

It would get so dark that it looked all blue-black outside, and lovely; and the rain would thrash along by so thick

87

that the trees off a little ways looked dim and spider-webby; and here would come a blast of wind that would bend the trees down and turn up the pale underside of the leaves; and then a perfect ripper of a gust would follow along and set the branches to tossing their arms as if they was just wild; and next, when it was just about the bluest and blackest—*fst!* it was as bright as glory and you'd have a little glimpse of tree-tops a-plunging about, away off yonder in the storm, hundreds of yards further than you could see before; dark as sin again in a second, and now you'd hear the thunder let go with an awful crash and then go rumbling, grumbling, tumbling down the sky towards the under side of the world, like rolling empty barrels down-stairs, where it's long stairs and they bounce a good deal, you know.

J. D. Salinger wrote about another boy with gifted tongue, who cherished his little sister Phoebe:

She was laying there asleep, with her face sort of on the side of the pillow. She had her mouth way open. It's funny. You take adults, they look lousy when they're asleep and they have their mouths way open, but kids don't. Kids look all right. They can even have spit all over the pillow and they still look all right.

And the best poets go back to childhood. May Swenson went back like this:

THE CENTAUR

The summer that I was ten—
Can it be there was only one
summer that I was ten? It must

have been a long one then—
each day I'd go out to choose
a fresh horse from my stable

which was a willow grove
down by the old canal.
I'd go on my two bare feet.

But when, with my brother's jack-knife,
I had cut me a long limber horse
with a good thick knob for a head,

and peeled him slick and clean
except a few leaves for the tail,
and cinched my brother's belt

around his head for a rein,
I'd straddle and canter him fast
up the grass bank to the path,

trot along in the lovely dust
that talcumed over his hoofs,
hiding my toes, and turning

his feet to swift half-moons.
The willow knob with the strap
jouncing between my thighs

was the pommel and yet the poll
of my nickering pony's head.
My head and my neck were mine,

yet they were shaped like a horse.
My hair flopped to the side
like the mane of a horse in the wind.

My forelock swung in my eyes,
my neck arched and I snorted.
I shied and skittered and reared,

stopped and raised my knees,
pawed at the ground and quivered.
My teeth bared as we wheeled

and swished through the dust again.
I was the horse and the rider,
and the leather I slapped to his rump

spanked my own behind.
Doubled, my two hoofs beat
a gallop along the bank,

the wind twanged in my mane,
my mouth squared to the bit.
And yet I sat on my steed

quiet, negligent riding,
my toes standing the stirrups,
my thighs hugging his ribs.

At a walk we drew up to the porch.
I tethered him to a paling.
Dismounting, I smoothed my skirt

and entered the dusky hall.
My feet on the clean linoleum
left ghostly toes in the hall.

Where have you been? said my mother.
Been riding, I said from the sink,
and filled me a glass of water.

What's that in your pocket? she said.
Just my knife. It weighted my pocket
and stretched my dress awry.

Go tie back your hair, said my mother,
and *Why is your mouth all green?*
*Rob Roy, he pulled some clover
as we crossed the field,* I told her.

These persons wrote of childhood at the height of their mature powers. If you are under twenty, you need even more than they to write of childhood. A writer requires about seven years of distance between him and the events he recalls. Then he is unfamiliar enough with them to feel the need to relate them fully for his readers and for himself. If he writes of yesterday's or last year's events, he usually remembers them so well he leaves them shrouded in his nearby intimate memory, which the reader does not share. James Boatwright, editor of *Shenandoah* magazine, says that few writers in their teens can write strongly of anything but their childhood. You may hope he is not right but you should start where you are most likely to achieve success. Do not search for tasks in which you will probably fail. Proceed, as this book suggests, from success to success.

> *But don't expect to write well about the love affair that you are in the midst of, or have just mailed a letter to break off. One principal figure in that situation you can't see. At least one. Probably two. You are "involved." You don't surround it. You suffer or you triumph; you do not comprehend.*
>
>   *Later, all those feelings will become your knowledge. They will be of your knowledge and your wisdom when they no longer possess you. Your subject must be something you possess and can move all the way around. The former feelings that come together in your sub-*

ject may include the most glorious or devastating that you ever had. And you will re-experience them. But you must emotionally enclose and dominate them.

SIDNEY COX

Consider the skill with which this high school student wrote of her childhood. Her name is withheld because she is writing candidly of her family.

BIRD

I sneaked back into my room, waited. I heard the light thud on the stairs. The floor creaked. The dress hangers swung squeakily on the door as it opened, then closed. I counted to ten, held my breath, listened. A soft shuffling sound came from the darkened room next to mine. Then with the squeak of springs came the shrill cry. A click. A spurt of choked sobbing began when the light went on. Rapid thuds sounded across the floor, door slammed, footsteps pounded down the stairs.

When the sound was gone, I crept from my bedroom to the stairway. Holding myself with my feet, I stuck my head through the bars and leaned down over the ledge. The room at the bottom of the stairs was dark, but I saw a light shining from the kitchen. Still, I could only hear a disturbed mumble and irregular sobs. My head was feeling heavy and since my position didn't let me hear the talk below, I inched back to bed without anyone else hearing.

I didn't think Suzie would act like that. She was a smart big sister, not the sissy type to get upset by a dead bird on her pillow. After all, the soft, smelly part had rotted off long before I found the bird. Now all it was was a delicate spine and skull with a few feathers sticking out at the neck. I liked it because of its pink and purple colors. No one else liked it. But my mother let me keep it when I told her I would keep it in my bedroom with my piece of driftwood. She didn't like my driftwood, either. Suzie had even handled my bird before. Now she had probably smashed its spine when she lay on it and maybe pulled some of the feathers off. She had been downstairs now long enough to stop her crying bit and to tell on me.

I heard someone; maybe she was coming. I started to go tell her that I didn't think she was going to take it so hard. But, no, it was a heavy, steady beat on the stairs. The sound came near my closed door. Silence. The beat, steady again, moved into Suzie's room. I fell asleep as the sound closed in on my room, but I woke up the next minute to see my father staring down. He had turned my bright light on, so I squinted up, looking sleepy and innocently asked what was going on. I knew that was a bad question when I saw my bird in his hand. He replied by asking where my driftwood was. I told him and he got it. And I told him I didn't see why everyone was making such a big fuss about the bird. He gave me the usual line about "never do that again." Then he told me how Suzie was really upset and that she was going to spend the night on our play room davenport. He left without really scolding me. He probably didn't see how my bird could scare anyone, either.

I didn't really believe that Suzie would stay on the davenport all night. And I thought she would want to come get mad at me herself. So I fluffed my pillow, lay down, and waited. All I heard was the garbage can lid slam down.

The humor of this story comes from the writer telling matter-of-factly of her childhood outrage at her sister's refusal to enjoy going to bed with a skeleton of a bird, yet at the same time letting the reader know that now she knows her sister had reason to be upset. The writer tells the reader enough, but not too much. She puts the reader there, listening for the sister's reaction down below. She makes the bird really dead, remembering "the smelly part had rotted off," and liking it "because of its pink and purple colors." She chose surprising attitudes to write about; so she keeps the reader off balance while telling him consistent and believable truth. She knows that bird and her family. When her father comes up the stairway, the reader probably expects a bawling out. Instead, father disapproves without scolding, and thus comes over as a real man, not a stereotyped parent.

This story is almost professional in its skill, but it could be polished further. It communicates sounds precisely: "a spurt of choked sobbing," "The beat, steady again, moved into Suzie's room." Almost every sentence makes the reader want to know what is going to happen next. And yet the repetition of *thud-thuds* and *squeakily-squeak,* all in the first paragraph, is weak.

Here is another young person's story about childhood:

ORANGE

A pitcher of orange drink fell over in the refrigerator and trickled out onto the floor, creeping along, where the tile meets the green of the living room carpet. I hate orange pop. It makes me think of our church picnics, which always had an over abundance of that too sweet nectar—the junk that kids consume by the gallon and end up vomiting up by the end of the day under some dwarfed tree in the corner of a baseball field. I was a champ at it—only I intermingled bottles of orange drink with cups of soft, white ice cream that slid down my throat (after the tenth or so) like chunks of plaster of Paris. Still I shoveled it in and then ran in the races. I won, of course, to the delight of my ego and the sorrow of my stomach.

Splash! We were in the creek. About a half dozen of Mrs. Sallay's Sunday School sweethearts couldn't make it through the day without plunging into the muddy creek while walking the narrow branches stretched from bank to bank. I never missed the fun, year after year. Was I sick by the end of the day! I remember clinging to the trunk of a very small friend, watching fat, bald shirtless men loudly oppose the young boys in softball. While the women squealed at flabby forms puffing around third base, I threw up my ten bottles of orange pop, now the gravy over my once-downed lumpy ice cream. The day was complete. I could go home.

GEORGIA TODHUNTER

A reader probably would not say that the writer of "Orange" was making up this story. It contains the authority of closely recorded fact: a "dwarfed tree in the corner of a baseball field," orange drink and white ice cream that "slid down my throat (after the tenth or so) like chunks of plaster of Paris." Parts of the story may have been made up but they are true to life, deeply. "Orange" is a fine piece of writing but probably would not be published in a magazine because it does not develop any incident through time, as does the following memory of childhood:

THE PIRATE SHIP

I can still remember the time two of my buddies, Jim and Tom, and I decided to leave home. We were all avid Captain Kid fans, and we decided to build a pirate ship and make our fortunes by looting and plundering other vessels.

After three agonizing days of searching for a ship, we discovered an old discarded casket crate drydocked in the cemetery. It was ideal. Just large enough to hold all three of us and yet small enough to make the fancy maneuvers demanded of a pirate ship. Finding our ship solved one problem, but getting it back to our hideaway created another, because it was well guarded by Mr. Snod, the grounds-keeper. We waited until he went into his office for lunch to avoid capture and then charged the ship and overpowered the sole crew member, Snod's angora cat.

We hoisted the ship upon our wagon, lashed it down securely, and set out of the cemetery full sail, knocking over two small tombstones due to the faulty navigation of Tom who was steering the wagon. This part of the operation went along without a catch until we started down a long hill a block away from my house. One minute we were towing the ship and the next minute it was towing us. About halfway down the hill, the ship got second wind and lurched ahead, breaking our grips on the rope.

Twenty crushed tulips and one trampled hedge later it came to rest in my mother's flower garden. Now more than ever, if we had a reason for leaving home, this was it.

We tried to fix the mangled tulips by breaking uncooked spaghetti sticks into pieces and inserting them into the stems, hoping to make them straight again. After twenty-five minutes of failure we gave up and dragged the ship into the back yard and tried to get it seaworthy before one of my parents discovered the disaster area in the front yard.

I went into the basement and rummaged around until I found some tar and old rags. Dipping the rags into the tar, we managed to seal up the slits in the ship. By now we looked more like the Bre'er Rabbit tarbaby than pirates.

Our mast and sail were made up of my mother's clothesline pole and a white sheet she had hung out to dry. We needed a Jolly Roger to identify our ship so we borrowed Jimmy's grandfather's V.F.W. flag. We nailed spikes into the bottom of the ship to prevent the sharks from eating us up.

All good pirate ships had a ram to destroy other ships at close range, so we had to have one, too. After a lot of fast talking I persuaded Tom to lend us his father's moose head which would serve as the battering ram. We needed a cannon for long range warfare and we found it in my father's pump-type fire extinguisher, which we first emptied and then refilled with soap water. This would blind the crews of other ships long enough for us to make use of our twelve-point battering ram.

At last we were ready. Tugging and straining, we lifted our coffin onto the wagon and embarked toward the river to launch it, taking the short-cut through Mr. Freeland's backyard and Mrs. Murphy's flower garden. The ship was now top heavy from the sail, and the moose head fell off the wagon every fifty feet or so. Every time our ship fell, the nails in it would gouge the ground.

By the time we had crossed Mr. Freeland's lawn and Mrs. Murphy's flower garden, they looked like battlefields ripped apart by bombs. We used everything in sight to cover these areas. Tables, chairs, incinerators, toys, wet laundry, lawnmowers, bikes, play pens, empty milk bottles, and a sleeping dog. But to no avail. Within minutes, Mr. Freeland and Mrs. Murphy attacked like dive bombers, forcing us to abandon ship and flee for our lives.

Where could we run, what could we do? Head toward my house and the ruined front yard, or surrender and face the wrath of Mr. Freeland and Mrs. Murphy? We never got to make a decision because we were intercepted by our parents, who had discovered the disaster in their front yard and were following our poorly disguised trail. Trapped, we surrendered and tried to explain our actions. It was useless. Our tar-covered pants were yanked off and we were flogged all the way home. Our ship was destroyed and we were confined to our room indefinitely, let out only to eat.

Whenever I see Jim or Tom today, we stop and look at each other with that knowing smile and say, "It woulda' floated!"

MICHAEL MAY

The writer chose his details skillfully: they never become tedious; they take the reader on the dry voyage. The ship metaphor is continued in the telling of the story: the crate is *drydocked*, the wagon faultily *navigated*, the crate made *seaworthy*, the flag is a *Jolly Roger*, they *embarked* toward the river. The story is more than just a tale of a day's play: it shows how kids become engrossed in playacting and run smack into their parents' world without realizing they come from another.

WRITING TEN: Choose from your childhood a moment you can't forget and write it down. Put the reader there as these three stories do. You may tell of the experience in simple narrative—this happened, then that happened—as did the writers of "Bird" and "The Pirate Ship." Or consider a persistent joy or annoyance in your childhood and find examples which illustrate the feeling as do the events in "Orange."

BEGINNINGS AND ENDINGS

Most good published pieces of writings have been created in several drafts—each version tighter and sharper than the last. What you see in print is almost never the first effort. No professional writer expects to dash off a piece of writing that is beyond improvement. Each version he thinks of as preliminary to another better version until finally he has had enough of drafting and says, "Done."

About eighty percent of the time, professional writers and editors find that the beginning of their first draft is no beginning at all. It is a mess, a series of false beginnings in which the starter's pistol goes off once, then twice, and the runners burst from their blocks only to stop and come back again. A writer must expect these bad starts because when he first meets his reader he has been thinking through *all* that he wants to tell him, not just the beginning of it. So he tells him too much—what concerns the end of the story or the chain of ideas, as well as the beginning—or too little, on the false assumption that the reader has just gone with him on this journey of reflection. In fact it cannot for the reader be a journey of memory. It must be a trip into an unknown woods in the partial dark where the stumps and branches leap at his feet and the hanging spider webs clutch his face.

Look at the first draft of your story. Is there some place on the first page where the reader could begin satisfactorily? Look for a spot where the story itself starts up, not simply where you began to write.

I write my first version in longhand (pencil). Then I do a complete revision, also in longhand . . . Then I type a third draft on yellow paper, a very special certain kind of yellow paper. No, I don't get out of bed to do this. I balance the machine on my knees. Sure, it works fine;

I can manage a hundred words a minute.
Well, when the yellow draft is finished,
I put the manuscript away for a while, a
week, a month, sometimes longer. When
I take it out again, I read it as coldly as
possible, then read it aloud to a friend
or two, and decide what changes I want
to make and whether or not I want to
publish it. I've thrown away rather a few
short stories, an entire novel, and half
of another. But if all goes well, I type
the final version on white paper and
that's that.

TRUMAN CAPOTE

In its first draft, "The Pirate Ship" began like this:

> I can still remember the time two of my childhood bud-
> dies and I decided to run away from home.
> Even today I'm still not sure what happened to bring
> about this idea of ours.
> Anyway, since we were all avid Captain Kid fans, we
> decided upon building a pirate ship . . .

The second sentence is all wrong because it confusingly returns the reader from childhood to today. The third shifts again to childhood with an apologetic "anyway," a word persons use in conversation when they have become mixed up in telling a story. The writer has the advantage over the speaker: he can unconfuse himself by rewriting his story until he gets it right for the reader. If he presents in the final draft confusion, he had better have intended to represent confusion or he is a lazy writer.

As "The Pirate Ship" appears in its complete and revised form, it begins competently and moves in a clear line. The writer introduces himself and his buddies, says they decided to build a ship, and then tells in ordinary narrative sequence how they searched, found, built, and launched their vessel—on land. What happened first, second, and so on. The revised opening is adequate. It might be more powerful written this way:

> My buddies Jim and Tom, and I searched for three days
> for a ship. We looked in Mrs. Grigg's junk pile beside her
> garage. The old steel swing wouldn't do, too heavy [and
> then more examples] . . . We were Captain Kid fans and

had decided to build a pirate ship and make our fortunes
by looting and plundering other vessels.

On the third day, we discovered an old discarded casket
crate . . .

This opening sounds more like a story and less like an explanation
or lecture. An opening should start something going. If possible,
arrest the reader with your beginning. Make him feel as if you've
pulled him over to the curb and are getting out of the patrol car.
Create tension, suspense, or surprise, or begin an action that carries
along the reader, making him continually ask: "What next?"

One of the simplest ways to create a good beginning is to look
down the first page until you find an arresting line and cut out all
that goes before it. Or move it into first position. Few writers, beginners or veterans, can throw a high hard one on the first pitch. They
have to warm up first, and they should not present their readers with
the beginning practice tosses they made in the bullpen. Anton
Chekhov is considered by many critics the best of all modern short
story writers. Notice how in his published draft—we don't know how
many earlier drafts he threw in the wastebasket—he began two stories:

MY LIFE

The director said to me: "I only keep you out of respect
for your esteemed father; otherwise you would have been
sent flying long ago." I replied: "You flatter me, Your
Excellency, in assuming that I am capable of flying." And
then I heard him say: "Take that gentleman away, he gets
on my nerves."

IN THE RAVINE (1900)

The village of Ukleyevo lay in a ravine, so that only the
belfry and the chimneys of the cotton mills could be seen
from the highway and the railroad station. When passers-by
would ask what village it was, they were told:

"That's the one where the sexton ate up all the caviar
at the funeral."

And here is Reynolds Price, author of the novel *A Long and Happy
Life,* beginning a story:

THE WARRIOR PRINCESS OZIMBA (1961)

She was the oldest thing any of us knew anything about,
and she had never been near a tennis court, but somewhere

around the Fourth of July every year, one of us (it was
my father for a long time but for the past two years, just
me) rode out to her place and took her a pair of blue tennis
shoes.

These three beginnings to stories do not go off like cannons, but
neither do they go *poof* like a puffball kicked in the woods. They say
something. They do not beg, or back up, or curtsey. Whether you
are writing stories, articles, editorials, or answers to an examination,
start solidly.

In writing an opening beware of the windy generalization:

Everybody likes hot rods and I am no exception.

Not true. Many persons detest hot rods and consider them the most
likely transportation to Hell. Don't turn off the reader by pretentious
or coy behavior. In the beginning you establish your voice. If you
begin squeaking like a monkey or thundering like an elephant, you
have ruined your chances with the reader, who will be astounded
later to find you writing in natural human voice. Beware of phony
introductions, voice changes, and unnecessary apologies.

An opening often gains by being new, surprising; but if your
writing is crammed with surprises all the way through, you may do
well to begin quietly and conventionally. You do not have to amaze
or stun or mystify your reader at the beginning. But you have to
avoid alienating him with emptiness, phoniness, or unsuccessful
attempts at humor. You may simply begin factually:

East High School is located two miles from the center
of the business district in Clarksville.

but don't use that fact unless it makes a point relevant to your story.
Later in this story, the distance from the school to the business district
should come up.

Think hard how your reader will take your first words. Consider
this opening:

**What's going on? This question might have gone through
the minds of the grocery store owners when the students of
Mr. McMahon's psychology class went to the different stores
for an assignment that was done over vacation.**

"What's going on?" is a question that might be asked by anyone in
any situation. Here the reader is required to wait too long before the
question gains any significance.

Revision: "What's going on?" said the grocery store owner when
he saw twenty-five students from Mr. McMahon's psychology class

walking up and down the aisles writing in their notebooks. They were carrying out an assignment during Thanksgiving vacation.

When you have found or created a good beginning to your story, consider its ending. At both ends of a piece of writing, a writer is driven to explaining, almost as if he wanted to give advice to the reader on how to read what he has written, and nothing is worse than advice. If the Explainery comes at the beginning, it is lost on the reader who does not know the story yet. If it comes at the end, it tastes like soggy bread. The reader has read the story and is insulted by being told what he has read.

The first draft of "The Pirate Ship" ended like this:

> And since we had taken the "short-cut" across our neighbor's lawns, I'd say that it was approximately four phone calls and one crushed fence later that our parents finally caught up with us.
>
> Our ship was contrabanded and we "pirates" were sentenced to three long weeks of reforesting various islands, along with a looooong lesson from the "Board of Education"!

When the writer read his first draft to other students, they told him they wanted to know more about what happened on the journey through the neighbors' lawns. They didn't like the tired joke about a Board of Education being used to spank the boys. It was a pun that didn't spring from the experience itself, a canned joke. Discussing his story with critics, the writer said, "We really were upset to be stopped by our parents. Why, even today, when I see Jim or Tom, we look at each other and say, "It woulda' floated!" The critics and the writer knew instantly that he had stumbled on to a fine ending.

Study the ending of "Bird." It asks the reader to guess the significance of the garbage can lid slamming down. The story ends: a lid is put on it.

Look over your story for a spot near the end which is exciting or surprising. Or consider stopping a little before you believe the reader expects you to. Near the end find a good detail, an example of one of the main feelings or ideas in the story and chop everything else off that follows it. Or move the good passage to the end position. Don't drool an ending. Wipe your mouth, say the last word. Leave the reader.

*[George Bernard Shaw often sent his
early drafts of his plays to his friend
Ellen Terry, the actress, for criticism.
Once she said she feared to suggest
changes on his manuscript. He wrote
back:]*

*"Oh, bother the MSS., mark them as
much as you like: what else are they for?
Mark everything that strikes you. I may
consider a thing fortynine times; but if
you consider it, it will be considered 50
times; and a line 50 times considered is
2 per cent better than a line 49 times
considered. And it is the final 2 per cent
that makes the difference between excel-
lence and mediocrity."*

chapter 12
sharpening

REHEATING a piece of writing after it has
cooled, tempering it, and sharpening it is enjoyable—if you know
how. Otherwise it may turn out worse, brittle or misshapen. Look for
the common sicknesses or dullnesses professional writers try to eliminate: Is-ness, It-ache, There-ache, excessive use of adjectives, adverbs,
and passive verbs.

Consider this column of opinion printed in a high school newspaper. Its first paragraph makes its point dramatically; its verbs are
vigorous and its adjectives full of meaning.

[THE FEMININE ERA]

**Waltzing down the corridor in a velvet-collared, ruffled
shirt, clutching a pink hairbrush, a teenager hurriedly
skipped into the school lavatory between classes and began
labor over a hair-do with side-swept bangs for four and a
half minutes of agony and disgust; the door was marked
"BOYS."**

5

Is this the beginning of a new feminine era today among the boys of our country?

As they walk down the hall fussing and swishing with their hair with an occasional pat on the bangs, it becomes more apparent that this is a generation of feminine men coming up.

Once it was the style for boys to carry small combs in their hip pockets; now it's brushes, brushes with pink and baby blue handles.

By a recent poll it was revealed that until a few years ago, a boy got up in the morning, ran a quick one-stroke combing through his hair, jumped into the same old pair of Levis he'd taken off the night before and headed for school in less than ten minutes.

Today, an act like this would be considered a tragedy in a boy's life if he wasn't allowed at least a couple of hours to himself for the care and parting of his hair.

It seems that of the both groups, the boys are more conscious than girls about subtleties of dress.

Although occasionally they are apt to go a little more overboard, when they begin wearing ruffled embroidered shirts and more cologne than girls do perfume.

Boys have adopted hair styles popular with the girls . . . The boys have joined the co-eds in going to the "mod" or "natural" look with moderately short hair and side-swept bangs that shade their eyes.

Today, it is not unusual for a receptionist at a beauty salon to pick up the phone and find out that it is a male customer who wants to make an early appointment to have his hair thinned, washed, set, and then sprayed for a big school event coming up. In some parts of the state, there are even special beauty salons for only the male customer.

Why this drastic change? Is it because the boys see the feminine world as a privileged one, and they want to join it too?

Is it the feeling that the demands of the traditional masculine role are more than they can tolerate and they are abandoning it? Whatever the reason may be, "BOYS," stand up and hold your role as a "MAN."

Through the first 38 lines, this writing makes a strong case. Then it asks several good questions which it fails to probe or answer. It ends in a thicket: asking boys to fulfill their traditional role without understanding why it may be changing or whether it should change or whether males were at other times just as feminine in personal habits.

The author, a girl, is quick to condemn boys for following feminine hair and clothes styles. She neglects to admit that many girls of the time follow masculine hair and clothes styles.

The column needs rethinking. But for the moment, consider only how its expression might be sharpened in lines 7 through 45. It suffers from Is-ness, a dullness marked by weak uses of forms of the verb *to be*. If *am, is, are, was, were, shall, will,* or *been* connects trite or empty adjectives or vague nouns, it probably needs replacing with a verb that carries more meaning. Often a form of the verb *to be* can be eliminated from a sentence without losing any meaning. Write down all uses of this verb in lines 8 through 46 and study whether or not eliminating them would strengthen the writing. Here is the way a professional editor might make such an inspection:

Lines 5 and 7: adequate *was* and *is*. Don't change.

Line 11: Is-ness. Revise sentence:

Original. As they walk down the hall fussing and swishing with their hair with an occasional pat on the bangs, it becomes apparent that this *is* a generation of feminine men coming up.

Revision. As they walk down the hall swishing and fussing with their hair, occasionally patting it on the bangs, they embody a new generation of feminine men.

Line 13: Is-ness (*was*). Revise sentence:

Original. Once it *was* the style for boys to carry small combs in their hip pockets; now it's brushes, brushes with pink and baby blue handles.

Revision. Once boys carried small combs in their hip pockets; now they carry brushes with pink and baby blue handles.

Line 16: Is-ness (*was*). Revise sentence:

Original. By a recent poll *it* was revealed . . .

Revision. A recent poll revealed . . .

Lines 21 and 22: Is-ness (*would be, wasn't*). Revise sentence:

Original. Today an act like this *would be* considered a tragedy in a boy's life if he *wasn't* allowed at least a couple of hours to himself for the care and parting of his hair. (34 words)

A difficulty in this sentence is that the expression "an act like this" doesn't refer to any words preceding.

Revision. Today a boy denied a couple of hours to himself for the care and parting of his hair would consider himself tragically mistreated. (23 words)

REVISING SIX: Circle other uses of the verb *to be* in "The Feminine Era." In considering possible revisions, try to eliminate empty nouns and verbs, and replace them with persons or things which act through vigorous verbs. The revisions exhibited above do away with these weak expressions:

> it becomes more apparent that this
> it was the style
> by . . . it was
> an act like this would be considered a . . . in a boy's life

Note that these expressions contain no power or color. They consist of abstract and lifeless words, necessary and useful at times, but here pale and empty.

One way to transfuse red blood into a sentence anemic with Is-ness is to substitute a metaphorical verb for *is*. For example:

Original. The poor dog *is* an inferior because he *is* not a symbol maker, says Western Man.

Revision. The poor dog *wags* his tail as an inferior because he *is* not a symbol maker.

Here the second part of the statement retains an *is*. If it were eliminated by saying "because he doesn't make symbols" the sentence would lose part of its balance and parallel construction: "an inferior . . . a symbol maker." So you can see that you should not eliminate *is's* wherever they appear without considering how they are functioning.

Shakespeare was a master of the metaphorical verb. In *Macbeth* he made Malcolm say:

> This tyrant whose sole name *blisters* our tongues,
> *Was* once thought honest.

Suppose Shakespeare had written with Is-ness:

> This tyrant whose sole name *is* a blister on our tongues,
> *Was* once thought honest.

Again, one use of the verb *to be* is enough in the statement.

REVISING SEVEN: In one of your past longer pieces of writing circle every use of the forms of the verb *to be*. Consider which need to be eliminated and revise the sentences in which they appear. Remember that Is-ness stands for a *weak* use of a form of *to be*. No writer can write many sentences in a row without usefully employing *is*.

It-ache and There-ache are dullnesses marked by unnecessary uses of *it* and *there*. They are often associated with Is-ness. Diagnosis of It-ache and There-ache in "The Feminine Era":

It-aches in lines 10, 13, 16 were eliminated along with the Is-ness. It-ache in line 24:

Original. *It* seems that of the both groups, the boys are more conscious than girls about subtleties of dress.

Revision. The boys are more conscious than girls about subtleties of dress.

There-ache in lines 37-38:

Original. In some parts of the state, there are even special beauty salons for only the male customer. (17 words)

Revision: In some parts of the state, special beauty salons serve only male customers. (13 words)

REVISING EIGHT: See if you can find other examples of It-ache and There-ache in "The Feminine Era." Often you will discover you have already eliminated them in dealing with Is-ness.

You are hunting for uses of *it* and *there* which do not carry solid meaning, but act merely as convenient handles for introducing other expressions. Sometimes they operate well as handles. They are hard to replace in these two sentences:

> It is cold out tonight.
> There are only four houses on the other side of the street
> on our block.

Too often, vague uses of *it* and *there* lead a writer to wasting other words as well:

Original. It is the task of the school to train all the students.

Such an It-ache as that may be cured by making a noun the subject of the sentence. At the same time, an editor would probably change the possessive construction "of the school" to "school's," a more informal but vigorous expression:

Revision. The school's task is to train all the students.

A sentence does not ache from a healthy use of *it* or *there*. For example:

> The ball rolled and rolled until it hit the fence.
>
> "He's sitting over there," said the witness, pointing.

In these sentences *it* represents the ball and *there* tells a place. These are different uses from those involved in *It is* and *There are*.

Now look for It-ache and There-ache in the longer paper you examined in REVISING SEVEN and make the needed changes.

Dullness also results from the excessive use of passive verbs.

Passive. It was brought to our attention by the manager that we had not sent out the invoice.

Active. The manager told us we had not sent out the invoice.

Passive. The play was a performance that was observed by George with amazing indifference.

Active. George observed the play with amazing indifference.

Passive verbs suggest that nobody is doing anything. Just sitting around being acted upon.

Passive. The object that was stepped on by me was a ladybug with lavender spots.

Active. I stepped on a ladybug with lavender spots.

Passive. The scheme was conceived by John at four in the morning.

Active. John conceived the scheme at four in the morning.

Dullness may also be imparted to sentences by excessive use of the verbs

make	go	get
have	move	come

They are not full of specific meaning. Circle each use of them in your writing and question it: can the verb be replaced with a more particular and meaningful one? For example, *making* might be supplanted by

constructing	gluing	joining	stringing
building	piling	digging	sticking

and many other verbs. Even these are fairly general; for example, a writer might say "I *cemented* two stones together" rather than "I stuck two stones together." Choosing more precise and vigorous verbs puts life into writing because life is particular, not general.

Like Is-ness, the shoddy use of *make, have, go, move, get,* and *come* leads to a frightening waste of words:

Original. This land *has* the appearance of being arid.

Revision. This land looks arid.

These verbs frequently seed sentences with unnecessary nouns.

Original. He finally *came to* his decision. He would run.

Revision. He finally decided he would run.

You should remember that these suggested revisions are made out of context. The last revision above saves three words from the original sentences, but if the author's purpose was to slow down the reader and delay the divulging of the decision, he might better use the original version, which carries a different rhythm.

Beginning writers often insist on establishing the ownership of an object with the verb *have* before they let the owner use the object. Good way to clog the story.

Original. He *had* a bicycle. He rode it to work every morning.

Revision. He rode his bicycle to work every morning.

The principle involved in sharpening is to fill words with precise meaning or get rid of them. Beginning writers splatter adjectives and adverbs like buckshot. Consider this passage:

> I summoned up courage and *boldly* set forth through the pathway. Suddenly loomed in sight five male patients sitting outside only a few feet from me. Too late to turn back, I consoled myself with the idea that an attendant was probably *unobtrusively* hidden from view but there, nevertheless, for protection.
>
> Then the thought dawned on me that I was in the wrong and didn't deserve protection because I was trespassing— there were blockades which I had ignored, set up in front of the pathway. The patients, perhaps sensing my *nervous* anticipation, *possibly* evident in my *faltering* steps and *nervous* eye movements, said "hello" to me.
>
> My *natural* reaction to this situation bothers me. In Psych class we consider mental patients just "sick people." I don't want to be guilty of sharing the *common* feelings of the *general* public.

Here in line 1, *boldly* is unnecessary with "summoned up courage" and "set forth," both expressions which imply boldness. In line 5, *unobtrusively* is unnecessary. Seldom does anyone hide obtrusively. In lines 10 and 11, *perhaps* is an honest word but the other italicized words overdo the notion of sensing nervousness. A sharp cutting is needed.

Original. The patients, perhaps sensing my nervous anticipation, possibly evident in my faltering steps and nervous eye movements, said "hello" to me.

Revision. Perhaps sensing my anticipation in my faltering steps and nervous eye movements, the patients said "hello" to me.

In line 13, *natural* is not an accurate word for what the writer wants to say. *Instant* or *stereotyped* would make more sense. In line 15, *common* is unnecessary. *Sharing* and *general* say enough by themselves.

Remembering the *repeat-and-vary* principle, the good writer avoids ruts. He does not allow himself to supply for every verb an adverb and for every noun an adjective until the pattern becomes monotonous and the words flabby. He avoids or changes dead patterns like these:

> He slowly walked up the stairs, nonchalantly pushed on the door, and casually entered the room.
>
> At the picnic were sticky-fingered children, rosy-cheeked mommas, and large-stomached fathers.

When he finishes his first or second draft, a good writer tests the adjectives and adverbs: are they pulling their weight? Do the other words around them render them unnecessary? See how freshly and powerfully Shakespeare uses an adverb in giving Regan, King Lear's daughter, these words about her father:

> 'Tis the infirmity of his age: yet he hath ever but *slenderly* known himself.

Powerful adverbs and adjectives are not beyond you. On the whole, the writer of "The Feminine Era" made her adverbs and adjectives count. *Velvet-collared* and *ruffled* and *side-swept* are doing their jobs. But in lines 26-27, the writer fell off the ship with the expression "a little more overboard." One can go overboard, but not more or less overboard.

A fundamental in using adverbs and adjectives is not to let one of them smother the effect of another strong word. Don't let your straight man steal the attention from the comic. If you write

She was *unusually* hideous.

you have lessened the force of *hideous* by making the reader attend to the weak word *unusually*. If you write

It was a tremendously tall skyscraper.

you have lessened the force of *tall*. In fact, both *tremendously* and *tall* are tired and should be replaced with words that fix the height of the skyscraper in actual or metaphorical scale.

I stood a hundred feet away and yet my neck ached from looking up to the top of the building.

This chapter has talked about weak uses of certain words. All of them may be used adequately or strongly by a skillful writer. Note in this beautifully phrased passage from "Self-Reliance" that Emerson uses many strong verbs but also forms of *to be*. He plants four adjectives within the space of seven words. He finishes with a sentence that carries the normally vague and weak verb *go*.

Travelling is a fool's paradise. Our first journeys discover to us the indifference of places. At home I dream that at Naples, at Rome, I can be intoxicated with beauty and lose my sadness. I pack my trunk, embrace my friends, embark on the sea and at last wake up in Naples, and there beside me is the stern fact, the sad self, unrelenting, identical, that I fled from. I seek the Vatican and the palaces. I affect to be intoxicated with sights and suggestions, but I am not intoxicated. My giant goes with me wherever I go.

The power of this passage comes from its ideas as well as from its expression. Emerson is true to his thoughts and feelings, and therefore his words carry surprise. The words that precede or follow ordinarily weak verbs like *to be* or *goes* are full of meaning—*intoxicated, giant, fool's paradise.*

Sharpening writing is not as black and white a matter as this chapter suggests. Many of the changes dictated here are debatable, and only a person considering the total context of a word or phrase can see whether or not it should be retained. Find ways of probing your sentences so that you see alternative ways of stating them. *Is, there*, and *it* frequently are wasted and breed other unnecessary words. But they are good words in their place. You will find writers as brilliant as Bernard Shaw using *it is* when the words are not absolutely necessary, as in the quotation at the head of this chapter:

> And it is the final 2 per cent that makes the difference
> between excellence and mediocrity.

This *it* doesn't ache much. It could be eliminated and the sentence written

> And the final 2 per cent makes the difference between
> excellence and mediocrity.

but the words *it is* in this passage act as emphasizers. They slow down the reader and make sure he gives attention to *2 per cent.*

The moral of this chapter is not to do away with all uses of the cited words, but to learn where to look for possible weak spots in your sentences. The writer of this book originally wrote the first sentence of the paragraph above in this way:

> Sharpening writing is not as black and white a matter as
> this chapter makes it appear.

Spotting the *it* in the sentence, and thinking about removing it, he saw that he could drop three words, *makes*, *it*, and *appear*, and substitute only the word *suggests.*

REVISING NINE: Look over two of your past free writings and attempt to eliminate from them weak passive verbs, empty verbs like *make* and *have*, the overuse of adjectives, and the unnecessary use of intensifying words like *tremendously* and *great big.*

. . . the point at which experience be-
comes form . . .

KENNETH CLARK

chapter 13
creating
form

PATTERNS

A RECENT TEXTBOOK on writing says:

> Since learning to outline is one of the most important
> steps—perhaps the most important—in writing well, we
> want you to make at least four outlines.

The man who wrote that must never have talked to a real writer.
Eight out of ten writers say they never use outlines and the other two
say they use them only in late stages of writing, in the second or
third draft when they have all the materials captured and need only
to rearrange them strategically.

In the first place, outlines freeze most writers. Professionals are
looking for ways of breaking up the ice and poking around in new
waters. They want writing and ideas to flow.

> *I have often at the beginning of a book*
> *found myself very uncertain what I*
> *would do, and appalled at the difficulty*
> *of knowing what to put where, and how*
> *to develop my incidents. I never have*
> *that feeling now because I have always*
> *found that there is some one point or*
> *other in which I can see my way. I im-*
> *mediately set to work at that point and*

> *before I have done and settled it, I in-*
> *variably find that there is another point*
> *which I can also see and settle, etc.,*
> *etc. . . .*
>
> SAMUEL BUTLER

In the second place—Wait a minute. The second place. By their form, outlines always imply there will be a second place. Maybe there won't be. Or shouldn't be. I.a., I.b., II.a., II.b. "Express all your points in the outline in the same style, all complete sentences or all phrases." The Outliners are full of stuff like that. They get a writer so interested in the form of the outline that he quits thinking of the writing he is outlining.

Yet a reader needs some form or he becomes confused, gets lost, gives up. Making anything—a table, a fishing fly, a piece of writing— involves a struggle between form and content. Only the dull assembly-line maker can avoid that struggle by drawing up a perfect plan, or outline, before he begins creating. Punched out, every one the same, no surprises anywhere. A good planner allows for departures from plan, sidetrips down alleys full of discovery. The best trip you ever took in your life—could you have written an outline for it beforehand?

Yet the reader and writer need form, some direction, some over-riding mood, or they will sense only chaos. When the folks at home send George on a trip, they expect more than a bagful of chaos spilled on the kitchen table when he returns.

Many professionals say that the more experienced they become, the more certain they are of where they're going before they start. But they still keep their eyes and ears open as they go, hoping for fortunate accidents.

Beginning, you may find a direction, even a conclusion, flowering in your mind. Then all you do is find experiences to embody it and bring it alive. But if there is not an example or experience clinging to the idea or direction when you first get it, the chances are you will never bring it alive. Better start with something already alive and kicking. A butterfly caught and squirming in the net, wings flapping wildly. Not a lot of preserved specimens lined up in the glass case neatly and systematically labeled.

But the glass case is good. Something to enclose the things flapping around in your mind and experience. Place something else with the butterfly. Does it go with him? Or does it contrast in some significant way? Is it a leaf in shape—half of the butterfly? And then a bird. Look at him. How do his wings differ from the butterfly's and the leaf's? Let these pieces of experience knock around against each other in the case and in your mind.

> *It doesn't matter which leg of your table*
> *you make first, so long as the table has*
> *four legs and will stand up solidly when*
> *you have finished it.*
>
> EZRA POUND

If what you are thinking about doesn't fit into a case, you may simply jot down the elements in a list, informal, like the one you take to the supermarket.

Any piece of writing needs a point. What that means is hard to say but easier to sense. Everyone knows the meaning of the word when he listens to a person talk on endlessly through boredom into sleep, and someone says, "He talked on and on but to no point." What *point* is and why it is needed can be seen by reading most term papers written in high school and freshman college classes. They have subjects but no points. For example, Harry Smithers writes "about Switzerland." His paper is dead already. The facts he has read about Switzerland or the things he has seen in Switzerland do not make a paper simply because they concern one country. What about Switzerland? Do any of the facts he has collected do anything to each other? Contradict? Surprise Harry in some way when compared with facts he knows about other countries? If he thinks he will write about Switzerland because the library has a number of books on it, or because no one else has written about it recently in school, or because he once heard that watches are made in Switzerland, his paper is doomed. When he starts in on a good piece of writing he will have an itch or he will never scratch hard, with purpose and enjoyment.

Switzerland might be Harry's subject, but never his point. To cover Switzerland would be to write an endless number of volumes, describing its government, postal system, watchmaking industry, role in European and world wars, people's dress, food, social customs—all with that dreadful emptiness of a travel brochure or a bad children's encyclopedia. Take this statement by a writer in a political magazine:

> The Swiss make watches, speak many languages, act as
> peace arbitrators, never commit themselves to the cause
> of right in any war, and act as holding companies for all
> sorts of high-level financial wheeling and dealing, aiding

persons all over the world in avoiding taxes and financial responsibility.

Maybe this statement is not true. But it is full of assertions, of points that could be pursued with genuine curiosity. It was not made by the Chamber of Commerce trying to attract tourists, but by a man puzzled and inquiring who said what he truly believed. If you came upon this statement as the opening paragraph of an article, you would probably suspect that the writer was going to take you on a journey.

An editor of a university press once said that most Master's and Doctor's theses submitted to him for possible publication were unpublishable. No one would want to read them, he said. Some contained ideas and material that could be brought together with point if the author could bring himself to see why anyone might want to know what he had found in his research. When he came upon such a thesis, the editor said he returned it to the writer with the query: "So what?" If the writer could rewrite his thesis so that it answered that question, he had made what could be justly called a book.

To construct a good piece of writing you need to go somewhere in it. If you haven't taken a journey, no amount of outlining or structuring can make the writing live. Whatever the type of writing—article, essay, story, case-history, poem—it must contain surprises and questions. Else it will remain dead for you and the reader. They must be genuine surprises and questions. Many beginning writers are affected by the worst, most gimmicky writing. They spin a long description of a man they have known, disguising who he is and where they have known him, and then in the last sentence they say: "There he was, smoking his pipe in the big rocking chair in the living room—my father." Surprise is valuable, but it must make a point or give truth to experience. This trick ending about Father does neither. If the writer told of a man exhibiting behavior shockingly unlike his father's, then as indication of the shock the writer himself felt, he might properly hold back the identity of his father until the end. The first-rate writer produces surprise after surprise for his reader, in his expression, in the events he records, in the thoughts he comes to through comparisons. But he does not play practical jokes on his readers.

What shape will you give a piece of writing? Or better yet, what movement? It needs a pattern. Formlessness is too hard on human perception. You will lose your reader if he has no hint of what journey you are taking him on. He needs surprise and wondering, but he cannot stand one question after another with no intimation of answer or direction. As a writer you need form, a limit which will force you to invention. Henry Ford did not say one day, "I think I will invent something great" and then build one of the first American motor cars. He was thinking about a form—a wheeled, self-propelled vehicle; and a purpose—faster travel on roads than was provided by horse-drawn carriages.

What is the right form of your piece of writing? There is no manual in which you may look up the answer. Like all good questions, this one cannot be answered simply. If you remember that a good piece of writing is composed partly through plan and partly through accident which the writer keeps himself ever ready to exploit, you may guess that a good form involves both discipline and freedom for the writer and the reader. It gives the reader a feeling that he can see the path at times, at other times that he has to work hard to open it up. Occasionally it will lead him astray on exciting side trips. Give the reader a small sense of direction for the journey, but don't keep nudging him in the elbow—This way! No! Over there! Now back again!

Professional writers are often mystified by the way they put together writing. They know it has a form but they seldom know its origin. They are afraid of outlining because they want things to happen to them as they write. Nevertheless their final draft usually possesses sure form, a movement that gives power to the events they have written about. Some emphasize freedom to discover. Some emphasize the need for plan. James Thurber said of Elliott Nugent, with whom he wrote the play *The Male Animal*:

> He could plot the thing from back to front—what was going to happen here, what sort of situation would end the first-act curtain, and so forth. I can't work that way. Nugent would say, "Well, Thurber, we've got our problem, we've got all these people in the living room. Now what are we going to do with them?" I'd say that I didn't know and couldn't tell him until I'd sat down at the typewriter and found out. I don't believe the writer should know too much where he's going. If he does, he runs into old man blueprint —old man propaganda.

Because Thurber wrote this passage doesn't mean that he never paid attention to the shape of his writing. He rewrote his stories dozens of times until he got them moving right.

Probably the reason professionals are so unsure in discussing form
is that good form always comes out of the materials of a particular
piece of writing. As he gains experience, the writer comes unconsciously to a sense of form for his materials. Always he holds in mind
a few simple, fundamental forms that will limit him wisely and
give his reader a sense of certainty among all the surprises he
encounters.

> *A plot is a thousand times more unset-*
> *tling than an argument, which may be*
> *answered. It is not a pattern imposed;*
> *it is inward emotion acted out. It is*
> *arbitrary, indeed, but not artificial. It is*
> *possibly so odd that it might be called a*
> *vision, but it is organic to its material:*
> *it is a working vision, then.*
>
> EUDORA WELTY

Here are a few such fundamental forms or patterns of movement.
They may be useful if you do not let them bind you. Allow one
to dominate your complete piece of writing and at the same time
introduce several of the others to shape small pieces of the same
work if you wish.

(a) *Simple Comparison.* X is different from B. You may show how
X's arms differ from B's, then the legs of both, the shoes, etc. Or you
may describe X completely and then B completely. As you make your
observations and as you write, keep thinking: So what?

(b) *Before and After.* It was *this* way once. Now it is *that* way.
You may emphasize the difference. You may ask why the difference.
You may tell how the difference came about.

(c) *The Journey.* I (he, or it) started here and went through this
experience or that country and came out there. Chronologically. First
this happened, then that.

You may present the whole matter as story, or occasionally interrupt to explain significance. Show. Give the story. Tell. Explain why
or discuss the significance of an act. But don't interrupt a story to
tell or comment unless you do so frequently and regularly.

The Journey pattern is useful in writing about ideas (as well as
events) which are apt to become confusing to the reader unless controlled. If it is your idea, you may show where it came from, how
you took it on, and what you did with it over the years or days. If
it means a good deal to you, the tale of your journey with it should

be exciting, for the truth is that the journey was full of surprises—traps, bogs, a mountain with a view.

(d) *David and Goliath.* David has only a slingshot and courage against a gigantic warrior armed with spear and shield and wearing a coat weighing as five thousand shekels of brass. Any little or deprived or disadvantaged person against great forces. Who will win?

(e) *Will It Work?* An idea, a plan, an invention new and untried, or old but now standing against the established order—a variation of the David and Goliath story. The odds are against it because it is not now the accepted thing. Will it win through?

In deciding upon a form, a writer constantly juggles

1. the needs of his materials (they may cry out for a certain treatment),
2. the weight of his purpose,
3. the limitations and potentialities of his medium (is it a letter, an article in a picture magazine, a paper to be read aloud or silently in class?),
4. the knowledge and needs of his audience.

The professional knows he is writing to other human beings, who can be bored, who are often insulted by gimmicks, who have normal human needs for rising excitement, for hoping that every trip they take will pay off.

THE HOOK

A good device to remember is the fishhook. It rises slowly and then hooks back, so it will dig in and stick. It is barbed. Its curve points back to its beginning, to remind itself and the reader where it came from.

In the light of these comments on form and movement, consider some of the writings in this book. For example, "Reed" in Chapter 8, is a Journey. A girl feels faint while playing her clarinet at a competition. Step by step she leads the reader through her travails, over to the judge's desk, to a chair for rest, and back to the performance where she takes up where she had stopped. She is much like the hero of the *Odyssey,* apparently modest yet actually prodigious. Visitors wander into the room as she starts playing the unfinished half of her piece. They come in like foreigners, and the judge, like Jove, must explain what is happening. The Hook is that the innocent, fainting girl changes into a successful performer and the dignified authoritative judge into a human being who "collapsed in a chair." Surprise.

Tension. It creates life. When it is not present, no movement—death. You know the person, old or young, who spills his story in great oceans of tedious and irrelevant detail. "Stop! stop!" you say to yourself. "You began telling me about how you fell out of the tree at Aunt Louise's but now you're listing the names of all the trees in her woods!" A good writer knows more than he presents. But he gives the reader only the intersection points where X and Y spark. Or where After is a surprise in relation to Before. Don't tell the reader that John or Algernon is a man unless the other one is a bear with long claws on all four feet.

So there are no sure-fire formulas for shaping a piece of writing. But the strong writer keeps the pressure of form upon himself. He keeps asking:

Where is this going?

Does it arrive somewhere?

Does it add up?

Is something happening between things here?

Have I made clear, directly or indirectly, why I wanted to write this?

What did I want to say? Did I get it said?

WRITING ELEVEN: Choose one of your free writings you like and shape it more powerfully. You may have to expand or contract it radically. Does it already follow one of the patterns discussed in this chapter? Can you improve it with a Hook?

WRITING TWELVE: Look over your story in which you remembered childhood and your case-history. Can you improve them with a firmer pattern of development?

In subsequent longer papers you write as you work through this book, try early to find a form that belongs to your materials, your purposes, your audience.

Life is not free from its forms.

WALLACE STEVENS

. . . childhood word-play, adolescent slang and double-talk, often derivative, but natural and exciting. In general the schools have made it their business to kill this kind of playful interest, and they have had the backing of society in this effort . . . most professionals with highly developed skills are fond of playing with those skills.

W. NELSON FRANCIS

chapter 14
playing
with
words

TOO OFTEN we act as if we were put on this earth to die. In conversation we paralyze each other with interminable repetitions, clichés, tedious details. Then we write down our dullness so it will live beyond the moment.

We could act as if we were put on this earth to live, to carry ourselves buoyantly.

Take phrases you have heard before and twist them to see what happens. Maybe nothing. Maybe something. Silly, like the words of a disc jockey on radio station WBBM Chicago?

Mostly fair in the morning followed by mostly cloudy in the afternoon followed by mostly evening.

Like most quick-minded word play, this statement started with no point and ended sharp. Not only does the twist "followed by mostly evening" delight because it surprises, but taken as a whole, it joshes weather reports, their dullness, their heavy repetitiveness.

Americans are taught in school to groan when they hear a pun.
Yet all the brightest writers love puns.

> ROMEO: I dreamt a dream tonight.
> MERCUTIO: And so did I.
> ROMEO: Well, what was yours?
> MERCUTIO: That dreamers often lie.
> ROMEO: In bed asleep, while they do dream things true.

The most intelligent persons play with words, seriously. Intelligent
readers and listeners laugh with them.

> BOOK TITLE: *Up the Down Staircase*
>
> PLAY TITLE: *Who's Afraid of Virginia Woolf?*
>
> TV COMMERCIAL: Who said you can't teach an old dog food
> new tricks?
>
> TV COMMERCIAL: Certs has the best taste I ever ate.
>
> NEWSPAPER ADVERTISEMENT: Where does Lazy Maple Bacon
> gets its remarkable taste and aroma? From some sap in
> Vermont.
>
> BUSINESSMAN IN CONVERSATION: You've buttered your bread.
> Now lie in it.

The word player takes the old and turns it. Like this:

> Join the Navy and see Norfolk.

Or this:

> He's three-square.

Or this:

> Life is just a bowl of pits.

These three twists on tired aphorisms and slogans were written
by a beginner in writing. Probably she heard the first one from a
sailor but the other two are hers. She took the mealy old paste of these
expressions and twisted them like pretzels. They came out crisp and
salty.

The secret of productive play is simple: let yourself go. All great
persons—artists, scientists, engineers, architects, cooks, designers—fool
around. If their play produces something usable, they use it. If not,
they feel no pain or guilt. You cannot feel guilty about play and
become a creative person. In this game you must be loose with
language. Sinful. Show no respect for the tried and blue. But do

not expect all your play to produce chocolate gems. Many mudpies, much unsorted, unexciting sand and gravel.

More often than you will anticipate, you will stumble upon hidden wonders, both nonsensical and sensical. Note that the girl's twists on old sayings made sense, possessed point. Join the Navy and see the world. Often the promise of romantic travel in the Navy sours in the drabness of a stateside training center. He's four-square. Often a man expected to be solid and trustworthy turns out missing one side. Life is just a bowl of cherries. Not usually. So the twists led to truth, as well as to fun. When E. M. Forster decided to publish a book of essays showing some of the faults of democracy in Great Britain, he named his book *Two Cheers for Democracy.*

WRITING THIRTEEN: Try playing with words.

1. Twist a cliché. Here are some clichés.

   (a) Everything is peaches and cream.
   (b) It is both a pleasure and a privilege.
   (c) It's raining cats and dogs.
   (d) They worked long and hard.
   (e) The woods was a white fairyland, covered with a blanket of snow.
   (f) He danced with the greatest of ease.
   (g) Please give me your undivided attention and keep a stiff upper lip.
   (h) Make a concerted effort. Don't run around like a chicken with its head cut off.

Think of seven more clichés and list them. Choose five from yours and those printed here and play with them. A student who felt worse than "something the cat dragged in" wrote "I felt like something that dragged in the cat." Henry Thoreau went beyond a cliché in this statement:

> If you have built castles in the air, your work need not be lost; that is where they should be. Now put the foundations under them.

And so did William Hazlitt:

> Miracles never cease, to be sure; but they are not to be had wholesale, or *to order.*

A college student twisted three tired expressions in this way:

> Home is where the garbage is.

Love Is a Many Splintered Thing.

I want a girl just like the girl that turned down dear old Dad.

2. Take figurative, metaphorical words and phrases literally. Look at some of your free writings, or begin a free writing and stop when you can twist a metaphor by reading it literally. Anne Haven Morgan was hearing "A bird in the hand is worth two in the bush" when she said this about bullfrogs in *The Field Book of Ponds and Streams*:

> The way to catch them by hand is to seize them very firmly by both hind legs, for a bullfrog "in the hand" is strong and apparently much larger than the same one in the pond.

In the following passage, note how a beginning writer took literally the metaphorical word *outgoing* and the phrase *on her shoulders*:

> **A girl friend once told me that I wasn't outgoing enough. I thought she was very wise, always cracking books—a good head on her shoulders. So while I was out going to house council, sorority meetings, and working on committees, she stayed home and worked on my boy friend—another good head on her shoulders. Of course this put me out quite a bit and I decided some drastic steps should be taken. I told her that she wasn't outgoing enough herself, so she took my advice and stepped out, going with my boy friend.**

> SHARON BUTLER

Write a paragraph or two in which you twist words in this way.

The word player is not so much playing chess as just playing around. He may decide to put the play to practical use, but he does not need to any more than he needs to publish his first three bad drafts of a piece of writing. The more you play with words, the more often you will find playful statements crossing over into serious expression. E. E. Cummings, an American poet, constantly sawed up his words and tacked pieces on them. He looked at the word *mankind* and decided to write it *manunkind*. Then he used that new word in the first line of a bitter poem about the evils man has committed in the name of progress. It begins:

pity this busy monster,manunkind

This was not simply a trick by Mr. Cummings. For years he had written against war and man's cruelty to man.

WRITING FOURTEEN: Play with titles of articles or books, with titles for your own writings. First study newspaper and magazine article titles. Note the puns, the newly created words. Here are some examples:

    (a) *How to Cheat on Personality Tests,* by William H. Whyte, Jr.
    (b) *A Problem of Design: How to Kill People,* by George Nelson
    (c) *Arms and the Boy,* by Wilfred Owen

"Arms and the Boy," a title of a poem, plays on the first line of Virgil's *Aeneid,* which begins: "Arms and the man I sing . . ." The poet Wilfred Owen is suggesting that the reader should remember that boys rather than men are often killed in war.

    (d) *The Beast in Me and Other Animals,* by James Thurber
    (e) *Bed of Neuroses,* by Wolcott Gibbs
    (f) *Golf Is a Four Letter Word,* by Richard Armour

The word play in all these titles is pointed. It makes a reader think twice and see significance. When Sidney Cox, a writing teacher at Dartmouth College, published a book of reflections and musings about writing—not a program of specifics for learning to write, he called it *Indirections: for Those Who Want to Write.* He was playing on the word *Directions.*

> *. . . the light of magic suggestiveness may be brought to play for an evanescent instant over the commonplace surface of words: of the old, old words, worn thin, defaced by ages of careless usage.*
>
> JOSEPH CONRAD

Try to write the truth in your language and at the same time let your words speak to each other. One day a student playing with words wrote:

> **November, and the cornfields are brown and broken and they rattle in the freshening wind. Meanwhile across the cornflakes heavy voices grumble the usual. A word of meaning drowns in a sea of crunch.**

When he handed this paragraph to a teacher, he appended this comment:

> I was just playing with words and sounds and pictures.
> Somehow it reminds me of T. S. Eliot's coffee spoons [in
> "The Love Song of J. Alfred Prufrock"]. Know what? I'll
> bet if the thing were printed, someone would analyze it.

Here the writer is dishonest. The passage is more than meaningless
sounds and pictures. In his play he must have had in mind tension
between the fresh wind in the cornfields and the stale breakfast
table conversation. It is a delightful and valid statement which makes
its point in a sidelong manner. If incorporated into a larger context,
it might become the most powerful paragraph of a paper. What a
writer says unconsciously may carry more meaning than what he plans
meticulously.

Much of Lewis Carroll's writing about Alice is sense rather than
nonsense. Playful sense. Before you tighten your belt, purse your
lips, and dry out your throat in preparation for impressing your audience, consider speaking playfully and seriously at once. Do you see
no virtue in writing lightly? Remember that the persons you write
to can avoid your writing more easily than your speaking.

Lewis Carroll is making sense in *Through the Looking Glass* when
he has Humpty Dumpty say:

> "they gave it me—for an unbirthday present."

Alice and he go on:

> "I beg your pardon?" Alice said with a puzzled air.
> "I am not offended," said Humpty Dumpty.
> "I mean, what *is* an unbirthday present?"
> "A present given when it isn't your birthday, of course."
> Alice considered a little. "I like birthday presents best,"
> she said at last.
> "You don't know what you're talking about!" cried
> Humpty Dumpty. "How many days are there in a year?"
> "Three hundred and sixty-five," said Alice . . .
> ". . . that shows that there are three hundred and sixty-
> four days when you might get unbirthday presents—"

In the same book Lewis Carroll is apparently not making much
sense in the first stanza of "Jabberwocky":

> 'Twas brillig, and the slithy toves
>   Did gyre and gimble in the wabe:
> All mimsy were the borogoves,
>   And the mome raths outgrabe.

Millions of persons have taken those non-words to their hearts. They like nonsense. What they don't like is nonsense written by persons who think they are writing sense. In "Jabberwocky," Lewis Carroll was making a kind of sense. In the later stanzas he plainly tells a satirical story of a Jabberwocky (dragon) being slain by a brave young knight. Lewis Carroll is making fun of pompously heroic knights. The hero becomes ridiculous as he takes

> . . . his vorpal sword in hand:
> Long time the manxome foe he sought—
> So rested he by the Tumtum tree,
> And stood awhile in thought.

After that puncture of the knight's armor, the reader can see that the first stanza is a setting of the physical scene for this knight's encounter with the dragon. It was a brillig day, and the toves and borogoves were out there in the wabe.

You can write so persons will enjoy reading your words. Why not do that? Something sinful about enjoyment? You landed with the Mayflower? Wear a wide-brimmed tall black hat? Put on a fool's colors and be wise for fun.

WRITING FIFTEEN: Write for twenty to thirty minutes. Start on something or someone you are fond of or despise. Say anything. Describe. Give your opinions. Say what others have said of this person or thing. As you write, listen to your words. Before you begin, read these examples of word play and use any of the methods that appeal to you.

(a) In Samuel Butler's novel *The Way of All Flesh*, Ernest Ponti-fex's tyrannical father says to him:

> "I must insist on two things: firstly, that this new iron in the fire does not distract your attention from your Latin and Greek"—("They aren't mine," thought Ernest, "and never have been.")

(b) "Do you think it's going to rain?"
> Tweedledum spread a large umbrella over himself and his brother, and looked up into it. "No, I don't think it is," he said; "at least—not under *here*. Nohow."
> "But it may rain *outside*?"
> "It may—if it chooses," said Tweedledee; "We've no objection. Contrariwise."

One difference between all this word play and much of the humor that we hear every day in conversation and on television is that it is making a point. It is not gag-humor, like these statements:

> My Uncle George reminds me of a rabbit. He has a hare-less head.
>
> We have a cow that never udders a word.

Sometimes a play on words may be clever and pointed but inappropriate to the occasion, to the subject being played with, or to the writer. For example, in a magazine advertisement a chemical-plastics company once depicted a room divider made of plastic cane, above a line of type reading "It's cane . . . and it's able." This is a play on Cain and Abel in the Bible, but as used here, it is all wrong. Those two names conjure up the great tragic story of brother killing brother. No reader wants to connect it with an industry merchandising its wares, especially when the two-page full-color spread showed two sophisticated couples lounging in a sumptuous room decorated with expensive furniture and a large Oriental painting.

As the author of this book was writing this chapter on word play, he was called to a bedroom to kiss goodnight a six-year-old girl and her visiting stepbrother, five, who was for the first time sleeping in the same room.

"It's pretty nice, isn't it," he said, "to have a big brother to sleep in the same room with you?"

"Yes," she said, "but it's nice to have a sister, too."

"Everything's nice in life," he said.

"Yeah, except liver," she said.

"And going to war."

"Yeah."

"That's another bad thing, like falling in the lake from a rope up in a tree."

"Or falling in love."

METAPHOR

Deep comparisons are only extended metaphors, one thing seen in terms of another. Ring Lardner, the American short story writer, wrote of a young boy observing a girl:

> He give her a look you could have poured on a waffle.

When a comparison is hooked together by the words *like* or *as* it is called a simile, as in these lines from the poet Henry Vaughan:

> I saw eternity the other night,
> Like a great ring of pure and endless light.

but the difference between metaphor (where one thing is directly said to be something else, as in Samuel Butler's metaphor, "Evaporation is an unseen heavenward waterfall") and simile is not as valuable to learn as how to make good comparisons, whatever they are called.

Some metaphors and similes:

> (a) Angus (speaking of Macbeth): Now does he feel
> His secret murders sticking on his hands;
> Now minutely revolts upbraid his faith-breach.
> Those he commands move only in command,
> Nothing in love. Now does he feel his title
> Hang loose about him, like a giant's robe
> Upon a dwarfish thief.
>
> WILLIAM SHAKESPEARE

> (b) . . . beyond him, one white sycamore straight as diving.
>
> REYNOLDS PRICE

> (c) A tree in spring is a double-barreled shot gun exploding.
>
> FIFTH-GRADE CHILD

Comparisons like these may seem so remarkable to you that you cannot believe they would visit you. But that is what good metaphors usually do. They come to the writer; he does not manufacture them at will. They come to all persons, at all ages. Frequently they come most perfectly in fast, free writing, as they did to the girl who wrote this quick description:

> I saw Chicago once. The heat *stood still* between walls formed by dirty *heaped-up buildings squeezed* tightly together. People walked under the "L" with greasy faces, not just white ones, but black and brown and yellowish-brown, eyes slanting up or down or straight across with

lines fanning from the corners as they squinted. **Even the hair piled high up on women's heads** *escaped* **in frizzy ringlets on the back of their bare necks. Children didn't hop on one foot or chase** *fleeting* **candy wrappers down the sidewalk, but walked** *like grandfathers,* **in order not to be** *strangled* **by the heat and soot. Red shirts and red dresses** *stood out,* **but everything else was grey, light grey or dark or dirty white, and everybody was too close to somebody or something. But at the end of the street the wind** *purred* **gently under the open sky and the sun** *smiled down* **on the** *green face* **of the lake.**

Most of the comparisons in this passage consist of simple personification of inanimate objects: candy wrappers are fleeting; hair escapes. Nothing remarkable about these, but four of the comparisons—

> Children . . . *walked like grandfathers* . . . the wind *purred* gently under the open sky and the *sun smiled* down on the *green face* of the lake.

strike with power. The first—children walking like grandfathers—gains power from freshness, originality. But the three metaphors which close the passage are not unusual. They gain force from smooth, pleasant sound and from the contrast the writer has built between their pleasant connotations and the unpleasantness of preceding words like *squeezed, frizzy, soot, heat, dirty white.* As always in writing, a word finds its meaning and charge more from the words that have preceded and followed it than from any one meaning ascribed to it in a dictionary.

Because all words on a page carry latent sound, most metaphors gain from sound as well as from the comparison they state. Shakespeare had his Prince Hal say:

> Falstaff sweats to death and lards the lean earth as he walks along.

So much is working in that sentence: the great metaphor of the fat man larding the *lean* earth would be enough of an achievement but Shakespeare creates a fine sound effect by filling the sentences with "l" sounds. Count them.

David Jones, the beginning writer who created the following comparison, also controlled the sound of his words skillfully:

> With dawn come the ducks. You aim at the first one flying
> by and shoot . . . and watch him fly away. You missed be-
> cause you forgot to lead the duck. When shooting ducks
> you don't aim where they are; you aim where they will be.
> You must lead ducks just the way a quarterback leads an
> end. He doesn't throw the ball at the end; he throws it over
> his head or in front of the end and if it is properly thrown,
> the ball and the end meet at the same spot.

In this passage, the segments of sentences rock back and forth in even lengths and then join *football* and *end* suddenly and finally with the words "at the same spot." *Spot* ends the passage with an explosive sound that echoes *shot*.

Beginning writers often shy away from figurative language, afraid they will fall on their faces with it. And they often do, because they make up metaphors and similes outside their experience. To find your metaphors and similes, look to your own life, what you know well. When you are moving through the everyday world and are arrested by a piece of cellophane tape plastered on the broken pair of glasses on your friend's nose, consider why it strikes you. And record in a notebook a precise description of what it looked like and what meaning it carried for you. Perhaps the tape looked dirty and ragged on an expensive pair of glasses. Then when you need a metaphor, this comparison may come to you with all the freshness of its particularity.

> *Falstaff to Prince Hal: Thou hast the*
> *most unsavory similes, and art indeed*
> *the most comparative, rascalliest, sweet*
> *young prince.*
>
> WILLIAM SHAKESPEARE

WRITING SIXTEEN: Record five sensory observations that strike you vividly and that you might use as comparisons at some later date. Do not choose what you think will impress others. Choose what hits your senses and holds you, for whatever reasons.

In a sense all language is metaphorical, stands for something else. The river runs. She smiles sweetly. The river is personified. Her smile is compared to sugar. As a writer you should become aware of the dead metaphor in language so you can exploit it. In *Walden*, Thoreau began writing this sentence,

> We meet at meals three times a day, and give each other
> a new taste

and he remembered the metaphor in the word *taste*. Because he did not allow the word to become abstract in his mind, he was able to finish the sentence in this way:

> of that old musty cheese that we are.

You can do this, too. Suppose you say that

> Aunt Helen was a plain woman,

Get on that word *plain*. If Grandmother was hard but exciting, you might continue your sentence this way:

> but Grandmother was the Rocky Mountains.

When you forget the dead and hidden metaphors in the language you may compose foolish sentences. For example:

> Changing the course of a fast, deep river would normally
> be a lost cause, but this is one cause the North High family
> cannot afford to lose hold of.

This is a metaphor used by a student editor to ask others to help him reform the school newspaper. In it, he forgets what he is saying and asks the readers to keep hold of a river. He should remember that water is impossible to grasp.

Here is an excerpt from a paint company's directions for using artists' colors:

> Where very thin glazes are desired, Liquitex colors mixed
> with the Medium may be quickly and lightly rubbed over
> the surface with fingers and thumb in the manner of oil
> glazes. On the other hand, unwanted color or glaze may be
> wiped off.

The writer committed a blooper in using the phrase "On the other hand." He forgot its dead metaphor. Just before that he is talking about literal fingers and thumb. Like a thousand other phrases in everyday language, "on the other hand" was once a brilliant metaphor. Now men use it so unconsciously they need to be jogged with the vaudeville gag: "On the other hand—she had a wart."

WRITING SEVENTEEN: Write two 10- to 20-minute free writings in which you talk of things you love. Let yourself describe them in metaphor and simile that come from your deepest knowledge about objects or processes or occupations. Don't be satisfied with simple, brief metaphors: "His face was like a sunny day." Develop a metaphor, let its parts speak to each other and create new and continuing comparisons, as this beginning writer did:

When I think of barnacles I laugh because if they were attached to my bottom I'd feel important—like the Queen Mary. Maybe I ought to think like this when I take a bath and slide across the porcelain ocean at the end of a narrow day.

Alice didn't dare to argue the point, but went on: "And I thought I'd try and find my way to the top of that hill—"

"When you say 'hill,'" the Queen interrupted, "I could show you hills in comparison with which you'd call that a valley."

"No, I shouldn't," said Alice, surprised into contradicting her at last: "a hill can't be a valley, you know. That would be nonsense—"

The Red Queen shook her head. "You may call it 'nonsense,' if you like," she said, "but I've heard nonsense compared with which that would be as sensible as a dictionary!"

LEWIS CARROLL

chapter 15

your subject choosing you

BY NOW A PERSON in the circle has probably said that once when he was writing, everything flowed together—his choice of events and ideas, the form in which to put them, and the sound of his words. This is what is meant by inspiration. Maybe it has happened for you. Then writing becomes effortless. That may sound romantic, but it is a fact in the life of working writers. Not all the time, but often enough that you would be foolish not to try to set up conditions which welcome this spirit, or Muse.

If you did your free writing truly and freely at the beginning of this course, you surprised yourself by what you wrote. Most persons need about three tries before they produce a strong passage. If you didn't amaze yourself in free writing, go back and try some more. It is a guaranteed activity: if you write fast—without thinking of spelling, grammar, punctuation, or form, and try to tell truths—sooner or later you will write something that moves you and others.

Then you will become more confident, begin to treat your own experience with respect, realize it is different from every other person's in the world—the ultimate source of your power as a writer.

Once you know in your bones where your power is, you can take Samuel Butler's advice, given at the opening of this chapter, and run with it. Write with it. Butler says that if you aren't called by a subject, do nothing. School often says you must follow the assignment whether you feel called or not. In the circle you will usually have more options than school customarily offers you. For example, you may be allowed to write three papers and turn in only one. But even if you are assigned a general topic, within that you can let a more specific topic choose you. This chapter will show you how to do that.

Here's a story by a student:

NEAT

The lake with unbroken waves had a flexible quality like a sheet of plastic food wrap. The moon was partially obscured by the leaves. Sparks and heat rising from the fire intertwined in the leaves, making them strain upward like a bobber pulling against the weight on a fishing line.

As I lay in my sleeping bag I watched the other kids walking around the camp. Their loud whispers were muffled by the crackling fire. I watched the jagged flames which made chaotic shadows dance on the distant trees. I heard an animal climbing a tree. Probably a coon, I thought.

A red light glided across the water. Lights on the other side of the bay were soothing as they flickered erratically.

The other kids' expressions changed from serenity to fright. A bright light shown on Bill and Lynn.

I pivoted on my elbow to face four lights. Two on each side of what I figured to be a car. I lay there for what seemed minutes, watching the lights rumble closer. More lights came. I tried to stand up and run, but fell. I was still in my sleeping bag. I struggled in a frenzy to unzip the bag, and fell a few times more. Finally I was free. The lights were terrifyingly close, and they hadn't slowed down. I took a couple leaps out of the path of the cars. The others were running toward the lake and swamp to get out of the way.

Someone seemed to have said, "Is he mad?" but I realized it was in my head.

The cars swerved to a scraping halt, ripping 'sod with their sliding wheels. Insignias on the car doors read "WEAVER COUNTY SHERIFF." A husky man jumped from one car and glared at me. In that familiar tone of authority he hurriedly asked, "What are ya tryin' to run for?"

I looked at my sleeping bag. Across the middle was one neat, fresh tread mark.

DENNIS R. WATSON

That story embodies the eight fundamentals of good writing. It is intensely dramatic, it moves from the quiet of the lake with un- broken waves to a tread mark that signifies the near death of the narrator. A sheriff's mind-set told him kids at a beach who run are guilty of something. This little incident, told with power, speaks to one of the current issues of the day: the attitude and manner of legal officers toward citizens. It is persuasive because it puts the reader in the situation, makes him feel the wrongness of a sheriff's actions rather than moralizes.

When Dennis Watson recorded that incident in his life he prob- ably didn't think he was writing a paper on one of the national issues of the day, but that's what he did. Once finished, his paper pointed the way for other students in the class. Another student de- cided to write about his encounter with a sheriff:

BIG SMILE

I woke up with a sick feeling in my stomach. I glanced out the rear window of the car: flying luggage. I yelled.

The car screamed to a halt. My brain started to func- tion. I remember hearing my uncle swearing. It took awhile for me to understand what had happened. The lug- gage rack had fallen apart. We looked at the contents scattered half a mile down the road. My uncle and I started to walk along, picking up things as we went. One of the suitcases was broken. The collection took about forty min- utes. In front of us sat three suitcases, a grill, and a water container—and the broken luggage rack.

Where to put it all? We were on vacation in Tennessee and the station wagon was full. Six people and our camp- ing equipment took up most of the room. We decided that the rack could be fixed if we had some wire.

At that moment a county sheriff's car pulled up. A fat man with glasses and a wide-brimmed hat got out. He said in a Southern drawl, "Anything I can do to help youall?"

We informed him of our problem. I was surprised to see a big smile break out across his face. He told us that he had some wire at his house. My three cousins helped load the bags into the car. We jammed in, but it was a tight fit.

As we followed the sheriff's car I began to wonder if we were ever going to make it to Memphis.

We drove a mile down the road. Then we followed the sheriff into a narrow driveway. The house was old but looked nice enough. He mentioned that we could go around to the back and he would be right out. I sat down on the grass still tired. I dozed a little.

When I woke about five minutes later the picnic table in front of me was covered with melons. There were muskmelons and watermelons. The sheriff had a big carving knife in his hand. The blade was curved and looked about a foot long. He was busy cutting melons into pieces. We were wondering why he was being so generous but decided he must be just showing Southern hospitality.

Then the sheriff took the knife and lifted it shoulder high. He started to come at me, slowly at first, but then fast. The knife seemed to get bigger as he approached. He kept coming. When he was about five feet away I panicked and ran for the car.

I jumped in, locked the doors, and waited. Nobody came. Thoughts of bloody knife wounds were going through my head.

Fifteen minutes later my uncle came back, followed by the rest of the family. I stayed in the car. The next thing I saw was the sheriff right behind them. As I met his gaze he gave me a cold hard look. The rest of them were smiling and dripping melon from their mouths. My uncle and the sheriff took some wire and tied the luggage rack securely. They then shook hands.

Everyone piled into the car. We drove a few miles. I couldn't stand it any longer. I asked if they weren't a little upset over what just happened. I was told that the whole thing was a joke. He was trying to scare me. I tried to laugh. All that came out was a cracked, broken sound.

MICHAEL ELLIAS

In "Big Smile," the writer stands off from the distant event and sees himself more objectively than he did at the time. He writes with the detail that puts him and the reader in the experience. He sees his own prejudice against Southerners and sheriffs, and in the act of writing about it so objectively, shows that it is now dissipating.

Think of your writing as possibly useful to yourself and others. In this class it is not simply an exercise to be done for teacher's grade. If a number of your fellow students write about law enforcement officers, they can take the class beyond the stock responses of "cops are good" or "cops are bad." Their writings may be sent to a social science class that is discussing the citizen and the law. If their accounts are honest and full of accurately observed details, they constitute evidence in one of the central debates of our time.

If your teacher knows a teacher in another part of the city, state, or country who is using this book, perhaps he can arrange to exchange papers with another class. Then you can see if the perceptions of law enforcement officers evidenced in your class echo those of young people elsewhere. Again, a step toward objectivity.

Powerful writing is often dangerous. When it compels and convinces, readers usually conclude it is telling truth. And truth about things that count in our lives has a way of spreading rapidly. For example, if you were a law enforcement officer and suspected that some young people were writing truly and vividly about encounters with law officers, you would be curious to see what they had to say. Or if you heard that law enforcement officers were making public reports of how the young people in your town conducted themselves on weekends, you would be curious to see what they had to say. So when you write about your experiences that touch national issues, you may expect some of your words to get around, even if they are not formally published. That is one of the reasons it's wise to try in your class to encourage accounts that show both positive and negative views of law officers, or whatever institutional representatives you are writing about. Not positive just to be nice, not "A police officer once kicked me in the stomach but most police officers are really very kind," but fully realized and felt experiences.

Before a writing on a national issue or any other topic can become useful, it must be read. If it is poorly done or half done, it needs to be rewritten or extended. For example, the following journal entry about a policeman is merely the bones of a good story:

> **The policeman that pulled me over was a really great guy.**
> **We were talking about school and he mentioned how much**

I'd grown in the last two years. He eyed my driver's license. I was overwhelmed when he told me he was going to give me a break this time. He only wrote the ticket for ten instead of fifteen m.p.h. over.

This paragraph needs to be a longer story. It could easily and naturally be extended by presenting the conversation between the policeman and the driver. Then the oppositions and the surprise would develop and build, as they did for the driver in the actual incident. The eight fundamentals of writing given in Chapter 3 need to be put into practice. As short as the statement is, it still wastes words. The words "really" and "only" are not needed. And the opening sentence is a *giveaway* which tells the reader what to expect and prevents him from experiencing the facts and developing the tension the driver felt.

Writing like this is private rather than public. It does not communicate to others. It is personal but it refuses to let the public know enough to judge the writer's judgment.

Samuel Butler said, "Let your subject choose you." He did that himself, as many professional writers do, because he wanted to put himself into the flow of words and experience and ideas that sometimes come to a writer free. You can do that and still be writing about a national or local issue. Think of the society you live in. Right now it is testing all its institutions. Thoughtful priests are leaving the church and getting married; thoughtful teachers are leaving established schools and setting up free schools; thoughtful men and women are living together without being officially married. And thoughtful priests are staying in the church and praising its conventional ways; thoughtful women and men are speaking up for traditional marriage; and thoughtful teachers are warning against the dangers of too much freedom in education. These are controversial times. You cannot have avoided experiences which touch some of the changes in church, law, race, school, marriage, the relationships between parents and children, government, the armed forces, war, bureaucracy, business, natural resources, narcotics, welfare, old age—the list is almost endless.

The experiences you write of do not have to be extreme: you do not have to have witnessed a murder or committed a crime. Perhaps you attended a wedding recently that took place in a pine woods and included rituals written by a bride and groom dressed in blue jeans. You were present at the breaking of centuries-old traditions. A report of what you saw is evidence in a national controversy. You need only tell what took place. If you wish, you can include your own feelings,

but that is not necessary. This is not the conventional school assignment which requires you to make "a concluding judgment at the end
of the paper expressed in not more than twenty-five words."

For example, here's a factual piece of writing which touches upon
the relationships of children and parents. You may want more than
the writer gives you, but what he gives is solid evidence, something
to ponder before coming up with suggestions for parents or children
looking for ways to live with each other.

STRENGTH

A little man parks his car in the shade of the tree in front
of our house. He walks toward me studying the house and
its surroundings. The lawn, the trees, the bushes. He kicks
at a weed sprouting up from a crack in the sidewalk. I remain in the porch chair as he comes closer.

He wears a gray pin-striped suit. In his hands is a brief-
case and *The Wall Street Journal*. A thin red tie rolls
down his fat stomach. His neck hangs out over the starched
button-down collar of his Arrow shirt. His pants are baggy
at the bottom; at the top he's poured into them. The belt
buckle is in the last hole.

"Hello Ron."

"Hi Dad."

"Where's your mother?"

"Makin' dinner."

"Did you get that faucet fixed?"

"Yes."

"Did it need a new washer?"

"Uh-huh."

"Good, better come in and wash up."

As he enters the house, the screen door squeaks. He
opens and closes it, searching for the insignificant noise.
Again I feel it coming.

"After dinner better find the squeak and oil it."

"O.K."

"Where there's a squeak, there's friction and where
there's friction, there's wear. Some day this thing'll fall
right off."

You've just met my father. Age 52. Roman Catholic,
married thirty years with six kids—three girls and three
boys. Employed by a big corporation as a systems analyst
with thirty years seniority. Lives in a fine house in a suburb

of Cleveland and owns two cars, a two-car garage, a trailer, and an oil well.

After high school he held three part-time jobs, one as an assistant manager in a grocery store while attending night school.

His father lived in the taverns and his mother, seeking only the companionship and love of her husband, followed him everywhere. They both died alcoholics.

My dad's theory is simple: work for the body, strict rules for the mind. Every Saturday he carried with him a list of chores we were to do. If we didn't get the work done, we had to do it on Sunday after church. Many times I stayed up Saturday night and worked on the car till 12:00 or 1:00 in the morning so I could watch the football games on Sunday. We fixed our own cars, made our own wine, re-shingled our house, painted our station wagons, laid our own carpeting, repaired our own washing machines, dryers, TV sets, and radios. For three weeks we worked in our basement to finish it off besides doing our regular chores. By himself my father has put in our basement bathroom, wired up our television antenna, and on one summer day shoveled a ton of topsoil from our driveway to the back-yard. I remember once he had to drill through glass but didn't want to buy an expensive diamond-tip drill. He used his fountain-pen, which had a diamond head, as a drill bit to fix a crystal chandelier.

Two summers ago a couple of cars smashed together on our corner and one of my friends came over and said, "O.K., you guys, fix these cars." It was meant as a joke, but still our reputation had made him think of it. Many of our friends hated to come over because my father either sent them home or put them to work. He wouldn't allow my older sister to wear blue jeans when girls started wear-ing them. About five years ago my brother lost his brand new hat, so my father made him wear a girl's scarf to church. He may have played catch with me about five times.

We couldn't listen to our radio or stereo on Sunday. Nor did we receive weekly allowances. He let my mother give us a nickel a week to put in the church collection. If our grades weren't good, A's and B's, we were not allowed to watch television during the week. In fact he moved the television set downstairs so it wouldn't interfere with our studying.

Up until two years ago I still had a bed time. Two summers ago I took Driver's Training and needed the family car to pass the final test. But he wouldn't let me use it. Within four months I got a job, bought a car, insurance, and a license just in time to pass the test. What had made me mad was that he had let my older sisters use the car not only for the test but for other things too. When I became seventeen he started charging me $20.00 a week for room and board.

My father has precedence over the lounge chairs which are both upstairs and downstairs, the newspaper, the *TV Guide*, and even the shower. If he and another person happen to be getting ready to take a bath or a shower at the same time, he gets it first because he pays the water bills.

I believe he hates city life. We travel a lot. We've been in every state in the U.S. but two, Alaska and Hawaii, even traveled all over Canada and Mexico. Yet he still doesn't change, whether at home or away from home.

One time my brothers, my father, and I hiked seventeen miles to the bottom of the Grand Canyon, a trip which would take two days. During the entire time he acted like John Wayne in his movies.

"All right, you guys, take five," or "Let's go, get a move on."

He rationed out the food and water. We got back at him though because for the last few miles he was gasping for air and saying, "Wait up, you guys." He didn't have that commanding tone in his voice any more.

Many times my mother has threatened to walk out and I remember how my brother and I would make plans to run away from home. We'd wait until everyone was asleep and then my brother would come over into my bed and we'd plan our escape. Get the suitcase down from the closet and pack up and sneak out to catch a bus for Texas. We loved Texas because that's where all the cowboys were. Pretty soon we'd just fall asleep, too tired to go anywhere.

My father had one weakness—cigars. Three years ago he was smoking eight cigars a day until his doctor told him to quit. Now he has gained at least forty pounds, which are endangering his health as well as aggravating his bad back and heart. Age is catching up with him now and he's beginning to loosen up. But there are things I'll never forget. I can't forget.

I love him.

RON B. RICHARDS

What do you think of that statement about a father? Chances are some of your fellow students will disagree with you. It is not a paper that comes to neat conclusions but it speaks from such depths of feeling that it cannot be quickly waved aside. You may remember it for several months. It will probably make you think of your relationship with your father or mother and help you see it more objectively. Those are not small accomplishments for a paper written in school.

Here is another view of parents and child encountering each other. Again it tells truth so faithfully that it demonstrates how both parents and child can view a matter with totally different perceptions.

BIG SWALLOWS

It was Saturday night. We were driving around deciding when we should go home. Hank and Ken were sitting in front of my car with Hank at the wheel. Both were drunk. I was sitting in the back with a couple of bottles of wine. One was almost empty. I finished it and tossed it out.

We had just left a party. Well, I think you would call it a party. It was more like a place to sit and drink or smoke. We only knew a few of the people. That was one of the reasons we left.

I sat in the back holding the other bottle of wine. It was hard to decide if I should drink it. I was seventeen and had been drinking for about two years but usually one bottle of wine was as much as I could handle. After glancing at my watch and seeing it was only ten-thirty I unscrewed the top—tilting the bottle, I felt the cold wine meet my lips. It turned into a warm glow the minute it hit my stomach. Taking big swallows, I finished drinking in about fifteen minutes. Suddenly my head was spinning and I was in a state of semi-consciousness.

The next thing I remember is being in our garage. Hank woke me up and told me he would walk home. He asked if I was all right and said we could ride around a little longer. I told him to go ahead home even though it was only twelve o'clock. We both got out of the car and walked to the side of the house. I was planning on using the back door. As Hank walked down the sidewalk he didn't see me fall into the bushes. I was out cold.

I came around what must have been about forty-five minutes later. My mind was jumbled. I glanced up and saw some lights were on. Numb and dazed I got up and walked into the house. Both of my parents were standing in the kitchen as I stumbled in, making a commotion. All I can remember is my mother yelling at me. They told me later that I just walked in and passed out on the couch. They had never seen me drunk before. I'm sure my mother thought I was tripping.

The next day I woke up at about noon. My stomach was upset and my head was still spinning. Staying in bed seemed like the best thing to do. I couldn't face my parents. They don't even drink. I kept thinking about what a wonderful relationship we had up until now.

After sleeping two more hours I began to feel better. I had to go out and see what my mother had to say. She was the only one home. I felt like a piece of petrified wood. The sickness in my stomach had turned to a nervous quivering.

I was standing at the faucet in the kitchen. I turned around quickly. My glance caught her standing behind me. I almost dropped my glass. Her stare was icy as I heard her say, "Is this going to be the type of thing we should expect from now on?" That was the extent of the conversation.

I watched the television for a while but couldn't seem to get interested. Then I tried to go back to sleep again. I managed to sleep about fifteen minutes. Time dragged by.

That night when my father came home we sat around the living room and talked. "What did you drink and where did you get it?"

My mother said, "Do you plan on doing this again?"

I said, "Probably."

She seemed near tears. "Just because everyone else drinks do you think you should?"

"Sure," I said. "It's no big deal."

Then my father cut in. "What about drinking and driving?"

I replied. "I try not to. Hank was driving last night."
The same thing never happened again. Not that I didn't
get drunk. It was just that I made sure they didn't see me.

JOHN R. SENDER

Most of the writings, including the one above, in this chapter are
printed with pseudonyms to protect the writer and others who might
be injured if their real names were used. Writing truths is an act
with consequences, usually good. But school has a way of getting you
to go at things backwards. It becomes hung up on authoritative statements because it wants to promulgate the Truth. And since authorities often speak the last word, that word is apt to be stated generally.
Therefore a student feels pressed to make general statements. If asked
to write a paper about Women's Liberation, for example, a boy
writes, "After many centuries of enduring male chauvinism, women
in America have finally begun to liberate themselves." That's his
statement of the general idea he's read in many articles. Or a girl
writes, "In the future, women will find themselves hired for jobs at
the same pay as men, and in general will be accorded the same rights
and privileges." And so on. Nothing there anyone wants to read at
this stage in the movement. "But how could I write any other way
about Women's Lib?" says a student. "I haven't read any books on
the subject. I'm not an expert."

But every person in the country has daily experiences which touch
Women's Liberation, which is simply a movement involved in changing the sexual roles of Americans. His father lives in relation to the
movement—he increasingly accepts and brings about changes or he
resists them, or he moves back and forth between the two positions.
His mother likewise. Every time the student—male or female—encounters the other sex, the experience is touching this subject. Examine yourself. If you are a man, are you treating women like sex
objects? If you are a woman, by your behavior are you asking to be
treated like a sex object? We need to have a current history of dating
behavior in this country, small accounts of this date or that date, or
the coming together of young people outside the custom of dating.
How do young people act toward each other through sexual roles?
Differently from the way older people act toward them? First we
should not generalize but begin writing the record, putting down the
evidence. Dozens and hundreds and thousands of little accounts of
the behavior—including the talk—of persons of the opposite sex together, working, playing, studying, meeting, sharing, or retreating
from each other. These stories are in your past experience and all
around you. For example, when I recently attended the National Boys

and Junior Tennis Championships, I overheard one of the waiting players—who looked to be seventeen or sixteen—say to one of his fellows:

"I'm not afraid to sit down next to any girl around here and put my arm around her."

"You aren't? Aw, come on."

"No, bet you a dollar I'll do it."

Just then a beautiful girl, who looked twelve, sat down on a bench far enough away that she couldn't hear the boys. She sat there silently, engrossed in the game before her, her clothes and hair perfectly groomed.

"See that girl? I'll do it for a buck."

She was the perfect target, fulfilled the stereotype of an American beauty.

"For how long?—thirty seconds? a minute?"

"No. That's too long. She'd leave. What would you do if you were her and somebody came up and did that? You'd be scared. You'd get up and leave. Just the arm around her—for a buck, OK?"

The talk went on. Later the girl left, unmolested.

That little incident, told simply and directly, is a full statement on the general topic of Women's Lib, and more valuable than some long generalizing papers that summarize or quote what a number of experts have argued on the matter. The tennis player unknowingly turned the act on himself. He admitted that any normal human being would feel attacked by what he proposed to do to a girl he did not know. He wanted to use this girl, any girl, to show off his maleness to his fellow players.

All around you are stories as good as that or better on the subject of Women's Lib. When you decide to write about a social controversy, maybe you will do better simply to examine your experience for an incident or relationship that has made you feel uncomfortable, released, excited, especially happy, and then ask if it is not material for a case-history that bears upon one of the central issues of the day. For example, here's an account from a student's journal written about the smallest of matters, a little animal.

DON'T FEEL BAD

I am sitting in the kitchen—facing the bathroom door. It's open just a crack, enough for some of the darkness from that room to pour into this one. It's early and no sounds are up yet. There is a tiny scratching though. It seems to be creeping into the silence like a genteel, soft joke. I know what it is—but I sit here still because I might scare it away or it might push the door open and run over my toes—I just watch the crack, wondering where did it come from. Is it really there? I plugged up the hole under the sink. It's probably just sitting there, nestled deep in the purple shag of the rug, peering at the other side of the same crack I am peering at. I wonder if it's pissed about the De-Con and all the holes I have blocked up, like the two in the living-room by the fireplace. That's silly—it doesn't have to be mad about that tall glass vase or the bookend. All it has to do is push a little, suck in, and it should be easy for it to squeeze by them.

It's probably not mad at all. It's probably just sitting in the bathroom trying to figure out a way to make it back to wherever it came from. Because I got up, came into the kitchen and turned on the light, it feels trapped in the purple shag. It doesn't have to feel bad, because I feel trapped by that crack. What if the door just slowly eased open? I'd probably be figuring out a way to get back where I came from, too. I wonder why I don't just go over there, break the crack by pulling the door open, and snap on the light. It's probably praying that I won't do just that, the same as I am praying it won't push the crack toward me.

Don't we both feel uncomfortable? I wonder if it snuggled in deeper at the thought because I just put my feet up on the rungs of the chair because of the same thought. Here we are—it and me—caught in the silence of a morning's yawn. We are sharing a time and a feeling and we are from different races of life. Maybe I should just turn off the light and go back to bed. It and I can't be suspended long in this unique understanding because this morning is about ready to sneeze her eyes open and then it and I will have to regress to hating and fearing each other simply because our understanding will be gone with the coming of the noise.

ANNE LAYTON

Trivial? The way a small animal's sounds affected this girl? Or sentimental because it gives animals the attributes of human beings? Maybe so to many persons, but right now there are many Americans who have begun studying and trying to follow Oriental philosophers who say that man and animal and rock and tree are one, together existing in this world, and they can get in touch with each other. Many of us on a walk in the woods at times have felt close communion with trees or animals. Is it possible that Oriental persons recognized the facts of existence better than we more scientific Westerners? Anne Layton's story suggests she possessed Oriental sympathies. The point here is that she did not read and summarize a number of books or articles on this "subject." She wrote down her own experience, about which she could speak more authoritatively than anyone else. Her story is a piece of evidence on which the controversy can be resolved or discussed with enlightenment. Hers is not the only evidence. Much more would be needed before a person should speak a final word on the kinship of animals and human beings. But not always do we need to speak final words, as school so often forces us to do. Often it is enough, and sometimes more truthful, to speak a word of experience that opens to other people new possibilities of living.

Never underestimate the record that is trying to be truthful to individual human experience. Frequently it is more convincing than a page full of statistics. At this moment in American publishing, magazine and book editors are increasingly printing thoughtful histories of individual experience. Seldom do they publish essays of ideas or summaries of trends unless they are accompanied by little stories or case-histories to give their ideas life and authenticity. Usually we are more persuaded by the record of a life than by a sermon, and the best ministers fill their sermons with little stories, as Jesus Christ did. And Buddha. And Mohammed.

WRITING EIGHTEEN: Write an account of the kind discussed in this chapter. You may get to it either way—by thinking of a moving experience in your life and seeing whether it touches one of the central issues of the day, or by thinking of a central issue and asking what experience you have had that touches it.

If you and your teacher wish, you may then write another account on a different issue. And another. The possibilities for writing innumerable papers are before you. With this method alone you can find topics for a dozen papers, enough to fill up the work of a whole semester.

*Look sharply after your thoughts. They
come unlooked for, like a new bird seen
on your trees, and, if you turn to your
usual task, disappear; and you shall
never find that perception again; never,
I say—but perhaps years, ages, and I
know not what events and worlds may
lie between you and its return!*

RALPH WALDO EMERSON

chapter 16
keeping
a
journal

MOST PERSONS write notes to themselves
(Get Kleenex and catsup. "I saw a rhinusahorus at the zoo"—Timmy's
report at dinner, which should be forwarded in next letter to Grandma) and each spring they wish they had a note from last year telling
when they first saw blossoms on the lilac bush. But they lose the
notes, which are written on torn bits of paper, the backs of laundry
slips, or the flyleaves of books.

An old cigar box will not do, because not enough of the notes
get put in there, and those that do are difficult to consult: one must
riffle through all of them to find one.

The answer is a journal instead of a box, a bound ruled book in
which to make instant and permanent entries. Many professional
writers keep one.

WRITING NINETEEN: Try keeping a journal for a week. You
may not be the journal kind of person—maybe you have a photo-
graphic memory or an aversion to recording anything you feel has
not been polished like a gem. But try keeping a journal for a week
and see. Here's a day from one of Henry Thoreau's journals:

Dec. 5, 1856. Clear, cold winter weather. What a contrast between this week and last, when I talked of setting out apple trees!

P.M.—Walked over the Hill.

The Indians have at length got a regular load of wood. It is odd to see a pile of good wood beside their thin cotton tents in the snow, the wood-pile which is to be burnt within is so much more substantial than the house. Yet they do not appear to mind the cold, though one side of the tent is partly open, and all are flapping in the wind, and there is a sick child in one. The children play in the snow in front, as before more substantial houses.

The river is well skimmed over in most places, though it will not bear,—wherever there is least current, as in broad places, or where there is least wind, as by the bridges. The ice trap was sprung last night.

As I walk along the side of the Hill, a pair of nuthatches flit by toward a walnut, flying low in mid-course and then ascending to the tree. I hear one's faint *tut tut* or *gnah gnah*—no doubt heard a good way by its mate now flown into the next tree—as it is ascending the trunk or branch of a walnut in a zigzag manner, hitching along; prying into the crevices of the bark; and now it has found a savory morsel, which it pauses to devour, then flits to a new bough. It is a chubby bird, white, slate-color, and black.

It is a perfectly cloudless and simple winter sky. A white moon, half full, in the pale or dull blue heaven and a whiteness like the reflection of the snow, extending up from the horizon all around a quarter the way up to the zenith. I can imagine that I see it shooting up like an aurora. This is at 4 P. M. About the sun it is only whiter than elsewhere, or there is only the faintest possible tinge of yellow there.

There are a great many walnuts on the trees, seen black against the sky, and the wind has scattered many over the snow-crust. It would be easier gathering them now than ever.

The johnswort and the larger pinweed are conspicuous above the snow. Some fine straw-colored grasses, as delicate as the down on a young man's cheek, still rise above this crusted snow, and even a recess is melted around them, so gently has it been deposited.

The sun goes down and leaves not a blush in the sky . . .

My themes shall not be far-fetched. I will tell of homely every-day phenomena and adventures. Friends! Society! It seems to me that I have an abundance of it, there is so much that I rejoice and sympathize with, and men, too, that I never speak to but only know and think of. What you call bareness and poverty is to me simplicity. God could not be unkind to me if he should try. I love the winter, with its imprisonment and its cold, for it compels the prisoner to try new fields and resources. I love to have the river closed up for a season and a pause put to my boating, to be obliged to get my boat in. I shall launch it again this spring with so much more pleasure. This is an advantage in point of abstinence and moderation compared with the seaside boating, where the boat ever lies on the shore. I love best to have each thing in its season only, and enjoy doing without it at all other times. It is the greatest of all advantages to enjoy no advantage at all. I find it invariably true, the poorer I am, the richer I am. What you consider my disadvantage, I consider my advantage. While you are pleased to get knowledge and culture in many ways, I am delighted to think that I am getting rid of them. I have never got over my surprise that I should have been born into the most estimable place in all the world, and in the very nick of time, too.

A day's record of observations and thoughts, from a journal which ran into several thousand printed pages. From these pages Thoreau put together several books, including *Walden*, a classic statement of the joys of self-reliant living which has been read for more than a hundred years in all parts of the world.

If a writer will go on the principle of stopping everywhere and anywhere to put down his notes, as the true painter will stop anywhere and everywhere to sketch, he will be able to cut down his works liberally. He will become prodigal not of writing—any fool can be this—but of omission. You become brief because you have more things to say than time to say them in.

SAMUEL BUTLER

Thoreau's entry for December 5, 1856 contained his usual miscellany of writing: simple notes of facts to mark the record of the year, observations of nature and men, thoughts. In your journal put down whatever strikes you. Think of it at once as private and public. You may be showing it or parts of it to others. If you find yourself recording such intimate secrets that you do not want them revealed, you can keep them in the book and copy out only those you want to show to others. The possibilities for entries are endless, as the following statement by Dorothy Lambert shows:

WHAT IS A JOURNAL?

Though a journal may be many things—a treasury, a storehouse, a jewelry box, a laboratory, a drafting board, a collector's cabinet, a snapshot album, a history, a travelogue, a religious exercise, a letter to oneself—it has some definable characteristics. It is a record, an entry-book, kept regularly, though not necessarily daily. Invariably some entries will be scrawled on the backs of ice cream wrappers, envelopes, paper bags, or programs, whatever blank surface is available at the moment. Some will be nearly illegible, written in the dark in the middle of the night. These entries can be recopied, pasted in, or dated and kept loose in the rear of the journal, but they are part of it; inspiration settles on one at the most awkward moments, not necessarily as one sits down to write with clean page, sharpened pencil, and open mind.

It is a record kept for oneself. As such, it is fragmentary, allusive, disjointed, uneven in quality. Nor should it be polished and unified; then it would be a collection of essays. What matters is the one entry in ten which sparkles, ready to be set in the ring of an essay or story or poem or letter.

Not only is it a record for oneself, but of oneself. Every memorable journal, any successful journal, is honest. Nothing sham, phoney, false. Who is there to kid? Yet euphemism, the word which hides the fact, is so much a part of the world; to break through the euphemistic mold of thought to honesty is very difficult. A journal need not be a confession, or a psychoanalyst's couch, however. Honesty lies in observing undeceived what lies about, not necessarily what lies within.

Finally, a journal is a place to fail. That is, a place to try, experiment, test one's wings. For the moment, judgment, criticism, evaluation are suspended; what matters is the attempt, not the success of the attempt. In a journal one practices the lines before going onstage.

A journal may be all gems, or all logs, or all plans and blueprints, or all test tubes, or all confession, or all collections of oddments—or it may be a marvelous hodgepodge of the old-fashioned general store. What follows are some ways of seeing, of thinking of a journal, and some suggestions of what to do with it. You may follow one suggestion consistently, or try all, or none. At least you will become aware of what is possible.

1. Think of your journal as a treasury, a jewelry box for gems and gold nuggets, for quotes (others' or/and yours), pithy ideas, epigrams, turns of phrase, insights, analogies, puns, aphorisms, nutshell wisdom. You will write little, but think much.

2. Think of your journal as a storehouse into which you pack canned goods (others' ideas), fresh fruit, nuts, corn, string, straw, K-rations—almost anything edible and useful, in preparation for a rainy day, when you can browse through your storehouse with delight and constant amazement at what is there. Like a pack-rat or the Collier brothers, don't stop to be discriminatory in your salvaging and collecting.

3. Think of your journal as a collector's cabinet in which you place or mount butterflies and moths, or glass figurines, or . . . What will you collect? salt and pepper shakers? stamps? model ships in bottles? oddments, little ironic quirks of life? Do you collect for others to see, or just to have?

4. Think of your journal as a snapshot album and you a roving photographer clicking a shutter on life. Light and dark contrasts, color, texture, angles and circles, portraits, landscapes: what will you photograph? Steichen chose faces and hands; Ansel Adams chose the Sierras. See life through a lens, telescopic, microscopic, or wide-angle, but a lens. In focus.

5. Think of your journal as a laboratory for experiments, blank pages waiting to be tried. Dissect. See what the insides are like, how it runs, how it's put together. Examine

minutely; see with a microscope. Mix test-tubes. Weigh.
Trace patterns; fix laws. Ask questions and set about to
find answers.

6. Think of your journal as a giant wardrobe which you
can step into and try on marvelous clothes. Put on others'
styles, look in the mirror, see and feel how they fit. Wear
what you like; change with the seasons; try on 49 hats and
buy none. Be Parisian, Ethiopian, or Hindi: experiment,
experiment. Even poetry, though by phrases, not rhymes.

7. Think of your journal as a drafting board. Blank
pages will become blueprints, plans for a house to live in.
Or are you drafting just window sills, or a whole cathedral?
Accuracy, careful detail, sharp lines, no smudges on the
pages. If you are an idea-person, what will you build?
Watch your idea-house grow, as you add on bedrooms for
the birth of new thoughts.

8. Think of your journal as a psychoanalyst's couch, a
confession. Lie down, and talk, talk, talk. Ramble on about
irrelevancies, or else list in order your sins. Repeat, go over
and over as you peel away each layer of onion skin to the
core. Explore your depths. Dreams, Fantasies, Truths.

9. Think of your journal as a tape recorder attached
directly to your brain. Record your stream-of-conscious-
ness, your associational thoughts. Don't fuss for words;
write as fast as you think. Use dashes, dots, skip lines and
spaces for "punctuation." Replay: can you find a coherence
in your thoughts? Emphasize and clarify such associational
leaps.

10. Think of your journal as a continuous but unmailed
letter to a specific, real person. Preferably of the opposite
sex, highly interested in you. Make every entry a love
letter, every entry an act of love. Or choose to write to a
close confidant. Or to your mother. Or possibly to your yet
unborn children. What would you tell them? no moralizing,
no mush.

11. Think of your journal as a letter to yourself. What
would you have yourself know? Or remember ten years from
now? Which self of your many selves will you choose to
write to? Or yourself as you *were*, say, at ten? Or yourself
as you will be? Will your other self/selves answer back?
Turn your journal into a dialogue or triologue with yourself. Argue, debate, reconcile.

12. Think of your journal as a history—memoirs—and you as a VIP: the average citizen. Write for an extra-terrestrial reader, or a terrestrial one of the 22nd Century. Let them know how we really lived and thought. Or else record the current world events, as filtered through your eyes, your consciousness, your concern. Record how history touches you.

13. Think of your journal as a travelogue, even though you may travel only through tunnels from dorm to class, like an underground man. See afresh, as if you were born yesterday, or recently distilled from another planet. Record the quaint customs, lore, folkways, speech patterns, super-stitions, magic, and miraculous sights of the local terrain. Be Livingstone, Margaret Mead. Or be Magellan; chart the unknown; fill in the map of your world.

14. Think of your journal as a religious exercise, one which might lead to a religious experience, or religious insight. Write it as a letter to God. A dialogue? Follow St. Ignatius' meditative methods: application of the senses; composition of scene. But write it down. Become all tongue, all eyeball, all nose; only hands; the world's ear. Be at the place, fly back to the time. Put yourself in other's feet; especially try those you can't stand, those who seem foreign to you. Use these meditative principles in areas not consid-ered religious; meditate on the secular. Write prayers, per-sonal prayers; write litany; write secular prayers, secular litany. Search for metaphors, new metaphors, for the in-effable, the wordless, the inexpressible. Reach out into the void, reach down, reach up, to find ways of telling others what you believe.

Mrs. Lambert's essay on journals is not a map, merely suggestions. Take one, take several, as you wish.

The great journal keepers have always distrusted their memories. When an idea strikes them for a piece of writing, they write it down even though it is only an idea, so far without the materials to give it body. Samuel Butler, whose published *Note-Books* are widely quoted, made such notes for writing he hoped to do some day. Here are three out of a long list:

1. Tracts for Children, warning them against the virtues of their elders.

2. Family Prayers: A series of perfectly plain and sensible ones asking for what people really do want without any kind of humbug.
3. The Sense of Touch: An essay showing that all the senses resolve themselves ultimately into a sense of touch, and that eating is touch carried to the bitter end. So there is but one sense—touch—and the amoeba has it. When I look upon the foraminifera I look upon myself.

If you are aware of the fabulous quality of reality, your notebook is bound to be exciting reading in spots. Here are excerpts from a number of student notebooks:

1

Mom to three-year-old: "Mary Jane, get out of your Coke!"

2

I have drained six cartons of lemonade and twelve glasses of tap water since this afternoon, and two quarts of milk. I have a fever but am on my feet, slushing off to class—reading, writing, and I get paid today.

3

My seven-year-old sister at a birthday party: "Oh, Momma, my feet went to sleep. It feels like salt and pepper mixed."

4

One of the salesmen at Sears absent-mindedly wore to work one shoe and one bedroom slipper. He didn't have time to go home to change, so he developed a limp for the day.

5

A white-haired old woman scooped up spilled dry oatmeal from a busy intersection after the bottom of her grocery bag had burst. She explained to one honking motorist that she didn't want to waste the oatmeal—she would take it home to her ducks.

6

My sister celebrated her sixteenth birthday yesterday. Her boy friend surprised her with a beautiful heart necklace. Later, a strange man surprised her at an intersection by pulling out in front of her car, and she rammed his car with hers, cutting her forehead, nose, and mouth. One scar under her chin is heart-shaped.

7

Last week I saw two guys walking down Western Avenue carrying on a conversation ten feet apart. I even walked between them. Interpersonal relationships are growing less personal but this was too much almost to believe. One of them, I suppose, had determined to assert himself, keep his pace and have the other come up to him. The other probably determined the opposite, so they walked along, making fools of themselves.

8

Charlie came home on leave today after eight weeks of basic training. He learned to kill.

My Uncle was gassed in the First World War and when I knew him he sat in a chair watching television all day and talked in a hesitating manner.

9

On the corner of a parking lot on Rose Street, a mailman stopped at the mailbox, unlocked it, opened the front, took the mail out, and sat down inside the mailbox while he sorted the letters.

10

It's the first day of school. It seems so empty. Oh, there's lots of things to do, but there is something missing. There is no one older. When we were sophomores and juniors there was always the big seniors. Now there is no one left. We're seniors, last year of high school. Is it really the fact that we're as big as we will get? Hard to say what's missing. It's lonely here.

In writing journal entries a person should begin by concentrating on what he says rather than how he says it. Entry 10 is carelessly written. The expression *there is* appears too often. Twice it led the writer to use a singular verb with a plural subject ("there's lots," which says in reverse "lots is"; and "there was . . . the big seniors" which says in reverse "seniors was"). But the writer put her finger on why high school students sometimes feel lost at the beginning of their last year. Since she solved that puzzle, she should not have said, "Hard to say what's missing." If she wants to publish the statement more widely, she should omit that sentence and improve the verbs throughout. If you look at your journal entries some time after you wrote them and find them in need of revision, you might cross out words and make changes for practice, but you do not need to. A journal is personal. If a teacher or someone else can talk you into publishing some of your journal entries, fine; but you should not allow your journal to be graded.

Here are some more journal entries:

11

I hate that sand dune. It looked down at me. I felt small. It seemed to be laughing at me as the wind from the lake blew over it. I hated it even more. I began to run up the side. The sand, like wet cardboard, under my feet. Heat. I could feel it conquer my throat. It was steep. Bushes and fallen tree branches served as handles. My legs were aching. Made me go faster. I fell. Made me feel like a dog crawling on all fours. I went on. The laughter got louder as the wind blew harder. Just kept running. Panting, until I found myself standing on the top of it. The lake and beach below looked so small. And the sand dune. Now that it was under me, it didn't seem so big either. My turn to laugh. Felt like God.

12

Moved. Just like that. She moved. I had known her for a long time. She had thick, curly eyelashes, long. Envied. Lise always grew her nails long, too. It was sort of awesome to look at them sometimes. They were curved and filed into a fine oval. No one at school said anything about it. No teachers. They didn't say anything. It's different now. Lise moved. She went to Grand Rapids. The nuns there were different. Strict. Scary. Lise was in typing. The nun said to trim the nails by the next weekend. She didn't. The nun wasn't to be ignored. Up to the desk. Lise had to cut off all her finger nails. Right then. Right there. It's too bad she moved.

When you write in a journal, keep your sense of a reader. That reader may be no one else but you, but so much later in time that he needs to be spoken to fully, to be put there. The writer of Entry 13 chose an incident involving deep feeling and wrote strong sentences, but she held back a little too much.

13

We went to the funeral and afterwards his grandpa asked me to go out to the house with all the other people. I did, and everybody ignored me. I think Kent did because after we went to the cemetery and the minister said the last words underneath the tent, Kent went over and sat in one of the limousines, leaving the door open, perhaps so I could come and say a kind word or pat him on the hand. I didn't want to. I lowered my eyes and walked right by him. I think he even said my name.

Benjamin Franklin tells in his *Autobiography* how he read and studied a passage of writing he admired, wrote down "short Hints of the Sentiment in each Sentence," and then several days later tried to reproduce the passage. Almost every professional writer has learned fundamentals in this way before developing his own style. No surprise here: long ball hitters have learned from imitating Johnny Bench and Hank Aaron, painters have learned from imitating Leonardo da Vinci and Van Gogh.

A good writer never plagiarizes from another writer, but he borrows obviously and he builds on what another writer has said. When E. E. Cummings wrote his great line "pity this busy monster,manunkind," discussed in Chapter 14, he may have got the notion of playing with *man* and *unkind* from Thoreau's lines in *A Week on the Concord and Merrimack Rivers*:

I love man—kind, but I hate the institutions of the dead unkind. Men execute nothing so faithfully as the wills of the dead, to the last codicil and letter. *They* rule this world, and the living are but their executors.

When Thoreau wrote in "Walking":

Any man can stop a hole to keep the wind away, but no other man could serve so rare a use as the author of this illustration did.

he was clearly alluding to lines Shakespeare gave to Hamlet:

Imperious Caesar, dead and turned to clay,
Might stop a hole to keep the wind away.

although he did not mention *Hamlet*. These two writers did not steal from Thoreau and Shakespeare. Cummings pushed further a

word play of Thoreau—if he borrowed at all; and Thoreau turned
a phrase of Shakespeare into half of a neat compliment to him.

All men must borrow from those who have gone before, but they
should understand what constitutes stealing from the printed page,
however difficult that act is to define. One does not always have to
use quotation marks. All men are created equal—the reader recognizes
the source. One can give the wise reader a hint that he is borrowing,
as Thoreau did when he borrowed from Hamlet. But one should not
take a series of words—say more than seven—from another writer
when they are distinctive and valuable in style or message, and allow
the reader to believe they are his own.

Student term papers often abound in such plagiarism. Speaking in
the most obviously alien voices, students write stolen sentences like
this:

> The nugatory effect of the prolix discussion was that the
> Treaty of Rackham was forever doomed.

This is calculated imposture, in writing called *plagiarism*. The most
responsible way to borrow is immediately to acknowledge indebted-
ness, not by footnote or quotation marks (although they are frequently helpful), but by naming the source:

> Burke said that . . .

WRITING TWENTY: After keeping a journal for a week, stop
for a week and then go back to its pages. Choose the entry which
most moves you, and work it up or cut it down until you have produced a small piece of writing whole and satisfying to you.

WRITING TWENTY-ONE: After one week's respite from journal writing, begin your journal again and make a daily entry or two
for two weeks. Choose an object, a place, a person that interests you,
and note it each weekday for two weeks—include weekends if possible.
Observe it daily. You will see it in different lights because the weather
has changed, the time of the day, the weather inside you. Write in
your journal what it looks like and what it makes you feel, on at
least ten different days.

Maybe you will find yourself writing a long description one day
and only a word or phrase on another day. Ask other persons who
have a chance to know this thing well, or to observe it frequently,
how it looks to them and makes them feel. Record the best answers
you get.

After all that looking and listening, put together from your best
journal entries a piece of writing about that thing. It may be several
pages long or a few compact lines of prose or poetry.

Nor use too swelling, or ill-sounding words.

BEN JONSON

chapter 17
writing second-hand

BELOW is printed a book review by Anatole Broyard, a reviewer for the daily *New York Times*. Remember what Miss Singwich, the English teacher in junior high, used to tell you about book reports? "Summarize the plot, name and describe the leading characters or principal theme of the book, tell the purpose in one sentence." If Singwich felt daring that day she might have said, "You may make your own judgment of the book, but reserve that until the end, and do not use the word 'I' anywhere else in your report." She was telling you to use no first-hand experience, and to be *scholarly,* as she understood the word.

Since the *Times* is the newspaper of historical record in the United States, you might expect Mr. Broyard's review would be dull and impersonal like a book report written for Miss Singwich. Here it is:

THE OBSTETRICS OF THE SOUL

DEATH AS A FACT OF LIFE
By David Hendin, 255 pages. Norton. $7.50

"I don't understand what I'm supposed to do," Tolstoy said on his deathbed—and neither do most of us. The conspiracy of silence with which we surround the subject of dying led Geoffrey Gorer, the British anthropologist, to coin the phrase "the pornography of death." But a "good death" is

an indispensable end to a good life—so crucial, in fact, that
a German writer called it the "obstetrics of the soul." To
die with dignity is important not only to the dying person,
but also to his or her survivors, who will always be able to
remember the one they loved in this light.

According to David Hendin in his "Death as a Fact of
Life," dying today is often rendered obscene by technology.
Many patients are kept alive when they are no longer
human beings, but simple circulatory systems, breathing
but otherwise unresponsive tissue. Under these circumstances, life may sometimes be more terrifying than death.
The dying person's relatives and friends are elbowed away
from him by machines. And since these machines interfere
with the natural course of decline, no one knows exactly
when death will come and the patient often expires with
only technology for company. In this connection, the author quotes Theodore Fox's famous remark: "We shall have
to learn to refrain from doing things merely because we
know how to do them."

Mr. Hendin quotes surveys to show that most dying people would prefer to talk about it, and are greatly relieved
when the silence is broken. I know that as I read his book,
I felt my own anxieties about death first articulated, and
partially assuaged. It *is* therapeutic to bring that imme-
morial enemy of ours out into the light. As the author
points out, for some of us the threat of death can have an
integrative rather than a disruptive function. It can make
us see our life as a coherent whole and give us an opportunity to sum it up emotionally and intellectually—to deny
the fashionable charge of "meaninglessness or absurdity."

Accepting death is not necessarily a form of resignation,
of giving up: it may be a positive reorientation. We can
look *back* over our life as well as forward to its end. We can
congratulate ourselves on what we have done and reverse
the old saw that "you can't take it with you." By renounc-
ing the terrible duty of pretending, Mr. Hendin says, we
can take the bandages off our fears and our feelings and die
with love instead of lies as the last thing we hear.

The author has done a brilliant and highly sensitive job
of bringing together the literature of death—from the need
for revising our legal, medical and psychological criteria to
the fact that the dead are forcing the living into an ever-

decreasing space. He discusses the science of cryonics, or freezing the body in the hope of future resuscitation (cost $20,000); the case for and against euthanasia; the need to train doctors to *face* death as well as fight it; the "hospices" being built for dying people, so that they can spend their last days in as homelike an atmosphere as their medical needs permit; the advantages of cremation and its relative unpopularity in the United States, and much more.

I found the chapter on "Children and Death" especially moving. Mr. Hendin knows how to evoke a feeling as well as most novelists and he is never, as far as I can remember, guilty of mere sentimentality in dealing with the most highly charged subject in our emotional repertory. Warning us against feeding inane euphemisms to children, he cites the case of a little boy who was told that his dead mother "went up into the sky." Shortly afterwards, the boy was taken on a visit by airplane and was very sad and disappointed because he had looked on every cloud but had not seen his mother. Informed that his infant brother had been picked up by God and taken to heaven, another child kept his windows locked, refused to cross open spaces and played only in the shade of trees for fear the same thing would happen to him.

Unacknowledged death haunts us far more effectively than the ghosts of our childhood. The author feels that the more fully it is faced, the sooner we are likely to recover from the shock of someone's death. If we do not make peace with them and separate ourselves from the dead through appropriate periods of mourning and grief, we may find it difficult to attach ourselves to anyone who might help replace them afterwards.

Though there is not a superfluous page in "Death as a Fact of Life," I found myself—emotionally, not morbidly—drawn to those passages dealing with the dying person. When Mr. Hendin speaks of the indignity of deterioration, I remember the humiliation I saw in my own father's face when he was a Rube Goldberg tangle of tubes and life-coercing machines. His difficulties were increased by his "stiff upper lip" philosophy that locked both of us in the anguish of all that we wanted to, and could not say. A terrible loneliness lurked in his eyes, but it was too late for him to learn or change.

What the author does not say because it may be beyond the scope of his intent is that our entire life is a preparation for our death, and we may expect to die well or badly depending on how we have lived. Freud told a story of visiting William James at the time when the American psychologist and philosopher had a brush with death in the form of a heart attack. He could not refrain from asking James afterward how he had felt about the prospect. James replied that he had lived his life and done his work. Death held no terrors for him. Edmund Bergier, the psychiatrist, remarks in one of his many books that, after a satisfying sexual experience with someone we love, it is natural to feel sleepy. I mention these two remarks because I feel that, somewhere between them, we may find the answer to one of life's most intimidating questions.

The New York Times, January 25, 1973

Maybe old Singwich would give Mr. Broyard a C for that effort. He started his book report with second-hand comments by Tolstoy and Geoffrey Gorer, and you can't tell whether they had appeared in Mr. Hendin's book or Mr. Broyard had swiped them from somewhere else. Then he tells about his "own anxieties about death" and at the crucial point, just before the end of the review, talks about his own father's death. He is constantly butting in on the author with his own ideas and feelings about death.

That's what Singwich might think, but many readers of this book review who have sat down and discussed their reactions have felt otherwise. They were moved by Mr. Broyard's report of how he was moved by David Hendin's book. They wanted to read it. And right away, before they could get the book in their hands, they discussed the way people face dying.

Like most good writing Mr. Broyard's review fulfilled the eight points presented at the end of Chapter 3. It did not waste words. It put the reader there, gave him a full example (about the boy told that his mother "went up into the sky") as well as a summary in paragraph 5 of what the book covered. It made things happen for the reader as they happened for Mr. Broyard when he read the book. It brought up some of Mr. Hendin's surprises: for example, the simple statement about not prolonging painful life: "We shall have to learn to refrain from doing things merely because we know how to do them." And the notion that death can be integrative rather than disruptive when we at that moment look at our life as a coherent whole. And Broyard went beyond Hendin to say surprisingly that "we may expect to die well or badly depending on how we have lived."

Mr. Broyard did not forget to judge the book: he pointed out that like a novelist Hendin evokes feeling, he is not sentimental, he does not waste words ("there is not a superfluous page"). But Broyard wove these judgments and the paragraph sketching the content of the book back and forth with his own response to it. He allowed himself to present some of his own experience on which his response was based. This weaving of the *objective* (description of what's in the object, the book) and the *subjective* (Broyard's own feelings and knowledge) provides a tension, and therefore a relief, for the reader. The review is not all the same, not all impersonal or egotistically personal. And it provided the fundamental of all good reviewing or criticism: enough evidence so the reader could begin to judge the reviewer's judgment.

Can you write like that? It's hard to do once you've learned how like an Engfish to swim in the dry water of school. Actually Mr. Broyard did his job naturally. He read a book, was moved by it, let his readers know how and why. Then he disciplined himself enough to sketch the book's contents so a reader would know what it presented beyond Mr. Broyard's special interests.

There are your readers out there—the rest of the class and the teacher. When you write second-hand, remember you yourself are always responding partly on the basis of your own experience, and your readers will be responding partly on theirs. So it's a second-hand experience, but also a first-hand one, and if you think of your readers, you'll remember they have hands too.

SHOWING WHY A WRITING AFFECTS YOU

WRITING TWENTY-TWO: Choose a piece of writing (book, magazine article, story, editorial, play, poem—makes no difference whether you read it in school or out) which moved you so much that you might naturally talk to a friend or classmate about it. Maybe you love it, maybe you hate it, maybe you have mixed feelings. But it hit you hard. Write a paper showing why and how it hit you. Let your reader see what in your experience or thinking made you excited by the writing. And in so doing, tell enough about the writing that another person who has never read that writing will see what hit you. This is not a book report. Don't try to summarize what you read. Don't try to cover everything in it.

Here is an example of such a paper, written by a college senior:

1

When I read *In Cold Blood,* our house was empty. One small reading light shone in the blackness of my musty den. It was late in the evening and the occasional creaking of the floors was the only sound. I swore I wouldn't read it again. It was a story of two men who committed four murders. This was what Truman Capote wished to show us, in the most factual language possible in a novel. The results were horrifying. They were not simply two characters. Capote let me know these men slowly, detail by detail, until I felt comfortable on a first-name basis.

I had never met two men who had shot four people in the head. They were men not unlike many students at this school. True, they had idiosyncrasies that were brought out, but they probably drank beer, brushed their teeth, and wore T-shirts just like I do. By the end of the book I actually felt sorry for them. They were human beings and capable of error.

How many eligible Perrys and Hickocks are in the dorm or my classes? If I point a pistol at a girl's head I am stupid, careless, and unsafe. If I move my right index finger one quarter of an inch, I become a maniac. One quarter of an inch is the measure of a madman. How many of us do not have one split second of weakness, one moment of unconsciousness when we do something completely irrational?

"I don't know why I did it. I guess I just wasn't thinking."

I believe that a man, any man, at the right place, at the right time, and with the right apparatus, will kill for no apparent reason. We are all capable.

This book scared me, bothered me, made me sick. I do not even know whether I liked it, but I know I'll read it again.

TIM SWEENEY

Here is the first draft of another such paper, written by a high school student. Its materials could be clarified and polished, but the critic and the work both come alive and encounter each other at a surprising point.

2

I've watched dirty little brats get up at 7:00 in the morning and play outside all day by themselves. Their mother works and so she can't watch them. They walk the streets by themselves looking for something to do. Anything that interests them they play with. You always read about kids playing in old refrigerators and getting suffocated. Their mothers didn't pay any attention to them.

I always swore I'd never be that kind of a mother. My kids are going to be happy playing in the yard so I can watch them. Kids aren't happy when they're neglected all day.

I read about Ulysses in *The Human Comedy* by William Saroyan. He walked around and amused himself all day. When he waved at the black man on the train, he marveled at life. This man was friendly. If he had been in his own yard, he would have missed the black man and missed his singing.

Ulysses would never have seen the boys steal the green apricots from Mr. Henderson's apricot tree. Ulysses would never have known that it isn't a sin for little boys to steal apricots. He would never have met Big Chris because he got caught in a bear trap.

I wanted to deprive my children of a childhood. My Ulysses would never know my love and he would never grow to be a man. His older brother would never reach manhood by delivering telegrams at night. I don't suppose I would ever wait up silently every night just in case my son wanted to talk. Delivering death messages isn't easy, and maybe he wouldn't even feel like talking. I'd deprive my children of life.

Now, if I could choose my future, I'd be poor. I'd work all day and my children would explore the city by themselves. At night I would come home and they would tell me what they saw. When my oldest son dies in war, my middle son will tear the telegram and I will invite a soldier who knew my son into my house.

The first time you try a criticism like this, you will probably fail to give enough of the work or of your own experience. In the following paper, the writer showed a fine understanding of the spirit of Huckleberry Finn, but she needs to include a few examples of how

Huck "did such a neat job" of running away. And she needs to say a little more about why and how in her own life "Everything has to be proper and formal."

3

Cam told me *Huckleberry Finn* was the only book he enjoyed reading this year. Isn't it the truth? Everybody tries to make more out of a story and ruins it. But the adventure and fun in this book are real. I've always been sort of a tomboy. So, I know what it's like to run off and enjoy the outdoors. Wouldn't it be exciting to go down a river on a raft? I love to be around water anyway. And there would be lots of camping, too. It makes you feel clean and healthy. Why didn't Huck run away sooner? That's not so important. It just seems like he did such a neat job of doing it, though. But something like a lot of blood and a mess would upset my parents too much. I would have to run away without mess. That's the trouble with our society today, though. Everything has to be proper and formal. It would be more fun if I could relax and be messy. How about running away tonight?

The following paper is an original and compelling comment on death. All it needs to be a great paper is a little more about how death appears in the novel.

4

On the Beach, by Nevil Shute, is a stimulating look at death with a touch of the feelings of people near the end.

This book comes to mind in this time because of life passing so quickly. As everyone would eventually die in *On the Beach*, so will everyone die in our world. The difference is in the cause. And in the time. Here during the past couple of days I have noticed a closer relationship between teacher and student. The way of the gatherings of classes is deeper. I have seen a teacher touch a student, me, when she doesn't ever touch anyone. Feelings are here now. They are open and my mind sees it. People will realize for a time that life is short and one must see every thing that one can. It's hard. Now it's doubly hard and very tense. But these people are closer. The librarian scolded me for talking and ten minutes later she came by and patted me on the shoulder. I am sensitive and in the air the eyes see the human feelings reaching out toward each other to hold for a while because there may not be a tomorrow for this person. In a time it will all pass away again and people will scowl at other people and strike out with whipped tongues and I will shudder at the sight of it and think of the memory of silence.

I will watch and be wary and then my day will come.

JAN OKEMURA

Like a number of writings by beginners printed in this book, Paper 4 needs grammatical polishing. The pronoun *it* is several times inaccurately or confusingly used. But the paper communicates feeling with subtlety.

Paper 5 more fully brings alive both the book and the writer's experience which intersects with it; but it, too, could be strengthened with more examples. Try to write a paper which achieves balance. And remember that what makes these papers provocative is their honesty.

5

Fleabags and flophouses, burleyque gals and bloody buckets. Strange words to those unaware of Skid Row, U.S.A. There's one in almost every city.

Sara Harris went to a Skid Row. She interviewed some of its inhabitants—prostitutes, drunks, addicts, and madmen; and in her book, *Skid Row, U.S.A.* reveals by a series of dialogues the people and the life they live.

Until I read this book five years ago, I hadn't even heard the words "flophouse" and "fleabags." I wasn't even aware that such fantastic people existed. People who live in 25¢ a night rooms. A Ph. D. who wore a Phi Beta Kappa key drank liquid black shoe polish as a substitute for expensive liquor. The utter abandonment of themselves so bluntly presented in this book shocked me and I didn't really believe it. But I asked a teacher about it and of course he affirmed that Skid Row was a serious problem. This made me want to take a better look at other people around me. I asked Mom to drive to the sections of town that would be considered something like Skid Row. She didn't want to, so I sneaked out and walked through town to the bars and dumpy hotels. A few men passed me, dirty and messy. Women in sloppy clothes shuffled by. One woman had on spiked heels that clicked and wobbled when she walked. I glanced quickly at their faces. The

> woman was a mask of wrinkles and stringy hair, of red
> eyes and orange lips, and I only stayed a few minutes.

This writer made his knowledge come home.

All of the five papers are presented here in their first drafts. You
can probably see a number of ways to polish them. In Paper 5, for
example, the third sentence gives away the conclusion and should be
omitted, so the reader will accompany the writer on his journey
and share his discovery. The next to last sentence should precede the
one that now comes before it.

When you write of something second-hand you should expect to
find more Engfish than usual in your first draft. Maybe the true words
came truly to you in a pleasurable flow, and there is little to be done
to improve them. But be wary. Before you read that first draft to anyone or have it read aloud, study the next three pages and then go back
to your work.

Mr. Broyard and the five student writers presented speak in voices
that ring true and strike the ear hard. Not any ear, but the ear of
an audience tired of the thick, pulpy language which we call Engfish.
You hear it from teachers in classrooms; you read it in the paragraphs
of second-rate scholars; you see it in the writing of high school and
college students who have imitated what was too much around them.
When Lareen Morgan realizes she is being interviewed for "Senior
Portraits," the high school newspaper column, she shifts into pedantic
gear and says:

> High school has encompassed many memorable, yet trying
> times.

You may have the urge to reply, "So has working in the fertilizer
plant." The word *encompassed* sounds impressive at first but on
second consideration the reader realizes it is so inflated it is about
to pop in Lareen's face.

When the college professor is asked to write an article for a
learned journal, he too often shifts into Engfish and says:

> Unquestionably the textbook has played a very important
> role in the development of American schools—and I believe
> it will continue to play an important role.

You may have the urge here to say, "So have spitballs." The professor goes on:

> The need for textbooks has been established through many
> experiments. It is not necessary to consider these experi-

ments but, in general, they have shown that when instruction without textbooks has been tried by schools, the virtually unanimous result has been to go back to the use of textbooks. I believe too, that there is considerable evidence to indicate that the textbook has been, and is, a major factor in guiding teachers' instruction and in determining the curriculum. And I don't think that either role for the textbook is necessarily bad.

The professor begins his statement with the weasel word *unquestionably*. The very point he is going to try to make in the paragraph he calls unquestionable before he starts. From then on he throws (*lobs* would be a better word; nothing has force in this paragraph) a bunch of dull generalizations in his reader's face. Something has played a *role* in the *development* of something. How many times have you heard that vague line? What role? An *important* role. What does that mean? What kind and rate of development? How did the schools develop as a result of the textbook? What a mishmash of educational language: "need established . . . many experiments . . . virtually unanimous result . . . considerable evidence . . . major factor." These are Weasel Words. They don't say anything for sure yet they keep insisting they are certain and unquestionable. The professor talks about impressive experiments but never mentions one. He doesn't think it is "necessary to consider these experiments" yet he employs them as the only evidence for his argument. Note his last sentence:

And I don't think that either role for the textbook is necessarily bad.

That's the only possibly exciting sentence in the paragraph. Someone has apparently said that using a textbook to guide teachers' instruction or determine the curriculum is bad. Who said that? Why? The writer needs to say, but he isn't fixing to say anything for sure. He won't give the reader anything he can examine and be sure about. He's just talking through his weasel nose.

Every writer talks weaselry at times. This language is hard to see because it is so common.

It was *sort of* a flop.
He was *kind of* a hero to me.
That, *incidentally*, is four fouls.
Going through the weeds there was *almost* like walking in a swamp.
His father, *by the way*, is a crook.

> *"I've got a sort of idea but I don't sup-*
> *pose it's a very good one."*
> *Winnie the Pooh (by A. A. Milne)*

In hurried conversation such weaselries should be forgiven, but not in writing, where the author has a chance to revise and tighten. The weakness of *sort of* and *kind of* is that they do not tell the reader whether the writer really thought "it" was a "flop" or "he" was a "hero." If the writer wanted to communicate that the play was not completely a flop but a failure only in the first act, he should have said so. If he wanted to say that "he" was a hero in one way but not in another, he should have told in what way. Otherwise, he should have simply said: "It was a flop" and "He was a hero to me." Usually *sort of* and *kind of* take the punch out of the words they precede. They lessen rather than increase meaning. If you scatter them throughout your writing, your reader will eventually suspect you don't mean anything you say. Note these weasel words:

> The *final* conclusions of the workshop.
>
> There is a *limited amount* of seating space.
>
> Throwing mud in her face wasn't *too* nice.
>
> Falling down the stairs isn't *exactly* fun.
>
> But being in that wreck was an *especially* devastating experience.
>
> Mary was a *remarkably* lovely queen.

Other words frequently used in weasel fashion are *relative, particular,* and *various.*

> This is a *relatively* minor matter and need not concern us long here.

If the reader doesn't know relative to what, he can't extract much meaning from *relatively.*

> This is a *particularly* fine example of social organization.

Fine already tells the reader the example is above ordinary. *Particularly* steals attention from *fine.*

> In his travels around the world, the captain has encountered many diseases in *various* countries and *various* environments.

This is straight cornmeal mush. Most readers would like it better fried crisp and served with hot syrup. If the writer wants to make his point with power, he should say "about two thousand diseases in fifty-six countries and in environments ranging from ice floes to tropical rain forests."

Most academic writing is loaded with weasel words and phrases; for scholars are taught to be cautious, to qualify. But there are times to be cautious and times to be bold. Watch this pedantic phrase weasel its way into an otherwise straightforward sentence:

> Last week the world was contained in a blue plastic egg
> filled with jelly beans and a set of rabbit teeth—*at least it*
> *was* for five-year-old Jack.

The author doesn't really mean to hint that anyone else's world beside Jack's was filled with that bunch of jelly beans and set of rabbit teeth, but she heard a weasel squeal somewhere and echoes it in her sentence.

As I write this chapter warning others of weaseling, I remember that when I was writing another text, an editor pointed out that almost always when I used the words *in fact*, I followed them with an unsupported personal opinion. Frequently writers try to make up for weak opinions by introducing them with one of the following expressions:

indeed	surely	honestly
obviously	certainly	frankly
of course	needless to say	sincerely

The most dishonest man I ever knew constantly prefaced his remarks with the expression, "I would be less than candid if I did not say—."

Writers are often dishonest with themselves: they speak apologetically, defensively, pompously, or condescendingly when they do not feel apologetic, defensive, pompous, or condescending. A teacher who once submitted a poem to an editor of a magazine, hoping for publication, referred to her manuscript in her covering letter as "This bit of fluff, modeled after 'The Children's Hour.'" Her comment sounds like the introductory remarks many persons make before they speak in a group meeting: "Now I don't claim to be an expert in this subject and what I have to say probably isn't worth much . . ." Then they make a fifteen-minute speech. One is tempted to say to the teacher: "If you think your manuscript is fluff, don't send it to the magazine"; and to the apologetic speaker: "If you don't think you are qualified to speak, don't speak. Or if you are qualified, don't waste our time telling us you aren't."

Whether a word is weaseling or not depends upon its context. If a writer brings most of his sentences alive with verbs crammed full of meaning, with details that speak to all of the reader's senses, he then can afford to use some of the paler, emptier words in the language: in fact his readers may crave relief from lines bursting with life. For example, Lois Phillips Hudson, in her short memoir "When the Fields Are Fresh and Green" (which appears at the end of this chapter), writes:

> At any rate, something important happened in the town
> and Edith sang for it.

Important is usually a weak word; *at any rate* is vague and almost meaningless, and *something* frequently shows a writer's lack of thoroughness in investigation. But here all the words are acceptable because Mrs. Hudson is demonstrating her honesty. In this faraway remembering of childhood she cannot recall every event or object clearly. An event stood out for the townspeople. Mrs. Hudson cannot remember why or how, so she is justified in using the vague word *important* to describe it. She is not vague in other parts of her story. A good writer learns what words and phrases lead him often into poor communication, but he does not try to achieve an absolutely pure diction. A sparing use of conversational tags like *very* or *too much* or *particularly fine* will not wreck an otherwise vigorous piece of writing. Nor will a little unnecessary repetition.

> *"What do you know about this business?"* the King said to Alice.
> *"Nothing,"* said Alice.
> *"Nothing* whatever?" *persisted the King.*
> *"Nothing whatever,"* said Alice.
> *"That's very important,"* the King said, turning to the jury. They were just beginning to write this down on their slates, when the White Rabbit interrupted: "Unimportant, your Majesty means, of course," he said, in a very respectful tone, but frowning and making faces at him, as he spoke.
> *"Unimportant, of course, I meant,"* the King hastily said, and went on to himself in an undertone, "important— unimportant — unimportant — important —" as if he were trying which word sounded best.

Some of the jury wrote it down "important," and some "unimportant." Alice could see this, as she was near enough to look over their slates; "but it doesn't matter a bit," she thought to herself.

LEWIS CARROLL

How much the readers know about a subject should affect the writer's decisions about cutting down his sentences. Samuel Butler, a strong advocate of tightening writing, said that diffuseness "sometimes helps, as for instance, when the subject is hard; words that may be, strictly speaking, unnecessary will make things easier for the reader by giving him more time to master the thought while his eye is running over the verbiage."

Nevertheless, most writers need to develop more ruthlessness toward their writing as John Ciardi, poetry editor of *Saturday Review*, said. It is theirs. They must initially love it. Finally, though, they must see it for what it is and remember that their readers are busy persons, and human beings, who are easily irritated by writing which does not get a satisfactory mileage with its words.

The ways of being untruthful about the world and dishonest with oneself are legion. But the effort to tell the truth is so exacting that once seriously undertaken, it becomes a habit. And one truth breeds another.

Not everyone who uses weasel words is a weasel at heart. If you read well the writings you examine and retain your essential honesty, you will use these expressions so seldom that your readers will not notice them. Do not strive for absolute purity; every person is born with an ego which at times drags him into a weasel's hole. The surest way to reduce weaselry in your writing to a forgiveable amount is to know what you are writing about and to find something to say you believe in. As you have seen, surprises then begin to appear.

WRITING TWENTY-THREE: Now that you've written a paper about a writing that you chose because it hit you hard (maybe you need to write two or three like that until you produce a first-rate criticism), try writing that kind of paper about a piece of writing you did not choose—the following story by Lois Phillips Hudson. Again, relate something in your experience or thoughts that touches something in this story. Show why you respond to the story positively, negatively, or with mixed feelings.

*Writing must be as immediate as life,
or there are no juices, no chance to involve yourself or others in your vitality.*

RAY BRADBURY

WHEN THE FIELDS ARE FRESH AND GREEN
Lois Phillips Hudson

*The boy moves through his life,
keeping a shy
Watch on the man who now assumes
his face.*

—DOUGLAS NICHOLS
Johnny Appleseed

While we are growing up, we become more surprised every year that we seem to other people to be changing, because to ourselves we seem always to be the same. And even while we exult in the higher mark on the closet door where we are measured every year, we feel an increasing apprehensiveness that a day will come when we will seem to have changed so much that nobody will remember who we are.

Thus, when we are still very young, we sense that our first memories of ourselves constitute the only reality by which we will always understand our existence. The problem is that nobody ever seems to see anything the same way we see it, and therefore the memories by which we place ourselves in time and space can never be verified by anybody else. This is the loneliness and the terror of childhood—not to see things the way anybody else sees them, not to understand why some things are "real" and some things are not.

My first hazy memories of myself were set nearly two thousand miles from the place where my second, verifiable memories of myself began. My father's business failed in 1931, and my family moved from Seattle back to a desolate half-section in North Dakota just before I was four years old. At that age, I would, in any case, have begun slipping from my first dreamy existence into my second "real" existence, but it was the drastic change of place that seemed to me, over the next few years, to have been the cause of all the changes in my existence. I had one possession that unequivocally connected me with all the parts of that first existence—all the parts I couldn't remember, all the parts everybody agreed I remembered, and all the parts I alone was sure I remembered. That possession was a doll with opening and closing eyes that I got for Christmas in Seattle the year before we moved. I took her with me wherever I went, and frequently she got left at the weather end of a long prairie trek when I had gone looking for something—gone out to watch in the haunted cloudless morning and found only beautiful emptiness. After a few years the poor doll's face grew pale under the prairie sun, and lined with the fine cracks of excellent crockery. But still she had the same delicate brows, the same private smile of a baby who knows she will never have to grow up.

I made a special point of taking her whenever my mother and I went to see Edith Bagley and Edith Bagley's mother, because when we went there I really needed company. Edith and her mother had a dark high parlor filled with dark high furniture that I had to climb up into but that I must never touch with my feet. After Edith and her mother and my mother had all watched me and my doll get settled without doing any damage, they left us to ourselves. Edith and my mother had gone all through school together and then through college together in Jamestown. Then they had come back home together and my mother had married my father and Edith had not married anybody. But Edith was talented in a number of ways. My mother always played the piano for her when she sang a solo, and usually when we went there it was so they could practice something.

In one corner of the parlor was a table that was covered, when Edith was not using it for her work, with an ecru lace tablecloth that hung down so that all you could see of the table was its four massive clawed feet flexing themselves over the roses on the carpet. The chair next to the table had lions' heads at the ends of its arms, and the lions were roaring without making any noise. It was clear to me that furniture like that could come alive at night when people were asleep, and I always tried to act wide awake when I was in a roomful of it. I wiggled and cleared my throat and did as many things as I could without having somebody tell me to sit still.

In another corner of the parlor sat old Mrs. Bagley, who did not, like the furniture, look as though she might be alive. The top part of her was gray and white with sweater and hair and skin and cloudy spectacles. The bottom part of her was gay in the way a new grave is gay—all covered with spots of color woven from wilted flowers over a shockingly high mound. The mound of her under the festive mosaic of her afghan was appalling because you couldn't imagine a regular body under there, with a stomach and hips and legs. What *could* have been under that afghan? Only once did I see any part of a body. Hanging below the multicolored yarn fringe was a brown cotton stocking that bulged far out over the top of a black, high-heeled shoe tied with tasseled laces.

The parlor smelled of a half-century of dust and cooking and of about twenty years of Edith's painting. I would sit in one of the great chairs, watching every minute to see that I didn't touch any part of any wooden animals, and try to think of something to say in case I was called upon to admire Edith's painting. It seemed to me unclean to paint flowers and thistles and twisting vines all over plates and cups that people were supposed to eat from and drink out of. I always felt a little sick when Edith answered the door in her smock, because I knew the smock meant she was painting dishes, and if she was painting dishes, I would have to say something.

Edith weighed almost three hundred pounds. That was what gave her wonderful volume when she sang. Her face was round like a plate, and it had a finger wave for a frame —just like the tendriled edgings on her plates. She had soft boneless hands, but they were facile and clever, as weak hands often are.

One day I watched them work for a long time. They were making artificial lilies for Easter Sunday in our church. The claw-footed table was heaped with piles of wire, stiff threads with yellow nodules at one end, fuzzy orange things shaped like tiny cattails, squares of green and white paper of the consistency of snakeskin, needles, thread, pliers, and instructions. Edith picked up one of the long wires in one of her limp hands. She twirled a strip of stretchy green paper around the wire. "See!" she said. "Now we have a stem!"

After hard study of her diagrams, Edith produced an Easter lily. It had long pointed petals of snaky white paper and enormous reproductive organs made of the threads with the yellow nodules at their ends. All the thread ends and all the petal ends were wired together at the center of the lily, and all the wires were neatly hidden in a calyx made from a little green wax cup. Then she made a calla lily, so she could try out the fuzzy orange pieces that looked like cattails. I don't know how many lilies she made before my mother came back from grocery shopping. All I know is that a sentence started repeating itself in my head. It was a simple imperative sentence, and one I had made a point of memorizing after reading the story it was in. "Stop, Little Pot, stop!" That was the magic command that nobody could remember for days and days after the obliging Little Pot got set off by some idiot who knew only the starting words and not the stopping words. The picture with the story showed the town's whole population eating pathways with teaspoons through the streets of waist-high mush.

Like the porridge nobody knew how to turn off, Edith's lilies inundated the little Community Methodist Church on Easter Sunday. Lilies jammed the vestibule, the aisles, the altar, the pulpit, the windowsills, the hymnal racks. Guarded by my mother on one side and my grandmother on the other, sitting in a safe church pew, I sank into that familiar lonely terror: everybody else's eyes were seeing something that mine could not see. To everybody else those things of wire and resinous snakeskin paper were flowers.

The year of that Easter was the hardest my grandmother and grandfather and all the other people on the prairie could remember. It was colder and windier and drier and hotter and dustier. When the meager harvest was in, Number 1 wheat sold for twenty-six cents a bushel. Finally a bleak frigid December brought the long year to an end. My mother told me not to expect much from Santa Claus. I'd given up believing in Santa Claus long before, and I know she must have known that. But it was less painful for both of us to pretend that it was Santa Claus who was poor.

That was the first time I had ever done any pretending of the kind that grownups did, and it gave me, oddly enough, that same feeling of lonely terror I had when I realized that I must be seeing something that nobody else saw—or that everybody else must be seeing something I couldn't see. I began to understand that most people simply decided on what they wanted to see and then saw it. They decided on what they wanted to believe and then believed it. And everybody pretended to believe what everybody else pretended to believe so that they could talk to each other. Santa Clauses ringing bells on the street in Jamestown did not believe in Santa Claus. Edith Bagley did not believe in her snakeskin lilies. They were all trying to make reality better for everybody else. And they were all trying to explain themselves to each other in order to try to make themselves more real to each other, in order not to lose each other. But the harder they tried to make the world real for each other, the more hopelessly they separated themselves from each other. It was even more lonely to be *deciding* what was real than it was not to have any idea of what might be real and what might not.

It made me feel very old—to believe in Santa Claus because I decided to believe. From then on, I would be responsible for what I saw and what I believed. I would make the decisions that created my existence and the decisions that created the world. The more I succeeded in believing what everybody else believed, the less real anything would be, because the things that are the most real are the ones that surprise us the most, and when everything must be decided upon and agreed upon, nothing can surprise us any more. We can never be surprised by the color of the grass or the color of the sky, and so they can never be quite so bright as they were in that first existence, when we were always being surprised.

And just at that time when I needed her the most, my dearest proof of that other existence, my faded cracked Baby Dimples, disappeared. I looked everywhere for her, but I did not admit to my mother that she was missing. I was afraid I had left her outside on the wrong afternoon and she had been buried under a five-foot snowdrift. If I asked about her, my mother might exclaim, "Oh, *dear!* You *didn't* leave her out on the day we got that awful blizzard, did you?"

There was also the possibility that my mother had allowed her to fall into the grubby eye-poking fingers of my little sister while I was away at school learning about reality. Then my doll would be like most of the other dolls I knew. At best she would have one eye stuck open and the other stuck shut. At worst, the whole mechanism would be turned over in her head and the only thing that would show through the eyeholes with their painted lashes would be a steel bar with rubber bands attached to two dull metal balls (the backs of the glass eyes) suspended in an empty china skull, rolling up and down, opening and shutting in hollow darkness. If she had suffered such an attack, and was now on some closet shelf until my father could find time to try to fix her, I didn't want to know about it.

I was pretty sure, though, that I must have left her outside. I spent a few dusky afternoons digging deep into the most likely snowbanks. I knew I wouldn't find her; I just wanted to show her or somebody that I felt as bad as she did about her being down there under the suffocating whiteness.

I still hadn't found her when Christmas came. That Christmas morning was the bleakest in my memory. There was no towering pungent tree like the ones from that other existence where Christmas trees grew on all the mountains, in all the parks, and beside all the houses. There was instead a tiny tree that had lost all its perfume while coming hundreds of miles from Wisconsin or Michigan. And under the tree, as gaily wrapped as if our decisions and our agreements and our responsibilities could always be made as beautiful as surprises, were sleepers and mittens and stockings and underwear—things I had been doing without during the first part of that bitter winter so that I could get them for Christmas. And, of course, because I needed them and because I was growing up now, I pretended that they mattered.

It seemed to me that our little family would suffocate from pretending in our little house that was so crowded by our little tree—like my doll under the snowbank. But my mother gave me a portentous look, as if to say that she knew you couldn't have Christmas without surprises and that nobody expected you to. She slipped out of the house and came back with a bundle in her arms—a bundle just the size of a new baby, swaddled in a precious furry pink blanket. The Christmas surprise! The Surprise that creates a universe of surprises every time it is born. She lifted a corner of the blanket so I could see the baby's face.

It was dead. It must have died while she left it out in the car, waiting to surprise us. Its cheeks were purple, like the cheeks of people found under snowbanks after blizzard snows have melted. Even its closed eyelids were purple.

"It's Baby Dimples!" my mother cried happily. "Santa Claus took her away and made her all new for you!"

I looked at the dead face again and saw around it the pen-like scrolls of Edith Bagley's plates. On the delicate brow and cheeks I recognized the dusty purple paste that Edith Bagley managed to use, in one spot or another, on all the dishes and cups she painted.

"Isn't she pretty now?" my mother pleaded. "You left her outside and she got all cracked and faded. Now look at her pretty red hair! Look at her healthy cheeks!"

I couldn't have said it to myself then, but I understand that even the master artificer which, in my little world, Edith Bagley was, could never bring surprise from one existence to another. Shock (a word I didn't know then, though I knew the feeling) no doubt was transferable; surprise was not. The glad surprise of a very young child that morning has come, that the grass is green and the sky is blue—and all without any decisions made by the child—that glad surprise, I have now come to understand, is what we beg our artificers for, pay them enormously for, especially at Christmastime. But they, being part of the grownup conspiracy to decide what is real, being, like the rest of us, helpless members of the second existence, no longer know, any more than the rest of us, what is real—what is surprising.

I say that I understood this, and the way I know I understood it is that I knew I was making a statement about my existence when I said to my waiting, heartbroken mother, "Yes, my baby is much prettier now."

I was careful, after that, to tuck my doll into her crib every night, and to do it when my mother was sure to see. Since I never took her out of the house with me again, it wasn't hard to find her to do the tucking in. There had been nights when even the long summer prairie evenings had caught me in the dark, with the panicked sounds of hard-pressed fecundity all about me and the weight of the heavy-leaved black boughs over me—there had been nights when I risked my life to search for her in the grove, so I could bring her safely home and put her to bed, grieving and promising never to forget her again. But in our second existence we don't grieve and promise with the same unqualified passion with which we grieve and promise in our first existence. We remember, in our second existence, how forgetful we are.

And so, now that my last proof of my first existence had been transformed into the first proof of my second existence, I no longer had to seek her or grieve for her or make promises to her. She was always there in her crib, with her purple cheeks.

Something important happened in the town that winter, not long after Christmas. Somebody got married or, more likely, somebody left for the West Coast and had a party in the town hall before they went. If a family was going to sell out, it was that time of year that would make them decide. Christmas and New Year's over. Nothing to look forward to but snow till April. No commitment to a crop planted. Winter feed for the stock about gone, because of the last summer's drought. Not much cream to sell and not much of a price for what cream there was. A time of year when the Pacific Coast temperatures, printed in the Jamestown *Sun*, seemed unbelievable. It didn't seem to matter where you were during these Depression years. After you'd been in one spot for a while, you decided things couldn't be quite so bad anywhere else, and so you moved. My own family had gone from North Dakota to Seattle and back, and we were destined to go again to Seattle in another couple of years.

At any rate, something important happened in the town and Edith sang for it. I still hated her so much that I could barely speak to her when we went to her upstairs house so she and my mother could practice the songs she sang. I sat in the chair with the lions carved on its arms and listened while they went over and over the songs, but only one of the songs said anything I could understand, and that's why I still haven't forgotten it.

Edith stood by the piano, her smock trembling over the vast regions where her emotions echoed and re-echoed themselves, until she herself must have lost track of them and could believe only what everybody believed—that she had, as compensation for her appalling obesity, for her appalling mother, for her appalling loneliness, a great voice.

Another thing I cannot forget (and this is one way you can distinguish your first existence from your second: never in your first existence do you wish you could forget anything) is the painful difference between herself and the girl she sang about, as she stood, wide as the piano, at the high-note end of the keyboard upon which my little mother played. The song she sang, the one I can't forget, had these words:

The roses all have left your cheek—
I've watched them fade away and die . . .

Oh! I will take you back, Kathleen,
To where your heart will feel no pain,
And when the fields are fresh and green,
I'll take you to your home again.

I know I understood that Kathleen was not ever going to see the fields again, because the song made me cry. It was the first time any song had affected me that way. I sat in the lion-headed chair where I had once watched Edith make the lilies with no perfume, holding my fists against my eyes, horrified at crying over something as silly as a song—especially the kind of song that Edith Bagley would sing—and even more horrified that somebody might catch me.

If anybody could go back, if Kathleen could have gone back, then nobody would cry over the song, but almost everybody does. We cherish our griefs over those green fields because our griefs seem to prove that what we grieve over must once have existed. It is good that all of us have these griefs. They do not separate us as do our beliefs.

Now that I am grown, I have discovered that our second existence does bring us one surprise—love. Now that I have children of my own, I try, as my mother did, to save their first existences for them, even though I know it is impossible. All the generations of us will go on forever trying to save the green fields for each other and we will always fail, but because it is for love that we try to do what is impossible, we redeem our second existence.

And in a way none of us ever really leaves those fields that made us. It is from those lost fields that we go on shyly, silently calling to each other. It is from those fields, forever sealed against the trespasses of our grownup selves, forever splendid with light falling like trumpet salutes through the old heavy boughs of the world, that each of us keeps his long watch on the people who come to assume his face.

. . . the crudest honest sentence is a re-sounding of experience. Have you heard a bright child describe an airplane crash? Have you heard a returned soldier describe his once-more-slept-in bed, at home? Sentences resound when experience is comprehendingly relived.

SIDNEY COX

chapter 18

controlling sound

WRITING APPEARS a soundless enterprise: the pen slides quietly across the page. And reading appears a silent act:

"Where's John?"

"He's curled up on the porch reading. I haven't heard a sound out of him all afternoon."

But one writer says of another writer, "He hasn't any ear," and he means the most damning criticism. For one of the chief resources of a writer is control over the sound of his sentences.

Scanning the printed page, most readers hear in their unconscious ear the sentences sounding against the echoing memory of all the words they have heard in conversation.

The following passage, written by a beginner, utilizes sound skillfully:

I COULDN'T STAY

I couldn't stay in the library with the rain pecking at its windows. The blackness outside invited me to lose myself in its depth. So I walked into it, letting the sharp spray tingle my forehead and tangle my hair. I walked slowly until my coat was damp and heavy and my knee socks slid around my ankles, making them itch. It was night and

nobody saw how the rain treated me. When I got to the
room, I listened to water splattering under the wheels of
cars and rinsing the stained sides of the brick buildings.
I wanted to sleep through the night and wake up washed
like the world on a new day.

SUE SMILTNECK

The girl who wrote this passage did not know how well she had
used sound effects. Most writers don't consciously create all of their
best sound effects. They write thinking of meaning, and their sensitive
ear helps them select words that strike other ears significantly. In "I
Couldn't Stay," note these sound effects:

rain pecking

*sh*arp *sp*ray *tingle* my forehead and *tangle* my hair

wa*ter* splat*ter*ing

ri*n*sing the stai*n*e*d* *s*i*d*es of the *b*rick *b*uil*d*i*ng*s

*W*hen . . . *w*ater . . . *w*heels . . . *w*anted *to* . . . *w*ake up
*w*ashed . . . *w*orld

It was a hard rain: the reader can hear it pecking and splattering.
Rhythms are set up by the repetition of consonant sounds (*tingle*,
tangle, etc.) in what is called *alliteration* and in the repetition of
vowel sounds (*rinsing*, *brick*, *buildings*) in what is called *assonance*.
Human beings like repetitions. They sense strength in the *repeat-
and-vary* pattern. All persons employ sound skillfully without being
taught. In a speech given to American teachers in 1966, Edmond
Wright, a British schoolteacher, pointed out that under extreme
emotional stress all persons speak in strong rhythm and often with
alliteration.

David! You're a *d*irty, low-*d*own *d*og!

He told students to write down what persons at home said under
stress: they found considerable alliteration. One student complained
that he didn't hear any, so Mr. Wright suggested he go home and
pour a glass of milk over his brother's head and then listen to his
father. He did. He heard considerable alliteration.

Knocking around in every person's head are the sounds of his
native language: spoken or muted echoes of what he has read, the
lullabies his mother sang him, the rich cursing of men hunting or
playing games, the formal rhythms of a trained voice reading in
church or synagogue, the skip rope song, the hurried swallowed

phrases of other children singing the "Star Spangled Banner" or chanting the "Gettysburg Address," the taunts they sang in the street:

Simpy Sam is a stupid old man!

Without trying, most persons can write rapidly such sound effects as these by a high school girl:

> **I like to go fishing. But I don't like to touch worms or slippery, slimy fish. They wiggle. I went with Anne three years ago. That was fun until she broke her promise and made me take the fish off. Then it swallowed the hook. It was terrible. It wriggled and writhed in the bottom of the boat. Then it just lay there. Dead.**

This is not an exceptional piece of writing. The seventh sentence suffers from It-ache. In the sixth, *it* refers to the fish; then suddenly *it* refers to the whole struggle of the fish with the hook. But in sound, the passage is strong. *Slippery* and *slimy* and *wriggled* and *writhed* alliterate with force and their sounds echo the sense of what they say. The last two sentences allow the record to run down appropriately, and *Dead* stands by itself, final—in its position, its shortness, and its two hard *d's*.

In the phrase "bottom of the boat," the writer has repeated the *b* sound skillfully. You may say that she did not mean to hit that sound hard and that it adds nothing to the passage because the *b* sound does not suggest *boat* or *bottom* as the *sl* sound in *slippery* and *slimy* suggests the squirming fish. True, but one of the marks of a strong writer is that through his sentences appears from time to time an occasional repetition of sound that gives his words a strength like the "bone" in spaghetti cooked not too soft by an expert Italian cook. Note this pattern of sound repetition in these next passages. The authors were probably not trying for any effects, but they achieved them nevertheless.

> Men are *h*orri*b*ly *t*edious *wh*en *th*ey are *g*ood *h*us*b*ands an*d* a*b*omina*b*ly concei*t*ed *wh*en *th*ey are no*t*.

> OSCAR WILDE

> It's like *wh*en you break up *w*ith a girl and you've explained all your reasons to her *wh*y. And *sh*e *s*ays, "I *st*ill don't *s*ee *wh*y it *w*on't work." And you've *s*een *it* ou*t* and you've hi*t th*e *b*lank har*d* col*d w*all of *s*olid no*th*ing.

> HIGH SCHOOL STUDENT WRITING FREELY

These passages get their bone from repeating consonant sounds. Vowel sounds also work their spell:

> These were softwooded trees, poplars, tulip trees, cotton-woods. There were fences around one or two of the houses, but mainly the yards ran into each other with only now and then a low hedge that wasn't doing very well. There were few good friends among the grown people, and they were not poor enough for the other sort of intimate acquaint-ance . . .
>
> JAMES AGEE

Here a highly skillful writer was trying to evoke the spirit of low-key joy felt by a small boy on summer nights. He did this partly by employing many variations of *o* sounds, and the *schwa* ("uh") sound that all the vowels take in certain words. Many American-English words carry with them a sound that supports the meaning they signify, as in this passage:

> **The door squeaked, then shrieked, and I felt my nerves frazzle once again, ragged nerves unraveled like the shat-tered end of the shoestring I couldn't get into the eyelet of my tennis shoe when I was a boy.**

Much academic writing suffers so from its empty abstract words that the reader never comes to the point of appreciating its repeti-tions of sound. For example:

> But besides these immediate practical advantages, important as they are, your membership in the Council enables you to function more effectively as a member of the English teaching profession. It does this by affiliating you with one of the most influential professional organizations for teach-ers . . .

Some bone of sound exists in that passage but no reader wants to hear once more together the tired words "function . . . effectively . . . affiliating . . . influential . . . professional." The above passage addressed to teachers may carry too many *f* sounds in too brief a space. Too frequent repetition of a sound may render a passage ridiculous. "Peter Piper picked a peck of pickled peppers" makes a funny tongue twister, but it will always tickle a reader with its little explosions rather than impress him with its meaning.

> *In the first place, certain sounds—the voiceless* s, *for example—possess a range of potential suggestibility, rather than a fixed or single capability. Thus, a prominence of* ss *is capable of suggesting certain classes of natural sounds (rustling, hissing, sighing, whispering) but not other classes (booming, humming, hammering, or groaning).*
>
> *In the second place, this power of suggesting natural sounds or other qualities is relatively* weak—*too weak to operate unsupported by meaning—and because of its range, is only* latent.
>
> KARL SHAPIRO AND ROBERT BEUM

The following passage, written by a college girl, not only reveals an ear for sound that fits meaning but suggests in its overall rhythm the way a little girl talks:

> **Ugly dorm food! Thick chili and dry crackers make a pasty lump. I used to eat some soda crackers plain when I was little. In our backyard we made mud pies and ate crackers. It was heroic action to eat four in a row without taking a drink from the hose.**
>
> **At my sixth birthday party we had to chew and swallow five crackers and then whistle to win a prize. Marlene Davis and I were the best. She had a big mouth and when she talked, white bubbles of spit came out of the corners. Naturally curly blonde hair kinked all over her head and dribbled down to her blue bug eyes. She was skinny, with scabby elbows.**
>
> **We started eating crackers at the same time. Cramming them in was easy, but gagging them down hurt. Marlene had a head start with all that spit in her mouth. She won, so I called her "skinny bug-eyes" and made her cry. Then I opened my presents.**
>
> JUDY SMOLIK

This description of Marlene utilizes another major sound device used by professional writers: the quick ending sentence, the short punch that surprises. A short sentence after a number of longer sentences varies the rhythm of a passage. Rhythm is a device involving sound, a beat or lack of beat, sensed in the ear, not comprehended intellectually.

Parallel construction often creates sentences or parts of sentences of equal length and thus sets up rhythm that becomes powerful when controlled and occasionally varied. In the following excerpt from a meditation written by John Donne, Dean of St. Paul's Cathedral in London in 1624, listen for the equal and answering beat of parts of sentences following upon each other:

> Who casts not up his Eie to the Sunne when it rises?
> who takes off his Eie from a Comet when that breakes out?
> . . . No man is an Iland, intire of it selfe; every man is
> a peece of the Continent, a part of the maine . . .

Part of the power of Donne's meditation arises not from the sound of its syllables but from the formality of its language. If you read the following paraphrase of a part of Donne's meditation and then Donne's lines, you will hear the informal language of conversation and then the sonorous language of the cathedral:

> The death bell rings for anyone who thinks it is ringing
> for him, and even if it quits ringing for a while, its effect
> upon him brings him to God. Everyone looks at the sun
> when it comes up. And no one quits looking at a comet
> when it flashes. Everyone listens to bells everywhere. But
> no one could possibly stop listening to his own death bell.
> No man can live separately by himself. Every person is a
> bit of the whole world and if any little part of that world
> disappears, he is affected by its disappearance, just as he
> would be by the destruction of a friend's house or his own
> house. Because he is part of mankind. Don't ask whom the
> bell is ringing for. It's ringing for you.

That version swings in places, for example: "Don't ask whom the bell is ringing for. It's ringing for you." But it lacks the majesty of Donne's original. Listen to him toll the bell:

> The Bell doth toll for him that thinkes it doth; and though
> it intermit againe, yet from that minute, that that occasion
> wrought upon him, hee is united to God. Who casts not up
> his Eie to the Sunne when it rises? but who takes off his
> Eie from a Comet when that breakes out? Who bends not
> his eare to any bell, which upon any occasion rings? but
> who can remove it from that bell, which is passing a peece
> of himselfe out of this world? No man is an Iland, intire of
> it selfe; every man is a peece of the Continent, a part of the
> maine; if a Clod bee washed away by the Sea, Europe is the

lesse, as well as if a Promontorie were, as well as if a
Mannor of thy friends or of thine owne were; any mans
death diminishes me, because I am involved in mankinde;
And therefore never send to know for whom the bell tolls;
It tolls for thee.

Donne ends comment upon the bell with a short powerful statement:
"It tolls for thee." It gains its power from the long rolling statements
which precede it. You may employ this device. Let yourself—or some
character you're giving words to—get wound up and go on and on,
and then stop suddenly with a clincher.

Note how Ralph Waldo Emerson does this in a paragraph from
his essay "Self-Reliance." He gains further emphasis by shifting
from Elevated to Kitchen Language (a device which will be discussed in Chapter 19).

> I have no churlish objection to the circumnavigation
> of the globe for the purposes of art, of study, and benevo-
> lence, so that the man is first domesticated, or does not go
> abroad with the hope of finding somewhat greater than he
> knows. He who travels to be amused, or to get somewhat
> which he does not carry, travels away from himself, and
> grows old even in youth among old things. In Thebes, in
> Palmyra, his will and mind have become old and dilapi-
> dated as they. He carries ruins to ruins.

These endings punch hard partly because of their meanings. If
what you say in an ending line is obvious and dull, it will not be
made impressive by being stated shortly. However, the reader may
be grateful even for a dull short sentence if all the preceding sentences were long. Just as professional writers learn to create flow in
their sentences—so they do not have to think consciously about it—
they learn to vary the length of their sentences. If a great many are
long, they habitually throw in a short one. And vice versa. They are
not afraid to throw in a piece of a sentence, a phrase, a single word;
and let it stand as a sentence. As they write, they hear the sound of
sentences as well as the sound of words.

Another way to create faithful and exciting sound in your writing
is to try to put down what you hear. The sound of a bullfrog? In
Walden, Thoreau calls it a *trump* and put it down *tr-r-r-oonk*! In his
Journals he describes the pigeon woodpecker's "whimsical ah-week
ah-week." In *The Field Book of Ponds and Streams,* Anne Haven
Morgan writes the American toad's call as "wheep."

When she heard the sound of traffic on a nearby street, a mother working in a beginning writers' course remembered her children's youth through sound:

HOME

At noon, traffic on Stadium transmits an even, steady sound, the passing of many cars blending together in a deep, harmonious hum. At two o'clock in the morning, a single car creates a gradual crescendo as it approaches, a diminuendo as it moves into the distance.

One car at night carries a lonesome, nostalgic sound. I am reminded of times I've lain awake waiting for teenagers to return. In the deep quiet of the country night I can hear the first faint sound of a car coming down the highway a quarter of a mile away, slowing down to turn the corner onto the gravel of our country road, the gradual increasing of sound as the car approaches; then a momentary lowering as it slows for the bump of the little bridge; an increasing again for the rise of the little hill where our house stood. I can remember lying tense and breathing lightly, waiting for the moment when the noise of the car would continue on past the house into the distance. Or— it would pause, diminishing abruptly as the driver pressed the brake and the car coasted with its own momentum into our driveway. I heard the final beat of the motor, the quick staccato of young feet, first on the porch steps, then on the stairs. Soon the hall light, always left on for the last one in, was snapped off.

My child was back under my roof again.

GERTRUDE ANDRESEN

Here the writer not only remembers sounds but evokes some of them by her choice of words and building of sentence rhythms. The statement

then a momentary lowering of sound as it slows for the bump of the little bridge

employs the word *bump* perfectly—a short word with a little burst and closure in it, coming in the middle of the statement so that it sounds exactly like what the writer is describing. Maybe *bump* was the only word that came to the writer's mind, luckily right in sound for her purposes. Maybe she also thought of saying *slight rise in the road, ripple,* or *protuberance,* and discarded them because they did not contribute anything in sound. Often a writer doesn't know how he achieved his good sound effects. Sometimes he doesn't hear them until a reader points them out. Yet they are there and he has a right to take credit for them.

You may train your ear by reading aloud good writing. Then when you read aloud your own writing you are more likely to hear skillful sounds. In reading a second or third draft you can change a word here or there.

To write fully, you must use all your senses. Remember how places and objects smell, the taste of the back of your hand, the touch of concrete, the sound of a laugh—an American's laugh, a Southerner's laugh, a Northerner's. Such variety.

The representation of sounds in words can become conventional and even trite—"bang!" "screech," "eek!" Here is a beginning writer recording sounds in fresh words:

> I like the quiet crackling of root beer foam; the swish, then flap of the net as the basketball passes through . . . squeaky popcorn; slept-on mattress . . . moccasins treading soft sand, crisp as toasted linen; steel door weightlessly slammed shut; secret roar of sea shell; whirr of a movie reel; the ps-s-s-t of freshly opened coffee . . . whirr and buzz of the WALK signal; a Band-Aid coming off . . . creaky wicker chairs . . .
>
> SISTER MARY LOIS GLONEK

WRITING TWENTY-FOUR: Put down in words a page of sounds you like and dislike. Study the passage above by Sister Mary Lois. Note her accuracy and restraint. She avoided the obvious and conventional representations of loud sounds. You may follow her direction or others. Like all symbolizing of experience through words, the representation of sounds is complex and subtle. Sometimes it is almost a precise rendering of actual sound; sometimes a satirical conventionalization, as in the *Batman* series—"Zowie! Blat! Pow! Bam!"

The most significant sound in life is that of other voices. The best writers seem born with an ear's memory for the way a person speaks, and if they write down the conversations of a dozen persons in one story, all speak recognizably differently. Maybe this is a natural gift, not to be learned. But you may try, at least, to see whether you have it.

Few, if any, professional writers put down conversation that is
absolutely and completely accurate in manner and extent; for it
would be boring. Most of us talk dully a great deal of the time.
But the skillful writer captures enough of the real tones and rhythms
and dialect of his character in writing to make them sound authentic.
Consider this passage from the first chapter of *Huckleberry Finn.*
Mark Twain varied the length of his sentences, the repetitions of
sounds within words, and the word patterns of a rural uneducated
boy from Missouri:

> Her sister, Miss Watson, a tolerable slim old maid, with
> goggles on, had just come to live with her, and took a set
> at me now with a spelling-book. She worked me middling
> hard for about an hour, and then the widow made her
> ease up. I couldn't stood it much longer. Then for an hour
> it was deadly dull, and I was fidgety. Miss Watson would
> say, "Don't put your feet up there, Huckleberry;" and
> "don't scrunch up like that, Huckleberry—set up straight;"
> and pretty soon she would say, "Don't gap and stretch like
> that, Huckleberry—why don't you try to behave?" Then
> she told me all about the bad place, and I said I wished I
> was there. She got mad then, but I didn't mean no harm.
> All I wanted was to go somewheres; all I wanted was a
> change. I warn't particular. She said it was wicked to say
> what I said; said she wouldn't say it for the whole world;
> *she* was going to live so as to go to the good place. Well, I
> couldn't see no advantage in going where she was going,
> so I made up my mind I wouldn't try for it. But I never
> said so, because it would only make trouble, and wouldn't
> do no good.
>
> Now she had got a start, and she went on and told me all
> about the good place. She said all a body would have to do
> there was to go around all day long with a harp and sing,
> forever and ever. So I didn't think much of it. But I never
> said so. I asked her if she reckoned Tom Sawyer would go
> there, and, she said, not by a considerable sight. I was glad
> about that, because I wanted him and me to be together.

The forty-year-old man who was writing this book spoke in the
voice of a boy. At times, he used adult words that Huck would never
have spoken, but he captured a youth's language in enough of the
lines to establish Huck's authentic voice and make it immortal.

chapter 19

writing reports and columns

THE LIVE CORE

MOST PERSONS expect two out of three lectures, reports, sermons, editorials, and presentations to bore them. And they do. So when they are told to write a report, they produce another boring piece of writing. They forget that one out of three reports they have read was entertaining, surprising, or exciting, like this encyclopedia entry on Davy Crockett, taken from *The Oxford Companion to American Literature*, 1965:

CROCKETT, DAVY (David) (1786-1836), born in Tennessee, spent a shiftless youth until his political career began (*c.* 1816) with his appointment as justice of the peace. He boasted that none of his decisions was ever reversed, because of his dependence on 'natural-born sense instead of law learning.' After being twice elected to the state legislature, he accepted a humorous proposal that he run for Congress, and to his surprise was elected, serving from 1827 to 1831,

and again from 1833 to 1835. Because of his opposition to
Jackson, the Whigs adopted him as a convenient tool
through whom to draw the backwoods democracy to its
standard. Davy was soon turned by skilful politicians into
a frontier hero, whose picturesque eccentricities, backwoods humor, tall tales, shrewd native intelligence, and
lusty pioneer spirit were all aggrandized. Whig journalists
were soon at work, and in short order turned out such
books, attributed to Davy, as *Sketches and Eccentricities of
Col. David Crockett* (1833), *An Account of Col. Crockett's
Tour to the North and Down East* (1835), *The Life of
Martin Van Buren* (1835), and *Col. Crockett's Exploits and
Adventures in Texas* (1836). With the exception of the
last, which is posthumous, he may have had a hand in all
these works, and he gladly claimed the *Tour* and life of Van
Buren. Swallowing the Whig bait, he enjoyed his sudden
rise to fame, and was glad to aid in propagating the myth,
which, however, removed him from office, since his constituents would not tolerate his desertion of Democratic principles. Piqued, he left Tennessee to participate in the war for
Texan independence, and a few months later died in the
heroic defense of the Alamo, adding a final dramatic chapter to his career. *A Narrative of the Life of David Crockett,
of the State of Tennessee* (1834) passes as his autobiography,
although the claim has often been disputed. In any case the
book has the robust manner attributed to Crockett, and
contains fine examples of the farce and exaggeration of
the tall tale.

This report includes a great number of specific facts—dates, offices
held, political parties, names of books—encompassing a lifetime, and
yet told in less than 350 words. Although James D. Hart, the editor,
was writing a reference book, he did not present simply a collection
of facts about Davy Crockett. He wrote the article with an angle:
Here is Davy Crockett, who became an American hero celebrated in
folk song and story. How did that happen? Did his life merit the
myth that has arisen about him?

Remembering his audience of educated Americans, Mr. Hart
did not begin the article by saying Crockett is a famous backwoods
hero. He expected his audience to know that, and he got right down
to telling how Crockett became famous. He omitted many facts about
Crockett's life, partly because he had to save words (he was writing

an 888-page reference work which names and describes thousands of persons, books, newspapers, and places), and partly because he did not want to divert the reader with facts not critical to his angle.

Mr. Hart did not think he was "letting the facts speak for themselves." He knew that all facts take on meaning because of their setting. He made his judgment about Crockett and chose facts which bore upon it. He presented Crockett as a man who rode luck to fame, allowed himself to be used by politicians, permitted his name to be connected to books that were in large measure not written by him, and deserved his fame as a skillful teller of tall tales.

> *Even the reporting of pure physical research findings, to cite an extreme example, is not unbiased. It is biased in favor of revealing the findings. In recent years the practical import and responsibility of such a bias has been felt deeply by atomic scientists. The question is not whether a communication is biased. The question is: toward what value system is the communication biased?*
>
> GERHART WIEBE

To write this report, Mr. Hart had to know a great deal about Davy Crockett. If he had known less, he would not have been able to find so many facts which touched his angle. Like all good pieces of writing, this report sounds authoritative partly because it implies the writer knew more facts than he employed—the iceberg structure, as some critics have called it.

When you write a report, know your subject. If it is a book, or books, you are writing from, you may need to read it several times, compare it with other books, and see what other persons think of it. Most of all, you need to test it in some way—does its experience or theory ring true to your experience, to your learning? Such questions will help you see more clearly what the book is saying. If you are writing a report from direct observation, you may need to ask questions to see how others see the subject. Talking with other persons about a book you have read or an event you have witnessed usually helps you see more than you saw on your own.

> *. . . I always try to write on the principle of the iceberg. There is seven-eighths of it underwater for every part that shows.*

> *Anything you know you can eliminate and it only strengthens your iceberg. It is the part that doesn't show. If a writer omits something because he does not know it then there is a hole in the story.*
>
> ERNEST HEMINGWAY

You should write a report with an iceberg of facts available to you, and you should choose and shape the critical facts to appear as the ice above the water. The professional report writer doesn't start writing until he has a large iceberg. He learns to sense when he has a sufficient core of materials and he learns quick, efficient ways of getting that core. For example, many sportswriters have available to them a running record of a basketball game, which looks like this:

UNIVERSITY OF TOLEDO VS. SAN FRANCISCO STATE

DECEMBER 19, 1960

SECOND HALF

TIME LEFT	TOLEDO		SAN FRANCISCO STATE
20:00		29	23
19:29			25 Williams jumper center of keyhole
18:46			27 Williams laid in set up
18:28	Lewis made layup	31	
17:43	Lewis one-hand jumper		
	beyond key	33	
16:06			29 Caranica drove for layup
15:56	Jones jumper side		
	of circle	35	
15:14	Galicki personal foul		Brown missed personal foul
15:03	Galicki laid in Jones'		
	pass	37	
14:43	Lewis' jumper side		
	of circle	39	
14:28	Pawlak personal foul		31 Caranica laid in setup
			Caranica missed free throw

This part of the game record shows only five minutes and thirty-two seconds of the action. An assistant or a representative of the teams may keep such a record, but the writer knows it will be available and he uses it. You may make a similar log of the activities you cover. Be prepared with whatever instruments you need to collect materials—notebook, tape recorder, 3 $\times$ 5 cards, camera. Gather whatever printed information is available—an agenda outlining the order of items in a meeting, lists of officers or speakers, minutes of last meeting, programs. Double-check all names for spelling. Learn as much as possible about the event before you go to it.

The writer who goes underwater and discovers the whole iceberg gives himself a chance to make the report fascinating to readers. He can discard the dull, the partially relevant, the tedious, and present only the bright, snowy peaks. Here is a report of a baseball game by Robert Lipsyte (*The New York Times*, August 5, 1966). Think of how many notes and records Mr. Lipsyte must have consulted while writing this story. His angle was not hard to find: the New York Mets (in ninth place) had beaten the San Francisco Giants (tied for first) while the Giants were using their star pitcher Juan Marichal. Lipsyte chose to tell his story concentrating on the relatively unknown Ron Swoboda, the Met who hit the winning home run, and to bring in the famous Marichal as his antagonist.

METS BEAT GIANTS 8-6, ON SWOBODA'S HOMER IN 9TH

Ron Swoboda, who won it in the ninth inning with a three-run pinch-hit home run, said: "It was a story-book game. Holy Cow!" And it was just that.

Most of the crowd of 41,038 at Shea Stadium sat stunned yesterday long after the Mets had beaten the Giants, 8-6. Swoboda's drive cleared the leftfield fence and the 22-year-old outfielder jogged around the bases in a mood he later described as "elation . . . the epitome . . . my greatest thrill!"

More than 24,000 in the crowd had bought their tickets just before gametime because the great Juan Marichal was starting for the Giants. For almost six innings they got what they paid for—perfection from Marichal and something less than perfection from the Mets.

The 27-year-old Dominican righthander, out of action recently because of a sore finger, had registered his 17th victory Tuesday night, by the official scorer's decision, after retiring the last four Mets. Yesterday, kicking high on a dusty mound, he retired the first 17 Mets.

3 OUTS ON 6 PITCHES

In the second inning, with six pitches, he put out the side so quickly that he had to wave his sleepy outfielders back to the dugout. In the third, facing Dennis Ribant, the busy little Met starter, he was worked for his first full count before Ribant lined out to Willie Mays, a well-hit ball that Mays had to hustle to catch and gave a few plaintive voices reason to holler, "Let's go Mets."

In the sixth, Ribant bounced one over Marichal's head for a single, and the crowd prepared to console itself with a brilliant one-hitter instead of a perfect game.

The Giants, meanwhile, were doing what was expected of a team that started the sunny afternoon game leading the National League and fresh from having beaten the Mets three times in a row. They scored a run in the fourth on Willie McCovey's 21st homer of the year, a run in the fifth on Marichal's double and Jim Davenport's single and a run in the sixth on Jim Hart's 24th homer.

GIANTS GAIN 5-0 LEAD

In the seventh, San Francisco made the score 5-0. Tito Fuentes drove one of Ribant's pitches into the leftfield corner. Larry Elliot dropped it in foul territory and examined it, apparently thinking the ball was foul, while Fuentes went to third, credited with a double. Ossie Virgil, who had replaced Davenport at third base, then singled and McCovey walked.

With the bases loaded, Darrell Sutherland replaced Ribant, and Mays singled home two runs.

In the last of the seventh, the Mets began to move at last. They needed three singles and a throwing error by Marichal to get one run. The people who had come to see at least a shutout went home.

Tom Haller hit a homer for the Giants in the eighth, making the score 6-1, but it was a wasted gesture. In the bottom of the eighth, the Mets charged.

Jerry Grote reached second on a two-base throwing error by Virgil, and John Stephenson, a 25-year-old catcher pinch-hitting for Dallas Green, the third Met pitcher, blasted his first homer of the season. Singles by Chuck Hiller, Al Luplow and Larry Elliot made the score 6-4.

In disbelief, the crowd froze.

HAMILTON IS VICTOR

Jack Hamilton, the winning pitcher, put out the Giants in the ninth. Then Marichal strolled back to the mound. He demanded that it be dampened because he was kicking dust into his own face. A little man with a green sprinkling can scurried out and dampened the mound.

Satisfied, baseball's best righthander pitched two balls and a strike to Ken Boyer. Boyer hit the fourth pitch over the fence for his 11th homer of the season, and Marichal was pulled out for some showering of his own.

"Let's go Mets." There was no plaintiveness now, no whine. There was hope.

Ed Bressoud, who had been playing an erratic shortstop for the injured Roy McMillan, singled to left. Ron Hunt, pinchhitting for Grote, bunted, forcing Bressoud at second. Stephenson, hero of the eighth inning, hit a wrong-field single to right. There was one out, two men on base, and the score was 6-5.

The roar was swelling now as Bill Henry, a left-hander, replaced Lindy McDaniel, a right-hander. The next scheduled batter, Chuck Hiller, was called back for a right-handed hitting replacement and Manager Wes Westrum said to Swoboda, "Get a bat."

Swoboda later admitted he was excited because "that's it, when everybody's relying on you." He kept telling himself to "stay loose" and he forgot that the last time Marichal had started against the Mets, on May 20, Swoboda had won the game with a tenth-inning homer against the same Bill Henry.

The first pitch was high; it would have been a ball if Swoboda, overanxious, hadn't swung and missed. The second was a ball, low and inside. The third, waist-high and fast, was thrown with the stuff that dreams are made on.

Although Mr. Lipsyte, the reporter, tells the outcome of the game in the second paragraph, 8–6, he then begins a story in which he builds tension: How and when did Swoboda do it? What was happening to the marvelous Marichal? How did the pinch hitter outshine the star? Frequently writers of reports build their story around such tension between two poles. A report of a laboratory experiment can be a suspense story: Will the scientist find the answer or won't he? Will his newly improvised piece of equipment work?

Mr. Lipsyte was writing a story of surprise, an upset. So he put the reader at the game, watching the expected happen: Marichal pitching a one-hit game for six innings. Thus he built tension for the Mets' rally. He could have provided many details about other Giants' players than the pitcher, but his angle made him present little individualizing details about Marichal, who was the Giant.

> In the second inning, with six pitches, he put out the side
> so quickly that he had to wave his sleepy outfielders back to
> the dugout.

Like all good writers, Mr. Lipsyte does not forget what he has said. He makes facts and words speak to each other. In the fourth paragraph, he shows how well Marichal was pitching:

> Yesterday, kicking high on a dusty mound, he retired the
> first 17 Mets.

In the fourteenth paragraph, remembering the dusty mound, he says that Marichal

> . . . demanded that it be dampened because he was kicking
> dust into his own face.

This is the great Marichal demanding. Mr. Lipsyte says:

> A little man with a green sprinkling can scurried out and
> dampened the mound.

Later, Mr. Lipsyte says

> . . . Marichal was pulled out for some showering of his own.

Dust, dampening, showering: the words speak to each other. In the last paragraph, Mr. Lipsyte says:

> The third, waist-high and fast, was thrown with the stuff
> that dreams are made on.

For Mr. Lipsyte, the comeback of the Mets was so great that it deserved an echo of Shakespeare's lines in *The Tempest* (IV, i.):

> We are such stuff
> As dreams are made on, and our little life
> Is rounded with a sleep.

The speaker is Prospero, a magician who commands the air and earth. Mr. Swoboda was a magician at Shea Stadium.

Here is an Associated Press record of the same game as presented in *The Kalamazoo Gazette* for August 5, 1966. Probably only part of the original wire-service report was used, for the account was printed in a roundup article including games of other teams. You can see how the extra space available to Mr. Lipsyte allowed him to bring alive the scene. His report in many respects is fresher and more dramatic than the AP account.

METS SHOCK GIANTS WITH SWOBODA'S PINCH HOMER

Ron Swoboda, unlike lightning, has struck twice in the same place, and Bill Henry has been left smoking.

Just two weeks ago, Swoboda flashed off the New York Mets' bench and jolted fireman Henry by slamming the veteran reliever for a ninth-inning homer that gave the Mets a 3–2 victory over the San Francisco Giants.

Thursday, the 22-year-old right-handed hitter reduced lefty Henry to ashes, again coming off the bench in the ninth with a crackling three-run clout that carried the Mets to an 8–6 triumph over the Giants.

"It was just like a fairy tale," said Swoboda, relegated to pinch hitting this season when the opposition starts a right-hander.

The earlier belt kept the Giants out of a virtual tie for the first place in the National League. This one dropped them into second place, two percentage points behind Pittsburgh, which hammered Los Angeles 8–1.

The Mets trailed 6–4 entering the ninth when Ken Boyer started the Mets' thunder with a homer off Juan Marichal, seeking his 18th victory. Lindy McDaniel, who took the loss, relieved and gave up singles to Ed Bressoud and John Stephenson. Then Henry entered and moments later Swoboda struck.

Marichal, who had beaten the Mets 17 times in his career without a loss and retired the first 17 hitters Thursday, thus managed to slip off the hook.

Willie McCovey, Jim Hart and Tom Haller homered for the Giants and Johnny Stephenson also connected for the Mets.

In this report, Mike Recht of the Associated Press achieved some style by using the metaphor of lightning throughout—"unlike lightning, has struck twice . . . flashed . . . reduced lefty Henry to ashes . . .

a crackling three-run clout . . . the Mets' thunder . . . Swoboda struck."
His angle was that Swoboda again homered against Henry. But in the
paragraphs printed by the *Kalamazoo Gazette* Mr. Recht's story does
not take on the excitement of Mr. Lipsyte's, which led up to a sus-
penseful last paragraph.

Readers expect more life from columns of opinion than reports of
events. But a column or short piece of opinion or comment on passing
events does not become strong simply because it exhibits more personal judgment and opinion than reports and other more objective
writings. It may easily be boring, flat, and without significance to
readers. Here is a discussion of happiness published in a school newspaper.

HAPPINESS

There are many different kinds of happiness. The meaning
of happiness can be defined according to a person, his en-
vironment and his heredity.

Let's narrow this word down to what happiness is to high
school teenagers. To one teenager, happiness might be a set
of "wheels," a "weed," and plenty of "petro."

This person seems to think that in order to be happy, all
he needs is a showy sports car, cigarettes and gasoline. Why
would he think this way? He might live in a shabby house,
not have much in the way of good clothes or property, so
he wants something more than the normal teenager, something he thinks he can be proud of and show off.

Another teen might decide happiness would be a good
education and a bright future. This person has most of the
"flashy" comforts of life handed to him on a silver tray.
What he really wants is to make his own future, the chance
to prove himself.

Is either opinion wrong? Happiness depends on the person. Two extremes were taken in this case, to try and define
what happiness really is. It all points out that to gain happiness there must be a certain amount of discipline along
with the desire. If the desire is great enough, this thing happiness, in any definition, can be obtained.

The point of this passage is defensible. Not everyone needs to strive for
the same kind of happiness. An old idea, though, and of little value or
interest to a reader unless brought alive with telling examples. This
writer seems not to have found an iceberg. She says that driving a

showy sports car may be a legitimate kind of happiness, but she doesn't reveal enough knowledge of what it's like to drive a sports car to convince a reader. Why did she pick this example? Perhaps because she just came back from an exhilarating ride in a car. If so, she should have taken the reader on the ride. If not, she has chosen a wrong example. If she has not talked to a young person who wants to "make his own future" and a chance "to prove himself," she should not use him as an example. If she has, she should reveal what he has done, what he hopes to do, how his aspirations and achievements make him impressive. If she doesn't know such a boy, why is she talking about persons who value a good education and look toward their future?

Most professional columnists write out of consuming interest in particular events, ideas, persons. They are given a regular space to fill each month or week or day because they write compellingly.

Here is a report that might well be the first of a series on the writer's summer trip to the Soviet Union. It could be printed in the school paper as a weekly column entitled "Foreign Correspondent":

A LITTLE SPOT

At 8:30 on a cool June morning we left our hotel, feeling full of eggs, dark bread, sweet rolls, cucumbers, and fruit juice, and started walking toward the mausoleum. Nine Americans, going to see a thing sacred to Russians. We had heard the rumors before, but still several members of the group took turns bringing them up. "You know it *could* just be a wax dummy."

"Yeah, I heard only his head and hands were saved—the rest is fake."

"What'd they do with Stalin? He used to be in there, too, ya know."

"They moved him underground, out of sight somewhere. Down to the dungeon with you, old man."

"Someone told me that the head and hands look *most* like wax. I bet the whole body is wax and everyone's getting excited and religious about a hunk of wax. What a joke!"

"But I know someone who saw him six years ago and again two years ago. She said she thought Lenin was smaller the second time. That means it's really a dead body; it also means Lenin's shrinking."

"Oh come on! How could it be a real dead body in there? He'd look a lot worse than just smaller by now."

"Naw, they got ways to preserve bodies—but maybe they aren't foolproof. A friend of mine was here last summer. He said there's a little rotting spot behind Lenin's left ear. He asked me to look for it."

As we turned the corner, we were in sight of Lenin's final resting place—a low red-brown marble building. There were hundreds of people milling about in the rain. They formed a sort-of line, dangling haphazardly over the red cobble stones of Red Square. Toward the front, the line was distinct, while near the end it looked as if people were standing behind other people, assuming whoever was in front was in line. This part of the line was a city block of crowd, connected to the main line in many places, spreading fan-like. Our guide left us at what seemed to be the end of the line, and went ahead. A fellow-American said, "Man, can you believe this crowd? I thought we'd be the first ones out here, especially since it's raining."

"I knew it would be crowded—I've heard it always is, even if it's below zero."

In a few minutes Nina, our guide, returned and moved us up in the line, up to where it was a distinct two-by-two line. We were visitors, and fast finding out the strong Slavic custom to push visitors to the front—to see Lenin, to see a parade, to get into a museum or restaurant sooner. As we were walking through patiently waiting Russians "We don't deserve it" flickered through my head. We took our new position, in twos, behind a family of Soviet citizens. The man was wearing a baggy grey suit, which reminded me of the late movies on T.V.; his wife wore a loose fitting print dress, which extended below her knees. Each had a hand on the shoulder of one of the children standing directly in front. The mother leaned over, crossed her arms on the far side of her daughter's neck, and gently whispered something in her ear. As she straightened up, they all looked back and smiled. The marble building was in full view now, wet and shining. Huge slabs of dark stone jutted out from the main building on both sides of the door and two guards, with guns, stood erect near the black granite. The closer we got, the quieter the crowd. I watched the family enter, and I followed them into the marble cave in a spirit of reverence. We were moving all the time, shuffling around Lenin, filing through, and out the door on the other side. Two guards stood at Lenin's head and all three had the same expression, stiff, unfeeling, with pursed lips. Lenin lay under a glass dome, slumbering peacefully on lush cushions. There were flowers under the dome with him, there were flowers outside the dome. A light from somewhere shone on his face. He looked waxy, pale, dead. I looked again; he looked asleep. He was tiny, no more than 4½ feet tall. The hair on his head was invisible, the same color as his skin, but on his face it showed ruddy-grey under his nose and from his ears to his chin. He wore dark clothing, dark shoes. His hands rested gently on his thighs—at any moment they might flop to his side. We approached the outstretched man from his right side, walked the length of his body next to the velvet guard rail, up shallow marble stairs, around his feet, down the stairs, along the left side of his body, and up to his head again. Not a sound but the echo and re-echo of our footsteps, a silent cough, and my own awed heart beat. I felt myself leaning slightly toward the rail, sneaking a peek behind his left ear. It was there, a small darker spot which could have been a shadow, could have been a mole, but something was there. Across the room near the entrance several women were crying, a few even crossed themselves. Did anyone else see them? I glanced back at the rest of my group as they passed Lenin's head for the last time and gazed intently at his left ear. We eased out the exit door. I looked over my shoulder at the endless, continuous double line of people, flowing through the entrance, and around Lenin. Outside the drizzle had let up and the line fell apart, quietly. Silence ended when someone in my group asked, "Did you look? Did you see it? What do you think— was it really *him*?"

"I don't know. I don't know that it matters."

KATE MACK

Most professional columnists are good writers to study because they often write of matters that other persons make boring. Kate Mack wrote professionally of her visit to Lenin's tomb; she shaped her experience into a solid personal-public piece of writing.

THE ALTERNATING CURRENT

Kate's column is lively because it employs most of the eight fundamentals of good writing, maybe all of them. And one other strategy of professional writers: the Alternating Current. Like James D. Hart and Robert Lipsyte, Kate shifts back and forth from a lowly to a bookish vocabulary, what might be called Kitchen and Elevated language. When we are talking informally in the kitchen with friends or relatives, most of us do not use the word *haphazardly* or such a phrase as *slumbering peacefully on lush cushions.* We don't talk about an *awed heart beat.* We don't speak in formal metaphor, saying that we *followed them into a marble cave in a spirit of reverence.* We simply say, "We went into the mausoleum after them." Instead of *gazed intently* we say "looked hard." Most of Kate's sentences are stated in Kitchen language: *to see a parade, to get into a museum or restaurant sooner . . . sneaking a peek behind his left ear.* So like most exciting writers, she uses Elevated and Kitchen language in the same piece of writing. This alternation keeps the reader awake, makes him sense a tension in the language. Bad preachers do not use the Alternating Current. They drone on in an unrelieved elevated vocabulary. Bad editorial writers do the same. They have no sense of the lightness that can be achieved in a writing that discusses a solemn subject in sober setting.

> We hold these truths to be self-evident . . .

This statement from the Declaration of Independence would be spoken by few persons in their kitchens, but

> all men are created equal

might well be there. Speaking of King George III, the writers of the Declaration said:

> He has plundered our seas, ravaged our coasts

in language again not of the kitchen, but the rest of the sentence might have been said there:

> burnt our towns, and destroyed the lives of our people.

You may understandably say that no one could keep up Elevated language through a piece of writing. But some persons try. In a good part of her column on "Happiness" the writer spoke in a voice foreign to the kitchen:

> There are many different kinds of happiness. The meaning of happiness can be defined according to a person, his environment and his heredity . . . Happiness depends on the person. Two extremes were taken in this case, to try and

define what happiness really is. It all points out that to gain
happiness there must be a certain amount of discipline
along with the desire. If the desire is great enough, this
thing happiness, in any definition, can be obtained.

"To try and define what happiness really is" is a statement that might
be said in the kitchen. But it is not used consciously as a contrast to
the more elevated language of the first part of the sentence. Note the
alternation of language in Robert Lipsyte's baseball article:

Kitchen	*Elevated*
they got what they paid for	perfection from Marichal
hustle to catch	plaintive voices
The people who had come to see at least a shutout went home	a wasted gesture
Marichal was pulled out	In disbelief
he was kicking dust into his own face	an erratic shortstop
There was one out, two men on base and the score was 6–5	The roar was swelling now

Elevated language is usually more precise than Kitchen language
and comes to us trailing associations different from those carried by
Kitchen language. In many ways it is superior as a vehicle of expression, but no one wants to hear it steadily throughout a lecture or a
column. The ordinary speech of the common man is our anchor, and
no good writer forgets it. Even a writer composing articles for a reference book remembers the value of alternating between these two languages—James D. Hart wrote his article on Davy Crockett largely in
Elevated language but he saves it from dead levelness by the word
shiftless in the first sentence and by quoting the vernacular employed
by Davy:

natural-born sense instead of law learning.

The rest of the article is filled with Elevated: *picturesque eccentricities, aggrandized, propagating, constituents, etc.* Mr. Hart uses an occasional Kitchen expression like "were soon at work" or "Swallowing
the Whig bait." Quoting a statement in Kitchen language is a good
stratagem for a writer who feels bound to maintain a sober, dignified
style, and sometimes he may through quotation point out a surprising
variation in the style spoken by one of the persons he is reporting. For
example, Mr. Lipsyte quoted the Kitchen language of Ron Swoboda:

"It was a story-book game. Holy Cow!"

and then revealed him using Elevated language in describing his mood:

"Elation . . . the epitome . . ."

Sometimes writers make a whole column or report out of what others have said. A good reporter is on the lookout for strong remarks from the persons he interviews. He does not use the dull statements that are made to him. For example, here is part of a column in a school newspaper, "Is Your Spirit Dead?" A dangerous subject—more space has been wasted in school papers trying to stir up spirit in a student body than on any other subject. And this column begins with two obvious and dead quotations:

> School spirit is "a desire, a wanting" to make a school great, according to Varsity cheerleader, Betty Uvan. "No one else can improve school spirit except the individual himself," she said.
>
> "I guess school spirit," explained junior Dave Mark, "could be defined as a feeling of pride or respect in all of the representative units of the school and a willingness to assume the responsibilities of citizenship at school."

What these students say is old stuff and the manner in which they say it is flat. But the following article is loaded with sparkling quotations:

> LONG HAIR WARMS THE HEAD
>
> Girls started a big mess and now the boys are going to finish it. What mess? Well, girls came out with short "Page-boys" and slacks. Now the boys are trying to put the barbershops out of business. Besides that they have now begun pouring themselves into the cloth straws called pants.
>
> How do people feel about this trend? Stay tuned to the next lines for the exciting results.
>
> Jan Pennold says, "I don't mind long hair that much. I think tight pants are cool as long as they're not too tight."
>
> Dave Mark: "Well, if they're intent on becoming girls, it's okay."
>
> Rod Senson quipped: "I think hair should be closely trimmed . . . about at the shoulders." About tight pants he said, "Fine, I like tight pants."
>
> Helen Sals, very disgusted, said, "Boys ought to look like boys; tight pants are disgusting, too."
>
> Hugh Rich: "Long hair looks good, but if it's not kept neat, it can start to look cruddy. I like tight pants as long as they don't go to extremes."

Mary Mann said, "For guys in a group long hair is okay because it's their gimmick, but guys not in a group with hair like that look weird; tight pants are okay."

Kit Pramm cheered for it but couldn't conjure up a flip for it as she said, "Oh! I think there's a certain extent that's okay, but past that long hair is unmasculine. Long hair's okay if it's clean." About tight pants she added, "Oh yeah! (but I don't think they should go to extremes)."

Fred Lance said, "Some people look good and others look terrible. I think it depends on the way they wear long hair. Tight pants are okay if you don't split them."

Carol Laurens said, "I don't like long hair, I don't like tight pants; not that I like baggy pants, but real tight pants are terrible."

Andy Charles said, "I don't think long hair looks too good; tight pants are okay."

Sam Rich fondly remembered his freshman year and said, "Long hair is great when a biology bug collection is due." And then he gave us this tailor-made statement: "Tight pants? Well at least you don't have to have them taken in."

Pam Miller said, "Long hair is okay as long as it doesn't go to extremes. I think tight pants are repulsive."

You've heard what these jokers and serious minded riddlers have had to say, but the worst is yet to come! Would you believe second worst? Well, this reporter thinks that boys look best in "Crewcuts and Skirts."

But don't you know that most people's conversation is flat as a pancake, dull as dishwater, and plain as Aunt Jane? If you're going to write true to life, don't you have to write as dull as that? Yes to the first statement and no to the second. Writing words always involves selecting words, and writers can be true while selecting the freshest words of others, not the stalest. And if their point is to show dullness, they can quote outstandingly dull talkers.

> . . . The lucky listen to those who have fun when they talk, to born mimics and story-tellers, to those whose words, literate or not, play with the people that they talk with, and keep, somehow, in play with the motion of their hearers' minds.
>
> SIDNEY COX

The Alternating Current is not difficult to turn on in your writing. The secret lies in the genuineness of its juice, the speech you already have in your unconscious memory. If you remember your native dialect—the language you learned at Mother's knee—and alternate that with the language of writing you have picked up through reading and listening to teachers in classrooms, you will find the current naturally coursing through your prose. Finding it is again a matter of honesty. What is your voice? Do you hear how you speak when you are not thinking of your language? Listen to the country, the Kitchen, the ball game, the streetcorner talk in your life. Introduce it sparingly into your writing. At the same time you will find yourself varying the length of your sentences, and that is another form of Alternating. You often talk in shorter sentences than those written in books.

The Alternating Current flows in this quick piece of writing: rich, full descriptions and then short iron, mannish sentences.

> **I used to hunt with Gramp. He didn't hunt like my father. We would walk along the cramped, hollowed-out cowpath. The bushes and weeds would push out at us from both sides. I always walked behind. It led along the murk-filled brown-greenness of the channel that connects his two lakes. I would wait for something to break. He taught me never to kill anything unless I was going to eat it. He helped my brother shoot a pigeon once. He would have eaten it if it had not smelled so much.**
>
> **When the hunting was poor, we would go down by the lake and shoot beer bottles that some ass had left behind. There were always some there. Gramp would sit on a rotten stump and remember. He used to shoot pickerel as they pulled their heavy egg-filled bodies up the narrow channel. He said that they would spawn near the roots of the silver-gray pussy-willow trees. They're gone now; so are the pickerel. He would sit and laugh. And tell how the warden had chased him for two miles up to his slate-gray house. He had hid in the barn until he had left and then fried the warm fresh pickerel on the old black stove that was the heart of the house on a cold misty morning. We all learned something from him although he never taught us anything. I never knew it until he left. Tomorrow is never the same.**
>
> TOM CRONK

This is the way writers keep their writing alive. Tom Cronk may not have known that he was following an age-old tradition, but he was.

Preachers use this method, poets, men who tell stories around pot-bellied stoves. If you open a book like *Ten Contemporary Thinkers*, a collection of modern essays edited by Victor Amend and Leo Hendrick, you will find that every third or fourth paragraph exhibits the Alternating Current. For example, E. M. Forster writes:

> What about Force, though? While we are trying to be sensitive and advanced and affectionate and tolerant, an unpleasant question pops up: does not all society rest upon force? If a government cannot count upon the police and the army, how can it hope to rule? And if an individual gets knocked on the head or sent to a labour camp, of what significance are his opinions?

Don't think for a moment that Mr. Forster doesn't know "knocked on the head" comes from the barroom and "significance" from the library. In the same book, Archibald MacLeish, former Librarian of Congress and poet and dramatist, says:

> The old words of freedom and revolution are still around, louder than ever, but somehow they are not the same. Revolution, which was once a word spoken with pride by every American who had the right to claim it, has become a word spoken with timidity and doubt and even loathing.

"Louder than ever" is Kitchen; "timidity" is Library, Elevated. Maybe "still around" is from the alley.

All of the ten contemporary thinkers in this book (including Robert Hutchins, George Orwell, Joseph Wood Krutch, Carl Becker, Walter Lippmann, C. S. Lewis, Julian Huxley, E. B. White) write part of their essays with the Alternating Current.

The lively writer creates tension in his sentences through many ways —employing the Alternating Current; moving between the general and particular, the long and short sentence, the expected and the unexpected. By reading his work aloud to himself and to others, he trains his ear so that he writes with variety. He does not write half his work in Kitchen language and half in Elevated language, but rather continually alternates them. Always he thinks of his audience and his purpose. If he is writing a satire, probably he does not alternate his style: he may be taking on the voice of a pompous fool and needs to stick to it. In some writing, he cannot afford to vary his language or he will break a spell, a mood.

WRITING TWENTY-FIVE: Write a report of a place, a person, or an event, maybe a short sketch of your grandfather modeled on the

Davy Crockett article. Or a report of an event you know a certain group of readers would like to hear about. Find an angle, cram in the critical facts, keep the narrative alive with Alternating Current.

WRITING TWENTY-SIX: Write an editorial or column of opinion. Find an iceberg of fact on which to base what you present to the reader. No matter how lofty your thoughts, you can base them. You will do better, probably, to begin with the core of experience and let yourself earn the idea or opinion. Remember how the column "Happiness" suffered from lack of underpinnings. Note how this little essay grows out of experience:

OLD CREEPY DEATH

It's rainy and cool outside and we waded through too many ankle-deep puddles before getting back to the dorm. Now my feet are cold. But that's nothing new. They'll stay cold until I fall asleep and can't feel them anymore. I wonder what it would be like to go to sleep with warm feet? Even on recent warm nights they've been carefully smothered under layers of blankets and quilts that have been folded down to the end of the bunk. It would be fine if you could ignore them, but I never can. You're all warm and comfortable except for those two awful extremities. They ache cold. And though they seem to be separate from the rest of me, they are persistent in keeping me awake.

I once knew a girl who wore sleep socks. They were regular wool socks except they had felt faces on the soles of them. One was a woman's face with cute little bow lips and long eyelashes. She offered to let me wear them and I tried to. But I couldn't stand it. I kept thinking of those faces on the bottom of my feet and of how I had one male foot and one female foot. I didn't like the idea of the two of them being alone together down there, especially on my feet. It was no way to get my feet warm. Besides, I felt bad when I had to make a trip to the john and walked on their happy-go-lucky faces. I don't like the idea of socks, anyway. Even if they would work. My feet feel bound and too restricted. So, maybe I've chosen cold feet.

But what makes me so conscious of them is what the cold feels like. I've always thought that their kind of cold must be how death feels. Like poems have told me how death and coldness creep up on you until you're completely cold and completely dead. So every night I thrash my feet around to make sure the cold isn't creeping up my legs. When I think of me dying I think of dying in bed while I'm sleeping so I won't know about it. And I can't help but think that I'll most likely die the night that I can't keep the cold limited only to my feet. That's why I hate them the most, the pleasant thoughts that accompany them. I put off sleep for a while each night to make sure that the rest of me is staying warm. But then, I've probably got it figured all wrong. Death will probably play a trick and the cold will work its way from top to bottom. But that wouldn't really be so bad, to have your nice, warm, cozy tootsies be the last to go. Because as long as my feet are warm I can feel warm all over and I could ignore old creepy death.

LOIS BERG

When you write reports and columns of opinion, use the Alternating Current if it is appropriate. Just because you may be writing your own opinion doesn't mean you can forget your reader. He's alive. He wants to be kept awake while reading.

The Alternating Current is usually more appropriate to columns of opinions than to reports, but you saw at the beginning of this chapter how it gave texture to a report on Davy Crockett. Nevertheless, many reports call for a less attention-getting style. A business executive may ask an engineer or consultant to visit a plant and report on the efficiency of its operations. A scientist may have to report on the behavior of fish used in an experiment. Often their reports should be highly objective, keeping the observer out of the sentences as much as possible. However, those who write and read such reports should never forget that any human report is a product of an individual's perceptions.

*Poetry is a response to the daily neces-
sity of getting the world right.*

WALLACE STEVENS

chapter 20

writing

poems

POETRY—ugh. "My heart is plunged in misery." Or, "Methinks I have seen your visage before."

Many people hate poems, would never think of writing one. Understandable. Too often teachers have assigned poems that speak in voices which sound pretentious and phony to readers unaccustomed to the language of another time. Meter—a regular beat to the lines—and rhyme make poems sound unlike ordinary talk, and therefore artificial.

Like bad poets in the past, many present-day students who write for the school literary magazine think that rhyme and meter alone make a poem. The result is "Sorrow, My True Story," that awful wail printed in Chapter 5, and many other creations printed in school magazines that are seldom read except by their writers.

The core of a good poem is made up of something other than these traditional poetic techniques, as is suggested in this paper written by a student:

POEMS

I grew up with a guy named Johnny. His nickname was Junior. He didn't wear clean clothes or shined shoes every-day. He didn't have his hair cut twice a month or even twice a year.

He left Stadium High School at the end of the third quarter of his sophomore year. He came back his senior year, about the fourth week of school, but I never really felt Junior was that interested in the school life. He and I were in the same English class.

One day our English teacher gave the class a small assignment. It was to be at least a half page long and was to be in a poem's form, and the topic was to be college, and it was supposed to be read at the end of the period.

This was the last period of the day, and she said after everyone read his paper the class could leave. Junior and I always sat in the back of her class. We were the only Blacks so we never wanted to participate in class discussions.

There were a lot of poems read, which said a lot about nothing and, just like always, we were last. I read mine first. I knew basically what this teacher liked. She liked those nothing poems, the type that made the world all pretty. I needed at least a "B" in the class to keep my grade up to standard so that was the type of poem I wrote. The class dug it.

Junior wasn't like that. He didn't care what a teacher thought about his writing. He wrote as he felt. His poem went:

> I think I'll go to college
> And mess with the broads and learn big words.
>
> Should I go to college
> And learn things my brother never heard?
>
> Should I go to college
> And wear thick glasses and never say "Hi"?
>
> Naw, I won't go to college.
> I'll just sit on the corner
>
> Drinking wine 'til the day I die.

Everybody in the class laughed but us. Everything we did in that class was funny. A month later, Junior dropped out of school. I wonder—was that funny?

EDWARD RANSOM

In 1800 the British poet William Wordsworth had the same notion as Ed Ransom. He got so sick of phony poetry that he wrote an essay condemning poetic diction and said that a poet should be "a man speaking to men." He added that poetry "takes its origin from emotion recollected in tranquillity." I would guess that if he were living today he might be disturbed by the lack of meter in the following poem written by a student, but he would say it fit his definition and would have some praise for it.

BUMPS

I knew a girl once
who had a '62 Falcon
with one headlight missing
and she believed that
you'd get less shock
from bumps
by driving over 'em fast.
So every afternoon
she'd pick me up after school
and we'd race off
looking for new bumps
to test her theory on
and she'd always be muttering
something about
cushions and suspensions.
And one Thursday
when we were finished
she dropped me off
at Tommy's Luncheonette, where
they had the best cheeseburgers,
and a bunch of guys
that were just hanging around
started making fun of her theory
and she got mad
and sped off . . .

And I never was exactly sure
how it happened
'cause I got the story
from a computer operator
who couldn't really be counted on
for correct facts
but they say
she was going
about 83 miles an hour or so
down Pleasant Street
when an old guy
in a Cadillac
pulled out
in front of her,
and he swore
on a Bible
that he never
saw her coming.

A simple way to define poetry is to say it is writing that uses all the strategies of prose but more fully and intensely. Most poets do not waste words. They employ more metaphors than prose writers. They control the sound of the words and the rhythm of sentences with more care. They try to wed sound and sense. They use symbols, flashbacks, flashforwards, dialogue—all without Explainery and Insistery. They play with words, making them speak to each other closely or wildly. They know that punning can be a deep delight rather than a bad joke. Good prose writers know all these strategies too, but they do not use them as intensely.

The principal difference between poetry and prose is compression. Most poems require the reader to work hard. Often he is expected to consider A and B and guess C without being given it. That's why poems are put down differently on the page from prose, which is lined up on both left and right margins. The shape of a poem on the page is a signal to the reader that he must slow down, do more guessing, often read through it a second time.

Once you know what poems are, you can presume they are easier to write than you thought. Many prose passages are so short and compressed they seem to be wanting to become poems. Look at your writings, especially in journals. You may find such passages. Here's one in which a student was remembering childhood:

> **If I were to write a book, it would be about spongy rubber balls. Without a doubt, spongy rubber balls are the number one pastime for children.**
>
> **You can ball them up and let them goosh out between the spaces of your fingers. You can play base-, basket-, and foot-ball inside. You can squish them up and cram them into your mouth, and then at the dinner table act like you're throwing up and poof—out comes the ball.**

That passage could easily be made into a poem. Cut it a little. Arrange it like a poem:

SPONGY RUBBER BALLS

You can ball them up
and let them goosh out
between your fingers.
Play baseball with them
and football—inside!
At dinner table
squish them up
and cram them
into your mouth.

Act like you're throwing up,
and poof—
out comes the ball!

John Milton, author of one of the most successful long poems ever written, *Paradise Lost,* said that poetry is more "simple, sensuous, and passionate" than rhetoric. That's a pretty good working description of most moving poems. Here again are prose passages which were made into poems:

NAME

If he asks me
to say my name
in class
one more time,
I'm going
to make up
a new one.

SCHOOL LANDSCAPE

All
those
empty cars
in the parking lot
look
   so
      left
        there.

Many of the best modern poems are *sensuous,* as Milton put it. They appeal to the senses. Their objects and actions are not abstracted but presented concretely, as in this love poem by a boy:

CHEEK

      Her cheek
      is as
      smooth
      and
      cool
      as the
   other
     side
of the
pillow.

That poem makes you feel the girl's cheek and the pillow. Another student wanted to say he often felt wanderlust. He followed Milton's advice when he wrote:

ABILENE

A lot
     of times
I want to be
     on the outskirts
of Abilene
     and slap my pants
and make
     big clouds
       of
     dust.

In fact he wrote that sentence as prose in his journal and here it has been arranged as a poem. To consider what is meant by being sensuous, think of how this poem might have been written if it were not simple, sensuous, and passionate but cold and abstract. The same thought might have been expressed like this: "Often I get the feeling that living here, going to school, is more than I can take. Then I wish I were far away in some of the places I have been at moments in my life when I felt really wonderful."

Wordsworth and Milton praised emotion and passion in poetry; but they, like many good poets today, did not exclude ideas from their poetry. Here's an idea poem by a student:

GREAT

Fifteen-cent
hamburgers and
guys carrying
around 6-transistor
radios listening
to the world
series do not
a great
nation
make.

Like good prose, good poetry carries surprise. Fifteen-cent hamburgers as a test of a great nation. Or maybe a common, ordinary feeling like the cars in the parking lot looking left there, but surprising that the writer would say that. No one else has said it before. "Sorrow, My True Story" in Chapter 5 cries out and shouts but doesn't surprise as much as this little poem:

BURN
May
the
flames
of
love
burn
your
heart
to
a
crisp.

More passion in that poem than in the wailing one. And so much
more compressed. It carries a cliché, *burned to a crisp;* but it is somewhat saved by being used with such a high-flown phrase as *flames
of love.* Still there is surprise in that short poem. Most beginning
poets who write of love or boredom usually do nothing more than
bore their readers. Here is a poem on lonesomeness which is simple
but not sensuous. The passion which lies in it must have been recollected in tranquility because it is expressed in a surprising way:

TWO
A jet
just divided
the sky
in two:
half for me
half for you.
I wonder
who you are.

The above poem controls its sound skillfully up until the last two
lines. It repeats a *j* sound, emphasizes *i* sounds in *divided* and *sky,*
rhymes *two* and *you,* repeats or parallels *half for me, half for you.*
Most of the other preceding poems were made out of prose sentences
or paragraphs and sound prosy. They do not control the rhythm of
phrase, the interior sounds of words; they do not employ alliteration.
The following poem carries a whole sound to it, as if the speaker
felt so strongly she had to talk in rhythmic phrases and words that
can be read aloud smoothly and softly:

MEETING

Love and I met today.
It was just a casual acquaintance,
        not one of those candle lights in Rome,
Just a walk in the rain.
Maybe it was just the rain I was in love with,
But we made it through together
        and if it was the rain
I hope it storms soon.

This is not a sensuous poem. It does not make you feel or see
the rain or the person walked with. But it surprises and it controls
its sound. And happily, though it is slow, casual, and almost mel-
ancholy, it speaks humorously in the last line. One suggestion: drop
the second use of the word *just*. Poet, don't forget—compress,
compress!

In all the poems presented here, Milton's suggestion that poetry
is *simple* is evidenced. Nothing fancy. No parading of the writer's
vocabulary, no insisting with adjectives and adverbs.

WRITING TWENTY-SEVEN: Try writing a short, simple poem.
Maybe your journal carries a passage that wants to be a poem. Look
to your experience and don't for a moment let the word *poem* make
you forget truthtelling.

Nothing said here was meant to imply that writing within bound-
aries—like those imposed by meter and rhyme—is bad for a poet.
Some of the most powerful poems have been written within tight
conventions. But this chapter is meant for beginners and persons who
do not consider themselves poets at all. If you wish to see what working within limits does for your expression, you might try writing the
Japanese verse form of *haiku*. Here's a sample written by an American
boy:

Afternoon sunlight
splattering through swaying tree-
tops, butters the ground.
        TOM THAYER

The haiku is an old verse form in Japan. It consists of three lines
of five syllables, seven syllables, and five syllables, without rhyme.
Traditionally it presents a small happening, moment, or notion in
the life of nature in which a simple thing is observed so closely or
in such a juxtaposition with other natural events that it comes across
newly, surprisingly. As you can see, it is another country's institu-

tionalized form of a fabulous reality. Again, it has a sudden ending, usually requiring the reader to find its significance on his own. Here are two haiku by Japanese poets:

> One man
> and one fly
> waiting in this huge room.
>   ISSA

> I sit like Buddha
> but the mosquitoes
> keep biting.
>   OEMARU

These poems do not follow the 5-7-5 pattern because they are translated and the translator cared more about the naturalness of phrasing and idiom in English than about the syllable pattern.

Here's another haiku by an American student, this time cheating on the form, giving only four syllables to the first line:

> A fly circling
> A half-filled glass of Kool-Aid—
> His sweet, liquid grave.
>   MEGAN REESE

WRITING TWENTY-EIGHT: Write three haiku poems. If you wish, depart from natural subjects and write of man-made things or events.

You can go on to write rhymed, metric verse. Robert Frost is a fine model because he was able to find rhymes that don't sound corny. His lines are almost irresistible in sound. They do not slavishly follow the accented pattern and often they sound like relaxed conversation at the same time they are disciplined by a somewhat regular beat.

By now when you write anything, you will probably think first of truthtelling. After that, when writing poems, think of compression. It helps you attain intensity, so essential to poems, as Milton hinted with his "simple, sensuous, and passionate." Intensity may also arise as it does in any good writing because the poet has talked of things which together surprise the reader but finally make sense to him. The skilled poet may press and press upon one point or feeling without being monotonous. Consider this poem by a student:

TAPS

1 plus 5 = 6
I am 6. Remember that.
8 plus 3 = nothing that I know of.
I am not eleven anything.
I skip that one. The teacher is mad.
Why don't you do your work?
She taps her red pen on my head. Hard.
I do not cry. I am a big girl. I go to school.
Do your work, says the cruel gleaming-teeth teacher.
She taps her red pen still more on my head.
One-two-three-four-five-six-seven-eight-nine-ten-eleven.
Now I know eleven. I do the problem, finish my work.
Now I understand eleven. I hate eleven.
I am a big girl. I will not cry.

PEGGY HOWARD

Peggy intensified her poem by pressing and pressing, on numbers. That is her subject. But she goes beyond citing addition problems and the number of times the teacher tapped on her head to say "I am not eleven anything." She uses short sentences, she repeats numbers, she builds the emotion (becomes passionate). She uses parallel construction in short hammering clauses: "Now I know eleven. I do the problem, finish my work." She repeats the word *eleven* strongly, not monotonously. It is a superb poem, employing the eight fundamentals of good writing. It makes the reader work. Only once does it come out and state its point: with the word *cruel*. Dropping that word would make the poem better, force the reader to see that the final hatred in the poem is directed not against the number eleven but against a tyrannical teacher.

Here's a poem by a high school junior that asks a great deal of the reader:

BOOKSTORE

I purchase a dream at the counter
of peeling linoleum,
of scarred wood,
place a dirty quarter
in the sweating clerk's hand,
politely hiding my repulsion at the touch
of his calloused palm . . .
and start down the aisle.

I edge past a smiling old man
engrossed in an illustrated calendar
from Sweden,
two teenage girls giggling over a confession magazine,
a fat woman reading an ad for reducing candy,
and a pimpled boy with a comic book.

They step aside for me,
not looking up to see my face,
to see my skin hidden by makeup,
to recognize our common reality.

Only the bell on the door
is obliged to say farewell, tinkling tinnily.

If you read that poem at the same rate as you read prose, you may have to try it again before you understand. That's part of the poetry contract: a reader is expected to slow down when he sees signs that the poem before him is put together like a puzzle. And he is not to feel ashamed or outraged if he has to read it twice. And two readers may find different meanings in it. If the difference is extreme (for example, if one reader believes that "Bookstore" says that old men who read girlie magazines are alien and disgusting and the other reader believes that the narrator is putting herself in the same class with him) then either the poem is written badly or one of the readers has read it badly.

"Bookstore" is subtle and surprising in its thought. It might be still better if the writer had not so frequently put an adjective before her nouns. Such a technique makes for monotony in expression; it creates sing-songy description. But "Bookstore" is so fully a poem —displaying many of the strategies open to poets—that it is a good one to discuss with your classmates. How do you read it? What do you get from it? What cues lead you to your meanings?

For centuries in China part of the test for bureaucratic officials to be admitted to office consisted of writing a poem. These officials were men. Most of the published poets in the Western world have been men. Yet most of the poems written in schools have been done by women. Same old story: women don't get the praise and the publicity. But in American schools boys usually are afraid to write poems because they may be thought effeminate. A wild circle of irony. It's time everyone started writing poems that demand truthtelling. We might have less Engfish in government, business, and organizations of all kinds—maybe less lying. The best poetry is often hard, lean, and muscular, like a good tight end or a middle linebacker.

Here's a poem by a high school boy. He wrote it the day after
he had heard that three young people in his school had been killed
the night before, two in one auto crash, one in another.

THREE DEATHS

What's the use when the kids are all gone?
Why the drawn faces for kids gone along?
I wanted to bang my head on the wall
        and fight for more lives.

What are the steps for events such as these?
        Trillium grows along the river
        where birds beat deer to the water
        and yesterday was such a nice sunset.

But when will I know of this death?
        Breath of steam ices the cracking cold sunshine
        where penguins wouldn't look too lost
        and snowshoes walk among the trees.

I'm not sure if I'll take a walk today.
I'm sick of knowing only the knobby outdoors
        when the state of these kids is dead,
        and I know of no way to play with that.
                                        MARK PATTULLO

Now two examples from a professional poet, William Carlos
Williams, who writes strong sounding lines. The two poems differ
from each other in sound. They move differently. That is one of the
effects a writer can achieve by controlling sound.

THE DANCE

In Breughel's great picture, The Kermess,
the dancers go round, they go round and
around, the squeal and the blare and the
tweedle of bagpipes, a bugle and fiddles
tipping their bellies (round as the thick-
sided glasses whose wash they impound)
their hips and their bellies off balance
to turn them. Kicking and rolling about
the Fair Grounds, swinging their butts, those
shanks must be sound to bear up under such
rollicking measures, prance as they dance
in Breughel's great picture, The Kermess.

POEM

As the cat
climbed over
the top of

the jamcloset
first the right
forefoot

carefully
then the hind
stepped down

into the pit of
the empty
flowerpot

Dr. Williams' mastery of sound should come as no surprise to readers who know he was a poet. A practicing M.D., he wrote poems in his office in between seeing patients or on the way to visit them at home.

In "The Dance," Dr. Williams writes only two sentences, listing again and again a few nouns joined by prepositions, or a verb form ending in *-ing*. Once he says they go round and round, his parts of sentences repeat and repeat and thus go round and round themselves:

the squeal and the blare and the tweedle
a bugle and fiddles
their hips and their bellies

One way he gets the parts of sentences to swing is to join them with *and*, a word he uses six times.

Read aloud, the poem almost flies off the page, because Dr. Williams has employed so many sound effects—alliteration and assonance, the repetition of *ound* in *round, around, impound, Grounds, sound.*

Dr. Williams' second sentence is not actually a sentence but a jamming together of the parts of several sentences which do not keep straight their subjects and verbs. For example, the shanks are not "swinging their butts"; the dancers are. Dr. Williams knows what a sentence is, but here he deliberately violates grammar in order to increase the feeling that the speaker is himself breathlessly swinging around and around rather than reciting a carefully composed statement at a speaker's podium.

In the second poem about the cat, Dr. Williams has arranged his words to slow down the reader as he speaks the lines. Instead of the constant repetition of words ending in *-ing*, he uses many words ending in sounds that stop rather than prolong sound: the word *top* not a word like *new*, the word *jamcloset* not a word like *see*. Also

many of his words begin with hard sounds: *cat climbed, flowerpot.*
In "The Dance," he wanted beer-drinking peasants to swing in
circles; in "Poem" he wanted a cat to step precisely and carefully.
The sound of words is the poet's business. He must be able to control
it as a pitcher controls a curve.

Let yourself write with the feeling of swinging freely and hearing
your words as you write. Then you'll get the parallel rhythms and
alliteration and the right sounds of voices. You can always shorten,
tighten, expand, change here and there. This love poem has the right
sound for what it says:

LOVE POEM

Every hitchhiker
silhouetted on every freeway exit
suitcase shoulder-slung
leaving every city
is you.

"Pick me up, hey,
give me a lift, I'll go
anywhere."

I would send out fleets.
                    COLLEEN ANDERSON

This chapter has been designed to get you over any fear or animosity
you might have had toward writing poems. It is an introduction and
nothing more. Hundreds of other remarks could be made about the
nature of poetry and its strategies.

WRITING TWENTY-NINE: In your journals look for short, con-
centrated passages that might be turned into poems. Or try your hand
at writing a poem out of your experience. Look at the first version
you have written. Then cut it and cut it. Leave not one word that
an intelligent reader will not need. Here, for example, is the first
draft of a poem:

Fiery red hot coals
glowing in an old fire
on a bland summer night
me
        staring
                wanting
to touch one
but the beautiful coals
that look so soft and orange
        would burn.

Consider what might be cut or rearranged. Be tough on your poem. Most poets write a poem and revise it, let it alone for a few days, and come back to it. They drop lines, stanzas, words. They rearrange. The revisions frequently number eleven or more. Here is a cutting and rearrangement of the above poem:

> Fiery coals
> glowing soft and orange
> in an old fire
> on a bland summer night
> me
>   staring
>   wanting
> to touch one.

Compress your poem. Intensify it. Make the reader work.

irony. 2 a: *the use of words to express something other than and esp. the opposite of the literal meaning.*

Webster's Seventh New
Collegiate Dictionary

chapter 21
writing indirectly

YOU DON'T HAVE to write in a straight line that runs right at your reader. You can shoot words off on a diagonal, a little off target, and expect the reader to see where the bull's-eye really is. Making a point indirectly gives it surprise.

You may turn upside down what you say. Exaggerate. You may say exactly the opposite of what you mean. Take up a serious subject lightly or a trivial subject heavily. A funeral is no place for jokes, but a writer can write humorously about funerals. Evelyn Waugh did and called his novel *The Loved One,* a story about an ostentatious burying park in California. You may joke about poverty. Jonathan Swift did and called his essay "A Modest Proposal for preventing the Children of Poor People from being a Burden to their Parents or the Country" (by roasting them as food for the rich).

Here are some of the ways a writer speaks indirectly:

(a) *A writer may play dumb,* pretend to be holding one opinion while tipping off the reader to his true, and often opposite, opinion.

In chapter seventeen of *Huckleberry Finn,* Samuel Clemens, talking through Huck, speaks so indirectly, yet with such a straight face, that many readers don't see what he is saying in this description of the Grangerford house and family:

> It was a mighty nice family, and a mighty nice house, too. I hadn't seen no house out in the country before that was so nice and had so much style. It didn't have an iron latch on

the front door, nor a wooden one with a buckskin string, but a brass knob to turn, the same as houses in a town. There warn't no bed in the parlor, not a sign of a bed; but heaps of parlors in towns has beds in them. There was a big fireplace that was bricked on the bottom, and the bricks was kept clean and red by pouring water on them and scrubbing them with another brick; sometimes they washed them over with red water-paint that they call Spanish-brown, same as they do in town. They had big brass dog-irons that could hold up a saw-log. There was a clock on the middle of the mantel-piece, with a picture of a town painted on the bottom half of the glass front, and a round place in the middle of it for the sun, and you could see the pendulum swing behind it. It was beautiful to hear that clock tick; and sometimes when one of these peddlers had been along and scoured her up and got her in good shape, she would start in and strike a hundred and fifty before she got tuckered out. They wouldn't took any money for her.

Well, there was a big outlandish parrot on each side of the clock, made out of something like chalk, and painted up gaudy. By one of the parrots was a cat made of crockery, and a crockery dog by the other; and when you pressed down on them they squeaked, but didn't open their mouths nor look different nor interested. They squeaked through underneath. There was a couple of big wild-turkey-wing fans spread out behind those things. On a table in the middle of the room was a kind of a lovely crockery basket that had apples and oranges and peaches and grapes piled up in it which was much redder and yellower and prettier than real ones is, but they warn't real because you could see where pieces had got chipped off and showed the white chalk or whatever it was, underneath.

This table had a cover made out of beautiful oil-cloth, with a red and blue spread-eagle painted on it, and a painted border all around. It come all the way from Philadelphia, they said. There was some books too, piled up perfectly exact, on each corner of the table. One was a big family Bible, full of pictures. One was "Pilgrim's Progress," about a man that left his family it didn't say why. I read considerable in it now and then. The statements was interesting, but tough. Another was "Friendship's Offering," full of beautiful stuff and poetry; but I didn't read the poetry.

Another was Henry Clay's Speeches, and another was Dr.
Gunn's Family Medicine, which told you all about what to
do if a body was sick or dead. There was a Hymn Book, and
a lot of other books. And there was nice split-bottom chairs,
and perfectly sound, too—not bagged down in the middle
and busted, like an old basket.

They had pictures hung on the walls—mainly Washing-
tons and Lafayettes, and battles, and Highland Mary, and
one called "Signing the Declaration." There was some that
they called crayons, which one of the daughters which was
dead made her own self when she was only fifteen years old.
They was different from many pictures I ever see before;
blacker, mostly, than is common. One was a woman in a slim
black dress, belted small under the arm-pits, with bulges like
a cabbage in the middle of the sleeves, and a large black
scoop-shovel bonnet with a black veil, and white slim ankles
crossed about with black tape, and very wee black slippers,
like a chisel, and she was leaning pensive on a tombstone on
her right elbow, under a weeping willow, and her other
hand hanging down her side holding a white handkerchief
and a reticule, and underneath the picture it said "Shall I
Never See Thee More Alas." Another one was a young lady
with her hair all combed up straight to the top of her head,
and knotted there in front of a comb like a chair-back, and
she was crying into a handkerchief and had a dead bird
laying on its back in her other hand with its heels up, and
underneath the picture it said "I Shall Never Hear Thy
Sweet Chirrup More Alas." There was one where a young
lady was at a window looking up at the moon, and tears
running down her cheeks; and she had an open letter in one
hand with black sealing-wax showing on one edge of it, and
she was mashing a locket with a chain to it against her
mouth, and underneath the picture it said "And Art Thou
Gone Yes Thou Art Gone Alas." These was all nice pictures,
I reckon, but I didn't somehow seem to take to them, because if ever I was down a little, they always give me the
fan-tods. Everybody was sorry she died, because she had laid
out a lot more of these pictures to do, and a body could see
by what she had done what they had lost. But I reckoned,
that with her disposition, she was having a better time in the
graveyard. She was at work on what they said was her greatest picture when she took sick, and every day and every

night it was her prayer to be allowed to live till she got it done, but she never got the chance. It was a picture of a young woman in a long white gown, standing on the rail of a bridge all ready to jump off, with her hair all down her back, and looking up to the moon, with the tears running down her face, and she had two arms folded across her breast, and two arms stretched out in front, and two more reaching up towards the moon—and the idea was, to see which pair would look best and then scratch out all the other arms; but, as I was saying, she died before she got her mind made up, and now they kept this picture over the head of the bed in her room, and every time her birthday come they hung flowers on it. Other times it was hid with a little curtain. The young woman in the picture had a kind of a nice sweet face, but there was so many arms it made her look too spidery, seemed to me.

This young girl kept a scrap-book when she was alive, and used to paste obituaries and accidents and cases of patient suffering in it out of the *Presbyterian Observer*, and write poetry after them out of her own head. It was very good poetry. This is what she wrote about a boy by the name of Stephen Dowling Bots that fell down a well and was drownded:

ODE TO STEPHEN DOWLING BOTS, DEC'D.

And did young Stephen sicken,
  And did young Stephen die?
And did the sad hearts thicken,
  And did the mourners cry?

No; such was not the fate of
  Young Stephen Dowling Bots;
Though sad hearts round him thickened,
  'Twas not from sickness' shots.

No whooping-cough did rack his frame,
  Nor measles drear, with spots;
Not these impaired the sacred name
  Of Stephen Dowling Bots.

Despised love struck not with woe
  That head of curly knots,
Nor stomach troubles laid him low,
  Young Stephen Dowling Bots.

O no. Then list with tearful eye,
   Whilst I his fate do tell.
His soul did from this cold world fly,
   By falling down a well.

They got him out and emptied him;
   Alas it was too late;
His spirit was gone for to sport aloft
   In the realms of the good and great.

If Emmeline Grangerford could make poetry like that before she was fourteen, there ain't no telling what she could a done by-and-by. Buck said she could rattle off poetry like nothing. She didn't ever have to stop to think. He said she would slap down a line, and if she couldn't find anything to rhyme with it she would just scratch it out and slap down another one, and go ahead. She warn't particular, she could write about anything you choose to give her to write about, just so it was sadful. Every time a man died, or a woman died, or a child died, she would be on hand with her "tribute" before he was cold. She called them tributes. The neighbors said it was the doctor first, then Emmeline, then the undertaker—the undertaker never got in ahead of Emmeline but once, and then she hung fire on a rhyme for the dead person's name, which was Whistler. She warn't ever the same, after that; she never complained, but she kind of pined away and did not live long.

What you have read is a mild satire of the décor of a house and a strong satire of a sentimental little girl who wrote bad poetry. Obviously Huck thinks the house beautiful, but Clemens suggests with small cues that he does not. He might admire artificial fruit, but when he has Huck mention "where pieces had got chipped off and showed the white chalk or whatever it was," you should begin to suspect his intentions in this writing. Think of the whole picture: the mantel a garish display of painted scene; crockery birds, dog, cat; and turkey wings. On the table an oil-cloth spread displaying a spread eagle—more wings. The books: standard family pieces, revealing no individuality of mind in their choice, all perfectly piled as if never used. The pictures on the wall patriotic and sentimental. The room is as gaudy as a souvenir shop at Niagara Falls, and Clemens wants the reader to know this at the same time he wants him to see that Huck Finn is completely inexperienced in judging such matters. The room goes perfectly with Emmeline Grangerford's poetry, which Twain hits more directly in hard satire.

Clemens' indirectness enables him to make three points at once. He scores the Grangerfords' lack of cultural independence, shows his hero limited in experience, and slyly criticizes the American middle-class for its use of pseudo art objects in its homes.

(b) *A writer may directly say he doesn't understand, when he does,* as this high school student did in a poem:

> I wonder if the mail has come
>   (Not that I really care.)
> Our quarrel was really very dumb.
> I wonder if the mail has come!
>   (I shouldn't have said that 'bout her hair.)
> Should I have written? Do I dare?
> I wonder if the mail has come.
>   (Not that I really care.)
>
>   KATHY CURRIER

(c) *A writer may take on another character's views,* perhaps his own when he was young, and pretend he doesn't know any more now than he did then, as did this girl in an account of her childhood:

TOMATOES

I was four when I had my first encounter with a tomato. We lived in Santa Barbara in a gray house separate from our neighbor by a garden of green and black stripes. The old man, Mr. Swift, fussed in his garden each dewy morning and worried his tomato plants into growing green and tall.

One early summer morning I was playing in the outskirts of the garden and happened to notice ladybugs crawling on Mr. Swift's prize plants. I didn't want them chewing up the fruits of my dear neighbor's labor so I decided to help him. I knew he would thank me when he found out I had gotten rid of the speckled pests for him. The only trouble was I was afraid to touch the bugs, so I had to break off each leaf that had an orange dot on it. I had gone through six rows when my mother called to me through the screened window that lunch was ready. Mr. Swift never knew that I tried to help him because I wasn't able to finish my job. A mysterious telephone call during lunch upset my mother and she spanked me right in the middle of a fried egg sandwich and wouldn't let me go outdoors the rest of the day.

It's a wonder that poor Mr. Swift's garden ever grew. One evening after supper my mother sent me out in the yard to break up a tea party that had been going all afternoon. Three of my dolls lay asleep on the ground around the orange crate tea table, and I feared they would be sick because it had turned very cold. I bundled them in my wagon and was pulling them to the back door when I noticed the garden.

Someone had played a mean trick on poor old Mr. Swift. Each of his tomato plants was hidden under a sawed-off milk carton. I knew they couldn't breathe inside there and would die if I didn't uncover them. It didn't take as long as getting rid of the bugs because I could just kick over each box with my foot. It was dark when I finished and got my dolls in the house. My mother scolded me for tracking in mud; I had been too late though, because next morning all the plants lay wilted on the ground. My neighbor didn't understand when I told him they died because they couldn't get their breath—he said, "The wind did it." I don't think he was a very smart farmer.

I don't know if Mr. Swift planted tomatoes again the next year because that winter we moved to Nebraska. We lived on the corner one block over and two blocks down from Grandma's house. In the spring Grandma gave me some seeds so I could plant a garden of my very own and learn responsibility. I decided I would have tomatoes because I already knew all about growing them. Besides, maybe I could send some to poor Mr. Swift. Daddy helped me. He spaded up the garden and planted the seeds, and then I watched them grow. My mother let me use my allowance to buy a sprinkling can from the dime store so I could water my garden. Daddy showed me which were the weeds and I tugged them out by the roots so they wouldn't choke my tomatoes. My garden grew and Daddy put a tall slender stake for each plant to climb. I watered my garden four times the first day and at least once a month after that. My garden grew as I played with the three boys next door, but I never got any tomatoes to send to my old neighbor. My mother told me that the odd blue flowers on my tomato plants were called four o'clocks, and I picked a bouquet for her.

CAROLINE SIEBLER

When you write indirectly, you must be consistent in style and viewpoint. You cannot use the Alternating Current without blowing the whole electric circuit. You must take a position or attitude or mood or role and stay in it throughout your writing. You are working on at least two levels. On the first, you must move authentically at all times. If your name is Alice and you are traveling through a Wonderland, you must believe in it all the time. You may have doubts and express amazement at what you see, but finally you must believe. And the Queens and Humpty Dumptys you encounter must be naïve and small-minded at all times on the first level, no matter how cleverly on the second level you manage to make them appear normal human beings.

In the story "Tomatoes," the author maintains the child's point of view beautifully except in a few spots, such as when she uses the word "outskirts" and the phrase "fruits of my dear neighbor's labor." Look for others. When you play another role than your own, you must stay in a voice that is right for that role.

> *Either stick to tradition or see that your inventions be consistent.*
>
> HORACE

(d) *A writer may make fun of pompous or pedantic persons or milksop and toadying persons by mimicking their language and pushing it to further excesses.* This exaggeration is often called burlesquing. For example:

IMPORTANT THINGS TO REMEMBER

Some things in this course will be more important than others. The most important thing to remember is that the War of the Tulips was fought before the Treaty of Pootrecht. Other important battles were the Alley Ambush of 1412 and the Small Slaughter of 1303. These are all important, but not as important as the date of the War of the Tulips.

(e) *A writer may blow up a trivial matter so large that it bursts.* For example:

The students who support the campaign to bring greasy and crumbly potato chips back to our cafeteria have completely rejected the traditions of Rich Central and are attempting to maliciously destroy the unity of our school

> . . . They are undoubtedly using innocent potato chips as a guise for their plot to overthrow the Cafeteria Honor Committee and instill chaos, disunity, and trash throughout the school . . .

This was the method Jonathan Swift used in *Gulliver's Travels,* a cutting satire of the way adult human beings conduct themselves in every department of life. In one part of the book he blew men up and in another he reduced them.

(f) *A writer may exaggerate his case,* speaking excessively so that what he attacks seems not simply deserving of criticism but absolutely ridiculous. This method is often used by an essayist, columnist, or editorial writer. Here is Thoreau writing in *Walden*:

> And I am sure that I never read any memorable news in a newspaper. If we read of one man robbed, or murdered, or killed by accident, or one house burned, or one vessel wrecked, or one steamboat blown up, or one cow run over on the Western Railroad, or one mad dog killed, or one lot of grasshoppers in the winter,—we never need read of another. One is enough. If you are acquainted with the principle, what do you care for a myriad instances and applications? To a philosopher all *news,* as it is called, is gossip, and they who edit and read it are old women over their tea. Yet not a few are greedy after this gossip. There was such a rush, as I hear, the other day at one of the offices to learn the foreign news by the last arrival, that several large squares of plate glass belonging to the establishment were broken by the pressure,—news which I seriously think a ready wit might write a twelvemonth, or twelve years, beforehand with sufficient accuracy. As for Spain, for instance, if you know how to throw in Don Carlos and the Infanta, and Don Pedro and Seville and Granada, from time to time in the right proportions,—they may have changed the names a little since I saw the papers,—and serve up a bull-fight when other entertainments fail, it will be true to the letter, and give us as good an idea of the exact state or ruin of things in Spain as the most succinct and lucid reports under this head in the newspapers: and as for England, almost the last significant scrap of news from that quarter was the revolution of 1649; and if you have learned the history of her crops for an average year, you never need attend to that thing again, unless your

speculations are of a merely pecuniary character. If one may judge who rarely looks into the newspapers, nothing new does ever happen in foreign parts, a French revolution not excepted.

(g) *A writer may treat an act lightly that is ordinarily feared,* in order to reduce its power.

For example, Julie Beach, writing in a student newspaper, begins a column with these paragraphs:

> **For those students who have not yet reached the grand old age of eligibility for a driver's license, here are a few helpful hints to get them through the ordeal.**
>
> **First of all, get plenty of sleep the night before the test is going to be taken. It helps one get a passing grade if the road signs can be read clearly.**
>
> **When walking out to the parking lot with the policeman, try to remember where the car is parked. It doesn't pay to put him into a grouchy mood by walking around the lot for half an hour.**
>
> **After getting into the car, remember to unlock the door on the passenger's side. If a tapping noise is heard, don't be alarmed. It is only the officer knocking on the window, trying to get in.**
>
> **The key should now be placed in the ignition, then turned. If for some unknown reason it won't turn, take it out and flip it over; it was probably in upside down . . .**

(Reminder for persons working on tightening: in paragraph 2 the words "is going to be taken" could be omitted, and also the word "noise" in paragraph 4.)

(h) *A writer may turn upside down or outrageously distort the treatment of an event* in order to ridicule the straight, sober, or trite treatment it is usually given.

For example, sports writers frequently present a dull roundup of the year, in which they try to make every team's record look impressive. Steve Henson, sports editor for *The Torch* (newspaper of Rich Township High School Central Campus, Park Forest, Illinois, May 13, 1966), decided he had had enough of such trite stuff and wrote a spoof, part of which follows:

> **. . . You all remember Central's football team, better known as Bill Barz. Smashing through the season nearly undefeated (well, you can't win 'em all) Barz and his teammates beat up**

everybody (if not on the field then out in the parking lot after the game). Cinderella Quanstrom put on his helmet and glass slippers and really turned in a great season. We can't forget guys like Denny Zumbahlen and Larry Morris, who averaged 38 tackles per game—31 of them after the whistle had blown.

The Olympian Gridders were undefeated at home, using the advantage of the home field, the home refs, and Central's own Mr. Matheny running the scoreboard. It was simple—how else could you beat somebody 51–0? "Football Player of the Year" has to go to little 6′8″, 295 lb. Bill Barz, to go along with his other awards of all-conference, all-area, all-suburban, all-state, and all-world . . .

The varsity cagers were a great team, though, and exciting to watch. Hundreds of records were set during the season. Hot Dog Madderom averaged about 40 points per game and set a game high record when he tossed in 68 points against T. F. South. Randy hit on an amazing 22 field goals in that game in only 97 shots from the field. His best performance was in the Oklahoma game. Randy really scored and made several fine passes. Ed Younker tied the world record of falling asleep during a game (17 times) and Bob Moyer hit the most number of free-throws without a miss by a manager: 2 (also a world record). Bob Ewing grew the longest beard by a 6-foot forward in the entire South Suburban area . . .

The Rich Central golf team has not been up to par this spring. Don Richmond, the "most consistent performer," really tore up the course at Olympia Fields last week, with a 67; in fact some fairways are still being repaired. He shot a Country Club record 58 last Saturday, with an eagle on the 5th hole, birdies on the 7th and 8th, and by forgetting to play the back nine . . .

One of Steve Henson's strategies in this column is to begin a statement in conventional manner and then end it with a kicker:

> . . . who averaged 38 tackles per game—*31 of them after the whistle had blown.*
> . . . He shot a Country Club record 58 last Saturday with an eagle on the 5th hole, birdies on the 7th and 8th, and *by forgetting to play the back nine.*

Another of his strategies is to present an actual fact and invent new facts which carry it to ridiculous heights:

> . . . to go along with his other awards of all-conference, all-area, all-suburban, all-state, and *all-world*.

The truth is that Rich Central teams had a good season; for example, the baseball team won the District Championship and the football team lost only one game. But the indirect writer does not speak pure and whole fact. He risks being misunderstood. Mr. Henson's spoofing is consistent enough to make most readers aware of his intent, but even though he said, "we remind you to not believe everything you read" one student complained in a letter, saying,

> You stated that *no* one ever went to *any* of the wrestling meets, and you did not even recognize the existence of a wrestling team.
>
> This proves you have never gone to a wrestling meet; regular, or any of their district, sectional, or state meets . . . So shape up, and apologize for the unjust insult you tossed to our boys, or don't call yourself a fair sports editor.

Answering that letter, Mr. Henson said:

> If you believed that I was not exaggerating when I said "nobody went to any of their meets" and that no wrestling team even existed, then you must have taken everything else in the column seriously too. You must have believed that I was not exaggerating when I said that Barz was 6'8" and 295 lb., or that Madderom scored 68 points against T. F. South, or that Zumbahlen and Morris tackled 31 men after the whistle, or that Ewing tossed the shot through the gym wall into the little theatre.

He shows by his answer that he realizes that indirect writing cannot alternate between straight and indirect expression. It must be consistent in its attitude.

At times all of us speak indirectly naturally and with ease. To a girl falsely modest about her pretty new dress, we say, "You look horrible, Anne, absolutely rotten." In sarcasm we say to a person who has assigned us an unpleasant job, "Oh, this is lovely work—I wouldn't want to do anything else." A common line spoken by a soldier in World War II to another soldier digging a ditch was: "Whatya gripin' about? You're learnin' a trade." We mimic the way a teacher acts or talks. In dozens of ways, we speak with double tongue, knowing closely our audience and sensing how far we can go in indirection without losing them. As writers, we can learn to sustain and unify a piece of indirect communication which cuts and cuts down, astounds and delights, cajoles and teases.

WRITING THIRTY: Write quickly a piece of indirect writing about something or someone you know well and feel strongly about. Whatever your degree of factualness or exaggeration, make your statement ring true. Do not attack or ridicule someone for something he did not do or say and cannot have done or said. All must be true, at least in the sense of being representative. Play with ideas, approaches, words. Then reconstruct, make consistent, tighten, sharpen, polish.

> *You writers, choose a subject that is within your powers, and ponder long what your shoulders can and cannot bear. He who makes every effort to select his theme aright will be at no loss for choice of words or lucid arrangement. Unless I am mistaken, the force and charm of arrangement will be found in this: to say at once what ought at once to be said, deferring many points, and waiving them for the moment.*
>
> HORACE, 13 B.C.

I am also convinced that the more you know about your craft, the freer you can be from it. My interpretation of freedom has nothing to do with sloppy or careless technique that is a caricature of freedom. To me real freedom arrives when the artist's creative instinct can function without limitation and without consciousness of technical means.

GABOR PETERDI

chapter 22
the
order
of
words

A CHILD OF SIX speaks as if he knew his meaning depends a great deal on word order. He wouldn't think of saying:

Of wouldn't he think saying.

And he wouldn't mess up the agreement signals in this sentence by using a word that signals twoness when it needs to signal oneness:

Johnny and Bill has his own bike.

And he wouldn't say:

It was nice of they.

because in the American grammatical system words like *he, she,* or
they preceded by prepositions signal their relationship by changing to
the object form (*him, her,* or *them*). Kids know this by the time
they're six or eight. But sometimes they run into an adult—maybe
a teacher—who is so worried about someone saying,

> You and me should go to the show.

that they say,

> She did not give it *to* you and *I*

when their unconscious and normal feeling for the signal would
make them say,

> She did not give it *to* you and *me.*

J. D. Salinger made his hero Holden Caulfield, in *The Catcher in the
Rye,* talk in this highly self-conscious ungrammatical way:

> I think I probably woke he and his wife up . . .

When Eudora Welty said that beginning and professional writers
have the same troubles—not being serious or truthful—she might
have added that they both have the same troubles with grammar.
Most editors find little that is grammatically weak about the writing
they edit, and when they do, the weaknesses are usually confined to a
few troubles to be expected in the writing of anyone using the American grammatical system. Frequently they involve (1) confusing word
order, (2) lack of clear signal by pronouns, and (3) verbs that do not
signal which nouns they belong to.

In reading over the first draft of your writing, look first for these
possible weak spots.

Word order signals meaning:

Original. When green I love the woods most of all.

Is that when I am green (sick at the stomach) (Young, like a green
plant?), or when the woods are green? If the latter, the sentence
should read:

Revision. I love the woods when green most of all.

or

Revision. I love the green woods most of all.

Thoreau opened Chapter Two of *Walden* with this sentence:

Original. At a certain season of our life we are accustomed to consider
   every spot as the possible site of a house.

His grammar would have been slightly confusing had he written:

Misrevision. We are accustomed to consider every spot at a certain season of our life as the possible site of a house.

Now *spot* and *season* are too close to each other. The phrase *at a certain season* should be close to *accustomed.*

In your writing, place next to each other those words which belong together in meaning. In the following sentence, the words in italics and in small capitals belong together in meaning but are separated from each other in position:

> This task, which George found highly agonizing, *grew* under the heat of the afternoon sun *soon* to be *unbearable,* and he QUIT working at it steadily EVENTUALLY.

When the words are rearranged (and a Whichery removed), the sentence is improved:

Revision. Under the heat of the afternoon sun, this agonizing task soon grew unbearable and George eventually quit working at it steadily.

The new order makes more sense, but it reveals the sloppy thought on the part of the writer. If the task "soon" grew unbearable, then why did George wait until "eventually" (whatever that means) to stop working at it? Either the "soon" or the "eventually" should be eliminated. Better yet, the writer might tell the reader what he means by "soon" or "eventually." How many hours or minutes?

Not every sentence changes its meaning with a change of word order. For example:

Original. Our minds thus grow in spots . . .
Revision. Thus our minds grow in spots . . .
Revision. Thus grow our minds in spots . . .
Revision. In spots thus grow our minds . . .

American-English grammar does not do all its signaling of meaning by word order.

REVISING TEN: Examine your last two long pieces of writing for blunders and weaknesses in word order. Write down on a separate sheet of paper your weak sentences and your revision of them. Reading aloud will help you in this task.

All writers and speakers occasionally let one of the segments of their sentence dangle out on a limb where it can fall off the tree. The most distinguished example is probably a sentence in Thomas Jefferson's **First Inaugural Address:**

> About to enter, fellow citizens, on the exercise of duties which comprehend everything dear and valuable to you, it is proper that you should understand what I deem the essential principles of our government, and consequently those which ought to shape its administration.

What is "about to enter" is Jefferson, not "you," who are fellow citizens, or "it," which here is one of those vague words which can't enter anything. A dangling construction fails to make clear who is doing what.

> While walking back from my English class, a squirrel came up and stepped on my foot.

Squirrels returning from English classes will upset anyone.

More examples of dangling constructions:

> Not finishing dinner until 8:30, another problem was in the making.
>
> By subtly mentioning to one set of parents that it would be nice if we could all be together, they usually take the hint and invite others.

But enough of these sinful errors. The good writer masters grammar in order to control his words, and meaning is his target. In a given paragraph, he may use an expression that is technically a dangling construction but nevertheless communicates his meaning clearly. For example, here is the masterful English writer William Hazlitt beginning the third paragraph of his essay on Sir James Mackintosh:

> To consider him in the last point of view first. As a political partisan, he is rather the lecturer than the advocate.

The first sentence does not show clearly who is doing the considering, and the whole group of words is not really a sentence at all. But it works, and an editor would be a fool to change it.

The commonest word-order change made in manuscripts by editors is to bring together subjects and verbs which have been thoroughly separated.

Original. *Professor Rending*, in approaching his subject, stumbled in circles, like a drunk.

Revision. In approaching his subject, *Professor Rending* stumbled in circles, like a drunk.

The method here is to pull out the segment of a sentence which is properly introductory, such as

> When he was altogether prepared,

from the sentence in which it occurs:

> President Wilson, when he was altogether prepared, presented his plan to the League of Nations.

and put it at the beginning.

Revision. When he was altogether prepared, President Wilson presented his plan to the League of Nations.

Often, such rearrangement allows the writer to eliminate a wasted expression such as a Whooery:

Original. Queen Gertrude is a weak person, who is, in spite of her faults, held in high regard by the three men in her life.

Revised. In spite of her faults, Queen Gertrude is held in high regard by the three men in her life.

All writers slip occasionally in making clear the reference between pronouns and their antecedents and the agreement between subject and verb. Therefore editors routinely check for these slips and find them frequently:

> Sol and his buddy Georgie, who is his uncle's favorite baseball player, often *tries* to eat more than he can hold.

Revised. Sol and his buddy Georgie—his uncle's favorite baseball player—often *try* to eat more than they can hold.

> The haggling and the bickering and the many hours of long drawn-out close reading I had to do when I was tired— it was all too much for me.

Revised. The haggling and the bickering and the many hours of long drawn-out close reading I had to do when I was so tired were all too much for me.

Note that most slips in pronoun reference and noun-verb agreement occur in long sentences which interrupt themselves with qualifications and side-trips. Editors examine such sentences closely, expecting meaning may have slid into a ditch.

Commonly professional writers use *which* and *that* to refer to the the word immediately preceding:

> I like HAMBURGERS *which* are well done but not dry.

But increasingly these days, they are using *which* or *that* to refer to a whole action described in a number of preceding words:

> Renny approves of making changes now, which is all right with me.

You will do well to stay with the conservative practice of including a clear referent word immediately preceding *which* or *that* as in HAMBURGERS *which*. If you ignore this practice and create a sentence that cannot be misunderstood by your reader, let it stand; but the odds are against you. Note that if the example contained three more words,

> Renny approves of making changes now in the plan, which is all right with me.

the reader couldn't be sure whether what is "all right with me" is the whole plan or the changes. The reader's understandable interpretation of the sentence is probably that *which* refers to *plan*, the word immediately preceding it.

These little matters of reference and agreement are the higgledy-piggledy of grammar. More crucial matters exist. When you think of word order—the way words come together in phrases and clauses (pieces, hunks, segments, absolutes, whatever you call them at the moment)—think of how you may control it to bring your writing alive.

Try telescoping three or four sentences into one, so that the first reaches out and grabs part of those that follow. Here are three sentences too closely related to stand separately:

Original. Immediately Juliet sees the only solution to her problem. That solution is suicide. This is a highly illogical choice.

You can tack on to the first sentence the essential elements of the second and third sentences:

Revision. Immediately Juliet sees the only solution to her problem— suicide, a highly illogical choice.

Such tacking-on must be done with care. If the sentences preceding those above have suggested that the author is judging Juliet's behavior, this revision may be clear. But if not, the reader might take the sentence to say that Juliet sees suicide as a highly illogical choice, a meaning which would jar against the notion embodied in "only solution."

Study the Tack-On sentences of good writers. You will see they frequently write down a subject and verb (and sometimes an object of the verb) and then simply add nouns or prepositional phrases, or phrases beginning with verb forms ending in *-ing* or *-ed*:

(a) *It would become a sorcery,*
       a magic.

ARCHIBALD MACLEISH

(b) *There is a pulpit at the head of the hall,*
       occupied by a handsome gray-haired judge
          with a faculty of appearing pleasant and impartial
             to the disinterested spectator,
                         and
                         prejudiced and frosty
             to the last degree
             to the prisoner at the bar.

MARK TWAIN*

(c) *Each of us lives and works on a small part of the earth's surface,*
             moves in a small circle,
                       and
       of these acquaintances
             knows only a few intimately.

WALTER LIPPMANN

(d) *There were several ladies on board,*
       quite remarkably beautiful or good-looking,
       most of them, alas,
                   now dead.

IVAN TURGENEV

(e) *Let us arrange the contents of the heap into a line,* with
       the works that convey pure information at one end, and
       the works that create pure atmosphere at the other end, and
       the works that do both in their intermediate positions,
             the whole line being graded so that we pass from
                one attitude to another.

E. M. FORSTER

Occasionally an author uses the Tack-On method at the beginning of his sentence:

(f) Approaching Concord, doing forty, doing forty-five, doing fifty,
       the steering wheel held snug in my palms,
       the highway held grimly in my vision,
       the crown of the road now serving me (on the righthand curves),
                now defeating me (on the lefthand curves),
       I began to rouse myself from the stupefaction which
          a day's motor journey induces.

E. B. WHITE

Most beginning writers need to nudge themselves into Tacking-On more often but the habit comes naturally to many persons. These statements were written by high school students not coached to Tack-On:

It is the great American tradition to shed your
anxieties and slothfully recline at the rim of a pond,
       resting and
       letting your unattended pole slip in the motionless wet.

While playing tennis I feel a sense
of freedom,
of being able to release the pent-up emotions from
        hours, days.

Man, who could have been so useful, is now dead,
not physically,
but emotionally and mentally.

Another way of exploiting the force of word-order in American-English is to place a word in an unusual or dominant position in the sentence.

> *[Ask] How many words out of their usual place, and whether this alteration makes the statement in any way more interesting or more energetic.*
>
> EZRA POUND

In many sentences the position of most weight for a word is the end. Frequently you can punch a word by putting it last in a sentence.

> **I went up to get a friend to go to class with. While waiting for her to get ready, I glanced around the dorm room. There were clothes, hairdryers, curlers, pressers, strewn all around the six-girl room. On the desk sat a book entitled Social Disorganization.**

Note how the power of the statement would be lessened had the last sentence been written:

> A book entitled *Social Disorganization* sat on the desk.

Of Sir Walter Scott, William Hazlitt wrote:

> The old world is to him a crowded map; the new one a dull, hateful blank.

Had he placed his words in normal order, he would have written less forcefully:

> The old world is a crowded map to him; the new one a dull, hateful blank.

Hazlitt's version forces the essential words to the end of each word group, where they gather power and achieve parallelism. To move a word out of normal position is to surprise the reader.

Normal Order. He was a lost man.

Unusual Order. He was a man lost.

A writer must develop an ear for normal word order and respect that order. If he continually scrambles it, he will confuse his reader rather than surprise him. The principle involved here is the old one mentioned in Chapter 9: repeat and vary. Vary the normal pattern, but sparingly. And don't forget to create a pattern of expectation in the first place.

REVISING ELEVEN: Take two of your past writings, one free writing and one a planned longer work, and go over each word and sentence to see where you can change word order and improve the clarity or force of your statements. Write in the changes on the original so you and others can see what difference they make in the writing.

"He has got no good red blood in his body," said Sir James.

"No. Somebody put a drop under a magnifying-glass, and it was all semi-colons and parentheses," said Mrs. Cadwallader.

GEORGE ELIOT

chapter 23
observing
conventions

FROM THE AGE OF FIVE onward most Americans know and practice the social conventions of their region and economic class. They say "thank you" and "you're welcome" and they eat with or without napkins or finger bowls or whatever is proper to the persons they associate with. Their ego is involved. They want to be liked, to feel right in the social circle they choose for themselves.

But most Americans don't know the publishing conventions of the educated world. They have been taught commas and semicolons as they have been taught "please" and "May I introduce my brother—" but each year in school they learn them for a test and forget them the following day. Why? Because they never expect to have their writing published, or even dittoed and passed around the class. Their ego is not involved.

But the torture of being required each year to learn again what they never learned and aren't going to remember once again this year is slow and unbearable. *Semicolon* becomes a dirty word. Like Mrs. Malaprop, they confuse *apostrophe* with *parenthesis* and *hypothesis* and *apotheosis.*

What should they do if they're sixteen or sixty and haven't learned the American conventional system for aiding readers in understanding the meaning of printed rather than spoken sentences? About the only chance they have is to study sentences in print and deduce for themselves the system. If they look to a textbook for rules, they will forget them again quickly and painfully.

If you're in this unhappy group of persons laden with guilt about commas and italics, begin observing. Construct generalizations which explain why certain mechanical conventions of print are used in the right-hand column of sentences below. For your convenience the left-hand column presents sentences naked and innocent of most punctuation or other signaling devices. Look at them first. Make your guess at what they need in the way of signals. Then study the signals printed in the right-hand column, which follow the normal conventions of writing published in most magazines or books. Note that they do not follow newspaper conventions, which are different from those of books.

DIALOGUE

Well, if we went to Raleigh we could get Mr. Isaacs Christmas candy. Before she could answer Mamas footsteps passed in the hall overhead so she said Don't you reckon we ought to stay closer-by than Raleigh? He turned to her. Look—are you sticking with me or not? She looked and said Yes. Let's go then. She scraped their dishes and left them in the sink and said I'll get my coat. Where from. My room. All right but come straight back.

"Well, if we went to Raleigh, we could get Mr. Isaac's Christmas candy."

Before she could answer, Mama's footsteps passed in the hall overhead so she said, "Don't you reckon we ought to stay closer-by than Raleigh?"

He turned to her. "Look—are you sticking with me or not?"

She looked and said "Yes."

"Let's go then."

She scraped their dishes and left them in the sink and said, "I'll get my coat."

"Where from?"

"My room."

"All right, but come straight back."

REYNOLDS PRICE

SEMICOLONS, COMMAS, PERIODS, DASHES, COLONS

Learn these marks in this order if you want to master punctuation quickly. The semicolon has only four or five major uses, the comma dozens. If you know a semicolon is not called for, you can bet wisely that what you need is a comma.

UNPUNCTUATED	CONVENTIONALLY PUNCTUATED
1. Well I agree you could say the atom bomb doesn't go boom	Well, I agree. You could say the atom bomb doesn't go boom;

it just obliterates a few hundred thousand people.

2. The world needs a little loosening of discipline and the schools need a little tightening of self-discipline.

3. He was no good for he had fallen apart at both the seams and the cuffs.

4. Renny a boy without guts was my enemy but Pedro a boy without guts was my friend.

5. I like Jackson Michigan Michigan City Indiana and Indianapolis Indiana.

6. It was a large city however I walked its streets without fear.

7. She was however a girl one could get along beautifully without.

8. Those days when Grandpa was a boy are long gone now the snows are deep and my Jaguar won't start.

9. In the last analysis Bertram doesn't measure up to the job.

10. Although a writer can lie about facts he should never lie about feelings.

11. When the moon comes over the woodshed behind the university library it feels out of place because Robert Frost is not there.

---

it just obliterates a few hundred thousand people.
(or):
Well, I agree you could say the atom bomb doesn't go boom. It just obliterates a few hundred thousand people.

The world needs a little loosening of discipline, and the schools need a little tightening of self-discipline.

He was no good, for he had fallen apart at both the seams and the cuffs.

Renny, a boy without guts, was my enemy; but Pedro, a boy without guts, was my friend.

I like Jackson, Michigan; Michigan City, Indiana; and Indianapolis, Indiana.

It was a large city; however I walked its streets without fear.
(or):
It was a large city; however, I walked its streets without fear.

She was, however, a girl one could get along beautifully without.

Those days when Grandpa was a boy are long gone; now the snows are deep and my Jaguar won't start.

In the last analysis, Bertram doesn't measure up to the job.
(or):
In the last analysis Bertram doesn't measure up to the job.

Although a writer can lie about facts, he should never lie about feelings.

When the moon comes over the woodshed behind the university library, it feels out of place because Robert Frost is not there.

What a sight it is, to see Writers committed together by the eares, for Cere-monies, Syllables, Points, Colons, Com-

ma's, Hyphens, *and the like? fighting,
as for their fires, and their Altars; and
angry that none are frightened at their
noyses, and loud brayings under their
asses skins?*

BEN JONSON

12. I liked working there in
the city next to the subway with
its rattle its earth jar its grimy
dirt that settled in the whorls of
the ear and transferred itself
from my sweating neck to my
white collar by nine each morning.

I liked working there in the
city next to the subway with its
rattle, its earth jar, its grimy dirt
that settled in the whorls of the
ear and transferred itself from
my sweating neck to my white
collar by nine each morning.
(or):
I like working there in the
city next to the subway—with its
rattle, its earth jar . . .

13. She is sweet notwithstanding her sour tongue and pretty
as cottage cheese.

She is sweet, notwithstanding
her sour tongue, and pretty as
cottage cheese.

14. I always found Archie that
sad bag of a man worth his
weight in tin.

I always found Archie—that
sad bag of a man—worth his
weight in tin.

15. We walked across the
square a place deserted by everyone but the familiar urchins who
were dipping their feet in the
fountain as if it were a cold day
in February.

We walked across the square—
a place deserted by everyone but
the familiar urchins, who were
dipping their feet in the fountain—as if it were a cold day in
February.

16. She was a beautiful plump
hen of a woman whose legs were
properly pipe-stems ending with
gigantic feet and I loved
her clucking and pecking her
squawking and fluttering.

She was a beautiful plump
hen of a woman whose legs were
properly pipe-stems ending with
gigantic feet; and I loved
her clucking and pecking, her
squawking and fluttering.

17. The Alsatians were losing
the Martian war quickly they
had no missiles or orbiting vehicles.

The Alsatians were losing the
Martian war quickly; they had
no missiles or orbiting vehicles.
(or):
The Alsatians were losing the
Martian war quickly: they had
no missiles or orbiting vehicles.

18. The General Velocipedes
car was a beauty stinking heater
buckling back wheels and valves
that needed regrinding after a
turn around the block.

The General Velocipedes car
was a beauty: stinking heater,
buckling back wheels, and
valves that needed regrinding
after a turn around the block.

SIGNALS FOR EMPHASIS

Conventionally, book and magazine writers and editors emphasize words with italics and quotation marks. When they use a word as an example of a word rather than as a regular part of a sentence, they usually put it in italics, which are indicated in handwriting or typescript by a single underline. (A double underline indicates small capitals; triple underline, capitals.)

19. The use of and is more difficult than most beginning writers realize.

20. Phrases like in terms of and with respect to can kill off an otherwise good speech.

The use of *and* is more difficult than most beginning writers realize.

Phrases like "in terms of" and "with respect to" can kill off an otherwise good speech.

More often than not, the words *say, call, refer to as* are followed by quoted words.

21. Those are what Mr. Wick calls "critical elements."

Frightened by Mrs. Clutched, their old third-grade teacher, many beginning writers use quotation marks around any word that would seem unusual in the sterile air of Mrs. Clutched's classroom. They say:

We had a "bunch" of good pitchers on our team and they used to "bug" each other constantly.

Nothing looks more square to an experienced editor or reader than this overuse of quotation marks. It implies either that the writer is a phony and won't admit that the words he's quoting belong in his vocabulary, or that the words *bunch* and *bug* are absolutely new to his readers in the use he has put them to. If they are slang, he should decide whether or not he wants to employ slang. If it is inappropriate to the subject and situation, he should not use it. If it is customarily set in italics—and there you can see the principle behind italics and quotation marks: to help the reader when he needs help, to inform him of what he is not apt to see on his own when he is reading in a healthy state of perception—then he should use italics or quotation marks.

NUMERALS

Unless numerals are being used in an article or book constantly, the professional writer conventionally writes in words those numbers that can be written in two words or one, and all others in numerals. He never begins a sentence with a numeral; for without an opening capital letter, a sentence looks as if it is part of the preceding sentence.

22. We counted twenty-four eggs within one hundred feet but there were 142 in the whole area.

If a sentence requires a number like 136 (written in numerals because it cannot be written in two words) and several other numbers, they are all written in numerals, for the sake of consistency:

23. ALWAYS: Three thousand and eighty-four men were ready; they each had 136 ounces of food, 32 feet of rope, 2 cans of suppressed napalm, and 12 rounds of ammunition.
   NEVER: In the cages were rabbits in groups of 4, 3, and 6. 7 of them were kept in the barn in a larger enclosure, and 413 in all the buildings combined.

TITLES

Quotation marks are not used around words that appear above a piece of writing as its title. That would be like writing,

My name is "John."

Exception: When the title consists of, or in part of, words borrowed from another source, those borrowed words may be enclosed in quotation marks. Even then, if the borrowed word or phrase is well-known, it need not be quoted:

To Be or Not to Be a Ham

Writers citing names of other published works are careful to follow a consistent signaling system. Usually they *italicize* (or *underline*) names of whole works—a novel, history, encyclopedia, anthology, play, magazine, newspaper. They *put in quotation marks* smaller parts of those whole works: a chapter, article, poem, newspaper report (its title is its headline).

24. Jerry Kobrins Why Gleason Got the Headlines is another star-centered article in TV Guide but Up at Yale by Neil Hickey seriously looks at what college students are writing that could raise the level of television drama.

Jerry Kobrin's "Why Gleason Got the Headlines" is another star-centered article in *TV Guide*, but "Up at Yale" by Neil Hickey seriously looks at what college students are writing that could raise the level of television drama.

25. The Old which is the first chapter of Renfrew's latest book The Gnu and the Auld is a masterpiece of humor.

"The Old," which is the first chapter of Renfrew's latest book, *The Gnu and the Auld,* is a masterpiece of humor.

SIGNALING POSSESSION

The apostrophe to signal possession is the hardest conventional sign to remember because it is slowly fading away in use. In formal names printed in capital letters, it is no longer used:

VETERANS ADMINISTRATION.

In the days before dictionaries began to establish conventions firmly (Dr. Samuel Johnson's *Dictionary* of 1755 solidified spelling and other writing conventions in England, and Noah Webster's *Dictionary* of 1828 did the same in America), writers often used the apostrophe to indicate plurals, as did Ben Jonson in 1640 in the line quoted in this chapter:

. . . Points, Colons, Comma's

(Capital letters were conventionally used in England and America then for most major nouns in a sentence), and in Chaucer's day (1400), possession was signaled by an *-es* ending on words:

As dide Demociones doghter deere . . .
That lordes doghtres han in governaunce . . .

Chaucer used no apostrophes for possession, although here the daughters in both lines belong to the fathers mentioned. Writing about two hundred years later, Shakespeare commonly used an *-s* ending to signal possession, but still without an apostrophe:

It was a Lordings daughter, the fairest one of three . . .
A womans nay doth stand for nought . . .

Conventions in publishing change like conventions in ladies' dresses but not as fast. At the moment, most printed books and magazines in the United States are employing the apostrophe to signal possession, even though it is no more necessary in most instances than in Shakespeare's day.

26. I got my moneys worth when all the ladies cakes were left in my car.

I got my money's worth when all the ladies' cakes were left in my car.

27. A womans nay doth stand for nought.

A woman's nay doth stand for nought.

28. Jamess trouble was not the Worthingtons trouble.

James's trouble was not the Worthingtons' trouble.

SCHOLARLY WRITING

Two common miswritings in scholarly work are the abbreviation for *page* or *pages* and the signal for paragraph indention.

WRONG: pg (pgs)   RIGHT: p. (pp.)

℘   ¶

Pg. may be some lazy person's abbreviation for *pig*, but it is not the conventional abbreviation for *page.* Understandably persons make the sign of a double-stemmed capital P to indicate *paragraph*, but the proper sign has nothing to do with the letter P. It is a sign used in illuminated manuscripts before 1440, then without such long stems, and still in use today.

Footnotes are a pain to writers, readers, editors, and printers; but some scholarly tasks require them so that scholar-readers may trace easily the steps through which a writer made his case. Like all conventions, footnotes are being constantly changed in form, usually in the direction of simplicity.

In footnotes, *Ibid.* means "the same as above." The following set of footnotes reveals a standard pattern. Why do some *Ibid.* entries include page numbers and some not?

1 Fred M. Oliver, *Love Problems of High School* (New York, 1939), pp. 33-34.
2 *Ibid.*
3 *Ibid.*, p. 101.
4 Karl Heimson, "The Courting Pattern," *New Ways in Education* (Englewood Cliffs, Texas, 1956), p. 555.
5 Oliver, p. 101.
6 Heimson, p. 420.
7 *Ibid.*, pp. 419-425.
8 William G. Looney and James Brass Smith, editors, *Thinking and Talking* (New York, 1965), p. 13.
9 George Walker, "Sex," *The Teacher's Magazine,* vol. 14 (June 1967), pp. 13-14.

Text of paper employing above footnotes:

> Fred M. Oliver, psychologist at Nendy High School, Oak Pond, New York, cites the informal conversation of students. Jane, a senior, says "I'm mad for you, John," meaning in the new dialect of her group that she has decided to take John's part in his quarrel with his girl friend Susan.[1] This new game, played at several high schools in the area,[2] represents a clever playing with words—taking old slang or in-group expressions and giving them their literal rather than traditional meaning. "Cool it" to these students means to open the windows or turn down the thermostat.[3]
>
> Conventional students in a Kansas high school do just the opposite. They develop a new language for love and dating which consists of giving new double meanings to the

commonest expressions, like "Wash the linoleum" or "Is it cold out?"[4]

Oliver[5] and Heimson,[6] however, both state explicitly that they admire high school students' ability to invent new language. Heimson presents six pages of new expressions created by students in a high school of only one hundred students.[7] Thirteen out of the twenty-five articles in a recent anthology on language center on the speech of American teenagers.[8] Parallels with these American developments have been found in Hungary by George Walker.[9]

This passage is footnoted in conventional form, but it is ridiculously overfootnoted. The reader couldn't stand that many footnotes in that short a space. The writer of these paragraphs is so overwhelmed by his sources that he has lost command of his own expression and line of development. If you are required to use footnotes, reserve them for documenting ideas or facts either so unusual and controversial or so detailed that they need to be credited to a writer. Footnote what readers are likely to want to check further.

A list of books, which occurs at the end of a paper, an article, a chapter, or a book, usually contains fuller information about the books: the publisher, number of volumes in a set, etc. In footnotes, names of authors are arranged in normal order: first name first. In a bibliography, they are arranged last name first, so that the order of the books in the list will be useful, easy to consult because arranged by author's last names alphabetically:

BIBLIOGRAPHY

1. Heimson, Karl. "The Courting Pattern," *New Ways in Education* (Englewood Cliffs, Texas, Pinetree Press, 1956), 158 pp.

The "158 pp." indicates that the volume contains 158 numbered pages, a way to show the reader how extensive the book is.

BIBLIOGRAPHY

2. Looney, William G. and James Brass Smith, editors. *Thinking and Talking* (New York, Mouth Press, 1965), 450 pp.
3. Oliver, Fred M. *Love Problems of High School* (New York, Kissinger Co., 1939), 413 pp.

In short papers documenting notes make more sense at the end of the paper than as footnotes at the foot of each page. Footnotes are hard to type at the bottom of the page—the writer can't gauge how much room he needs. And they are hard to set in type—the printer can't gauge the room either, and he must shift to smaller type as well. An intelligent alternative to footnotes used frequently in scientific publications employs parenthetical references: (2: 33-34), which means that the book referred to is number 2 in the bibliography and the references are to pages 33 and 34 in it. Part of the above text would then be written this way, referring to the piece of bibliography given above, which would be printed at the end of the paper or article. The paper would contain no footnotes:

> This new game, played at several high schools in the area (2: 33-34), represents a clever playing with words—taking old slang or in-group expressions and giving them their literal rather than traditional meaning. "Cool it" to these students means to open the window or turn down the thermostat (3: 101):

The wise writer and editor adopt a pattern of documentation of sources that fits the purposes of the writer and, as much as possible, of the reader. If the place of publication and publisher are not apt to be significant to the reader, the writer omits them from footnotes and supplies them only in bibliography. Almost always he gives page references and dates of publication because they are useful to the reader in locating material and in assessing the up-to-dateness of assertions and facts. All conventions need the help of common sense: the man who speaks outside in February with his head bare in order to observe a convention may find others soon observing his funeral.

Here are a few more models of conventional footnotes: For a book:

[1] George M. George. *The Georgeness of the World* (New York, George Book Company, 1918), pp. 33-34.

For a magazine:

[2] Margaret Mead, "Trends in Personal Life," *The New Republic* (September 23, 1946), 115: 348.

For a newspaper article:

[3] "College Dating Changes Pattern," *The New York Recorder,* June 2, 1952, p. 13.
[4] George Kriver, "Bronx Hospital Planned," *The Bronx Bomber,* June 3, 1967, p. 1.

For a government document:

[5] *Dating Problems in Urban High Schools,* United States Health Service Publication 1090 (Washington, 1953), p. 7.

For an encyclopedia:

[6] "Harvard University," *The Encyclopedia Britannica,* 14th edition.

For an excerpt from a book not read in the original but seen reproduced in part in another book:

7 Francis E. Merrill, *Courtship and Marriage* (New York, 1949), in Edwin R. Clapp and others, eds., *The College Quad* (New York, 1951), p. 74.

For a personal interview or conversation arranged by the author:

8 Interview with John Rogers, Dean of Men, Northside High School, Chicago, Illinois, April 4, 1967.

BORROWING WORDS

Conventionally the professional writer commands his words and those of others, but he never implies he owns the words of others. He inserts borrowed words naturally into his own sentences.

Wasting Borrowed Words:	*Commanding Borrowed Words*:
His dearest relative described him as "He was a great guy, full of fun, but gentle."	His dearest relative described him as "a great guy, full of fun, but gentle."

The professional writer does not refer to a statement he is quoting as a *quote*, for he is doing the quoting, not the author. He calls the statement a *statement*, an *assertion*, an *argument*, etc. He remembers that quotes do not speak, only persons.

For example, one quote states: "The Undersecretary rejected the budget proposals of the whole Council."	For example, an unidentified London *Times* reporter states that "The Undersecretary rejected the budget proposals of the whole Council."

The professional writer remembers that in conversation he must say "I quote" but in writing he indicates this act by quotation marks.

War Magazine says, and I quote, "Wretches strew the beaches in a lovely pattern."	*War Magazine* says, "Wretches strew the beaches in a lovely pattern."

If you respect your writing, learn the craft and learn the conventional systems of signaling meaning to the reader. But do not use these signals as a substitute for the order and clarity you must achieve with words. If you want the reader to become excited, you must write excitingly. You cannot force excitement by putting three exclamation marks at the end of your sentence! ! !

suggestions for teachers

Many teachers around the country have broken loose and found a way of enabling their students to write alive. By hit and miss they have constructed a whole enabling process. But what may work for them and their students may not be congenial to others. Here is the process I have patched together. I do not say it is *the* way, but it has been tested. Every element in it contributes to three essentials:

- raising the level of truthtelling in a class;
- inducing students in the first week to forget their English-teacher-inspired fears and find authentic voices in writing;
- creating a seminar in which students help each other learn the disciplines of the writing craft.

These are unusual accomplishments. I do not bring them about for every student, but usually for a majority of those in every writing class.

The following steps create a climate that encourages truthtelling and, in turn, live sentences:

1. I read aloud an example of *Engfish,* the stilted word-wasting language of the schools. Point out its weaknesses. Read aloud a truthtelling student paper that speaks with authentic voice.

2. Tell students: "No one speaks truth always. We all lie, consciously and unconsciously. I ask you to try for truths. I am going to try. You will be astonished by the difference that is made by a constant effort to raise the level of truth in this room."

NOTE: Every line in this litany is designed to help students feel like telling truths. To risk truths in front of the group. To write for every person in the room, not just for the teacher. In this program a steady effort to *protect feeling.*

3. I begin with free writing, the best passages of which I reproduce and bring into class. Read them aloud. Prohibit negative comments for the first few meetings. If a listener does not like a passage, he is to say nothing. That is not lying, simply refraining from comment.

4. On the first day I face the effects of grades upon truthtelling. One expedient is to ask students to store their returned writing in a folder or envelope, and at the end of the course present it for a grade. Those having the greatest number of writings that have scored with students and teacher receive the highest grades. But no grades earlier unless students ask to know how they are doing. Then I look over the folder and grade it as of that moment. A request for such early grading has seldom been made, because a constant evaluation of everyone's writing has been occurring in the seminar. Most students quickly find out how they're doing.

5. Ditto or otherwise reproduce the best writings and pass them out to all members of the class before having them read aloud. Announce that those who want a class response on a paper the teacher has not chosen for reproduction will be given that right.

The reproduction of papers is a burden, whether I retype the papers myself or ask students to write or type their best work on ditto masters. However the job is done, it is costly in time and money. But like the other steps described here, it enables students to reach readers with their writing. One expedient: I type ditto masters single-spaced in two columns to make them more readable, and thus save 50 percent on paper.

Because comments are made on papers in class where they count, where they can be judged by the writers as they compete for attention and belief, I do not need to waste time writing in their margins while I am reading them. Many studies have shown that written marginal comments have little effect. Late in the course I might write a note to a student I think is ripe for a certain suggestion.

6. Pass out a reproduced writing to the group and read it aloud, or ask a student to read it aloud, or suggest that the writer (unidentified) read the paper if she/he wishes.

After the paper has been read, ask the group, "Well, how does that strike you?" At that point my experience is to encounter silence. It seems to grow and spread through the room as I become more nervous, fearing the writer will take the silence as negative criticism. The members of the class sit, eyes down, tongueless. I have for nine years failed to realize why the eyes are down. The students are on the spot. They are quickly reviewing the writing, trying to sort out the reasons for their feelings. Sometimes unsure of their response, they are reading the work again to locate it.

And I am sitting there thinking, "Come on, you dumb people. Are you incapable of responding to human experience recorded truthfully?" For nine years I forgot that I had read the papers on initially receiving them, often typed them on ditto masters, and then heard them read again in class. So my students were encountering the paper for the first time and I for the third. I have made my sortings, enjoyed the opportunity for second and third revisions of judgments, and grown familiar with details.

Now I tell students that their reluctance to speak is intelligent and remind them of what they are doing during that silence. After a few moments for heads down—"Did anyone like anything in the paper?" If I get a number of positive responses, later, "Now, any suggestions for improvement?" Sometimes lively discussion erupts, sometimes continued reluctance; sometimes praise and help; sometimes confusion and pain.

The heads-down period is necessary: time to review first reactions, to collect thoughts and examples, to ponder a response that will be focused rather than fatuous, helpful rather than damaging.

7. I always ask students to comment on a piece of writing before I do. Teacher's comments later, or last. Otherwise students step back into traditional school where the game is to find out what teacher thinks and go along with it. Hour after hour, year after year, students have played that game. Even in this program they will revert to it unless the basepaths are obliterated.

8. I try to build the students' confidence and move the class forward on it. At first reproduce good writing so that students can advance from success to success. As the course proceeds with assignments, some students do not score. I ask them to do free writing again.

After they have received praise from the group, writers are usually strong enough to listen to others tell them that a subsequent work is weak in large ways. Eventually every writer must learn to use negative comments to improve her/his work.

9. When I give regular assignments (for example, "Tell an incident in your childhood that struck you hard"), I add that persons who find the assignment wrong for them at the moment can come to me and say they are writing on another topic of their choosing. I want to help people become powerful writers, not to make them jump through identical hoops.

10. Once or twice a semester I bring in a piece of my own writing done for one of the assignments, or for some project I'm working on, and allow it to be judged along with the work of students—without divulging beforehand who wrote it.

11. By subtle and direct means I let the class know that I am not asking for True Confessions. Truthtelling here does not imply, "I am baring my soul, and I must tell you that once I—" This book demonstrates the power of telling facts, of objectifying experience so a reader can live it vicariously and a writer can re-experience it. Thus

—objectivity, which is seldom the mark of True Confessions writing. My class is not designed to be therapeutic, but to produce strong writing. If it has a therapeutic effect, all right; but no psychiatrist worked in that room.

If I sense that a paper will be embarrassing or injurious when read aloud, I withhold the identity of the writer. Sometimes I ask writers about the wisdom of publishing their work to the class or outsiders. I am reminded of a girl I'll call Mary in one Shakespeare class who said she was afraid to write journal entries. Her sixth-grade teacher had once asked the class to write honestly whatever came to their minds. "I won't reveal writers' names." Mary wrote of her attraction to a boy who sat two rows behind her. The next day the teacher read aloud her paper as an example of poor sentence structure and organization, and chastised Mary before the class for "sloppiness." That was the end of Mary telling truths that counted for her in school.

School is the last place an objective observer should expect to encounter students speaking or writing truths that count for them. Unwittingly it is designed to nurture copycatting and phoniness. The Test-Grade System requires students to read a book or listen to teachers talk and give them back exactly what was said. The outcomes of doing exercises in the drillbook are expected to be exactly alike for every student. If instructors say, "Tell the truth," it is their truths that they usually expect to hear; and if they are given a disappointing or offending truth they are apt to say, "I'm sorry, but I'll have to give you a D for that."

What brings about truthtelling is a feeling that one is free to tell it, and that this act will occur in a room of nine or more persons (the response of a smaller number can be too easily dismissed as "friendly" or "prejudiced") who are trying to respond honestly. That one expert—the teacher—is not the sole responder and judge.

What brings about live voices in writing—the sound of individual human beings drawing upon all their powers—is a release through free writing at the beginning of a course and then a growing self-discipline in trying for truths.

In dozens of ways this process forces students to care for their writing. They have a real audience; they will become audience themselves. This double position is a responsible one.

12. If the class numbers more than twenty, I frequently break it into smaller groups for reading of papers. But I keep the whole group as the central testing ground, where I comment as well as the students, where I can speak to the whole class for ten or fifteen minutes when I feel, like a teacher, that I have something for all of

them. But I never sit in on the small groups. Students must perceive that the responses of their classmates carry weight.

13. Promise publication of the best writing: The dittoed two-column handout is itself a kind of publication. My students have frequently said, "When I saw my paper *printed* [it was actually only dittoed] in the handout, I could spot faults immediately." Thumbtack good writing on bulletin boards in the halls. Try to find resources for publishing a magazine or handout to be distributed beyond the classroom. As writers, the wider our readership, the more we feel pressure and desire to tell truths that count.

Those thirteen points make up the core of a writing program. Not all teachers will find them essential. I caution readers against taking this book blindly, chapter by chapter, assignment by assignment. More activities are provided than most students can satisfactorily carry out in a semester or a year if like professional writers they are revising and rewriting and abandoning some pieces. I wrote the book so that teachers could select those parts which make a program fulfilling and comfortable for them.

All kinds of writing are presented here, not to furnish a hodgepodge, but from an inner necessity. For all good writing—no matter what its type or form—has much in common with all other good writing. A precise statement of the parts of a vacuum cleaner and how to use it is more like Shakespeare's *Macbeth* than it is like a vague and lifeless description of a vacuum cleaner. A beginning writer would be mad to isolate a type of writing, like exposition, and concentrate on it as if the strategies of drama and story have nothing to do with his task. But that is what he is asked to do by most composition courses.

Instead of being required to follow all of the assignments in this book, students may be asked simply to write *in their own lives,* as they have real needs. A letter to a prospective employer—not the standard lifeless type but one that has powers that arise from experience. A biographical sketch required with an application to college or music camp. A journal of a student's plague year. The minutes of a meeting—this time human, not dehydrated, and terse as well as accurate. A letter to father, who is in Europe on a sales tour, asking for help in buying a new motorcycle—but not in an imagined situation, only if the writer is thirsting for oil and gas and the opening road. Chapter 15, "Your Subject Choosing You," shows how the students' experiences can act as self-assignments that produce papers which eventually touch national issues. The suggestions given there for topics could take students through most of a semester.

In this approach to writing, instead of seeing their errors paraded before them and the class, students are forced to look at their best work and go on from there—frequently from success to success. Like professionals, they are aiming to produce a number of strong writings, not thinking simply of periodically supplying a teacher with a paper to be graded. They write more than is presented to the group. They put aside writings which didn't go well after several tries. They take a short paragraph with good bones and put flesh on it. They add and cut drastically. They sharpen and polish.

They are advised to do these things by their classmates and teacher and textbook. They feel the pressure of possible publication. Some teachers using this book have begun exchanging a group of student papers with a similar class in another part of the city or nation, and then exchanging student responses to the writings. A way toward more objective evaluation.

This program combines freedom and discipline. Students begin to learn the discipline of the craft, to control techniques and strategies. That is a creative discipline, in which there is a need to shape one's materials to an end that may surprise the writer—the very opposite of the need imposed by the major discipline of conventional school, taking a test.

The most remarkable discovery of this approach has been that in free writing persons who think they have no skills frequently find themselves exploiting major strategies of writing: alliteration, metaphor, rhythm, parallel structure, telling details, a building of suspense, words speaking to words within the writing, dialogue, powerful endings. And before they have been instructed in them.

Probably two reasons for this emergence of language powers: the first is that free writing liberates students to use their speech competencies without fear of being nailed for faulty form. The second is that the act of writing so fast often moves them into a kind of trance in which nearby distractions fade and they focus on the act so that their words seem to be writing themselves. In that condition (which scientists have now isolated by a study of brain waves as most occurring when a person is drifting into or out of sleep) writers can remember their past experiences more fully and vividly. Part of that experience has been reading and listening to the cadences of the words of skillful writers and speakers. Much of what people have heard and read has been printed on their brains—the sounds of television-uttered sentences, the rhythms of film sequences, the economical humor of the cartoon characters in *Peanuts*—and at a propitious time they can pull up from this reservoir patterns of language and form useful to their purposes.

And then the conventions of writing—punctuation and paragraphing and footnoting. This book touches on them—in a new way —too. A good writer utilizes all the powers available to him. Some come to him free, and easy; others require study and discipline. This book furnishes training in both, but suggests by its arrangement that there is no use hammering away at mechanics before writers have moved real audiences with what they have had to say.

Traditionally, unwittingly, over the centuries school has become a place where you and I were handed things—usually statements or combinations of numbers belonging to school or "the authorities." We were to hand them back to teacher in the form of answers to tests or papers (collages of excerpted statements by authorities or summaries of what they had said). That was learning. Teaching was asking people to do that.

This handing back and forth of the ideas and experience belonging to school left no room for students' experience, which must enter the transaction somewhere or there can be no relevance in learning. I have put the words *you* and *school* together—*Youschool*— to indicate that one should carry as much weight as the other. School should not make you feel small. Ideally it involves the accumulated experience and wisdom of many you's, but it should exist for you, not you for it.

By *Youschool* I mean to specify not a place or method but a relationship, in which the students' experience counts as much as the experience of the authorities, or "school." A relationship in which these two experiences are brought up against each other, and their strengths and weaknesses compared, so their knowings, feelings, and insights speak to each other.

Traditionally school has said to students, "This work is preparing you for college" or "for graduate school" or "for life." In fact it is often preparing them to say things that do not count for them, things they do not feel attached to. There is no life in that classroom, simply preparation; and so the student work counts only for the teacher, and then only as something which can be graded.

Youschool turns all that around, but not easily, and not for everyone. In the past my writings have implied to some readers that a reform in education is simple to bring about. Nothing in this textbook is intended to oversimplify the difficulty of human beings working together. My latest book, *A Vulnerable Teacher,* documents how agonizing as well as joyful I have found the experience of trying to bring about *Youschool* for every one of my students.

K. M.

list of sources

Page

1 Robert Morley, on the Jack Paar show NBC-TV, February 12, 1965.

1 Quoted in Clara M. Siggins, "Then It Got Buggles," *College Composition and Communication* (February, 1962), p. 56.

4 Friedrich Nietzsche, *Beyond Good and Evil* (Chicago, Regnery, Gateway Edition, 1955), p. 77.

5 John Donne, "Satire III," *Poetry of the English Renaissance* (New York, F. S. Crofts, 1929), p. 482.

5 Eudora Welty, *Delta Wedding* (New York, New American Library, Signet Edition, 1963), p. 220.

5 Eudora Welty, quoted by Reynolds Price, "A Kind of Valedictory," *The Archive*, Duke University (April, 1955), p. 2.

6 Peter Ernani, "What I'd Like to Be," *Portola Portals* (n.d.) submitted by Mrs. Nancy Wakefield.

8 Samuel Butler, *Works* (London, Jonathan Cape, 1923–26), XVIII, 210.

12 Wallace Stevens, "Adagia," *Opus Posthumous* (New York, Alfred A. Knopf, 1957), p. 158.

13 Alfred North Whitehead, quoted in *The Practical Cogitator,* edited by Charles P. Curtis, Jr., and Ferris Greenslet (Boston, Houghton Mifflin, 1953), p. 40.

14 E. M. Forster, *Aspects of the Novel* (New York, Harcourt, Brace, 1927), p. 197.

15 Henry Moore, "The Painter's Object," *The Creative Process,* edited by Brewster Ghiselin (New York, New American Library, Mentor Edition, 1955), p. 77.

16 Alfred Kazin, "The Language of Pundits," *Atlantic Monthly* (July, 1961), pp. 73–74.

17 Wallace Stevens, "Adagia," *Opus Posthumous* (New York, Alfred A. Knopf, 1957), p. 162.

19 Anne Haven Morgan, *The Field Book of Ponds and Streams* (New York, G. P. Putnam's Sons, 1930), p. 199.

20 John Ciardi, "Work Habits of Writers," *On Writing, by Writers,* edited by William W. West (Boston, Ginn, 1966), p. 153.

21 Irma S. Rombauer and Marion Rombauer Becker, *The Joy of Cooking* (Indianapolis, Bobbs-Merrill, 1953), p. 451.

21 Joyce Macrorie, Trip Directions.

22 *Draftee's Confidential Guide,* pp. 9, 34–35.

24 Sidney Cox, *Indirections* (New York, Viking, Compass Books, 1962), p. 130.

25 William Hazlitt, "On the Familiar Style," *The Hazlitt Sampler* (New York, Fawcett World Library, 1961), p. 228.

25 Benjamin Franklin, quoted in Carl Becker, *The Declaration of Independence* (New York, Alfred A. Knopf, Vintage Books, 1958), pp. 208–209.

27 Wallace Stevens, "Adagia," *Opus Posthumous* (New York, Alfred A. Knopf, 1957), p. 169.

Page

31 Samuel Butler, *The Note-Books* (London, Jonathan Cape, 1926), p. 97.

32 Sir William Osler, "Teacher and Student," *Aequanimitas* (New York, Blakiston, 1932), p. 38.

35 Ray Bradbury, "Seeds of Three Stories," *On Writing, by Writers,* edited by William W. West (Boston, Ginn, 1966), p. 48.

37 John Ciardi, "Manner of Speaking," *Saturday Review* (July 2, 1966), p. 6.

39 Eileen Crimmin, "Bernie Little and His Little Four-Seater," *Hot Boat* (Spring, 1966), p. 31.

43 Sidney Cox, *Indirections* (New York, Viking, 1962), p. 131.

45 Frank O'Connor interviewed by Anthony Whittier, *Writers at Work: The Paris Review Interviews,* First Series (New York, Viking, 1959), p. 169.

51 Henry David Thoreau, *Walden and Other Writings* (New York, The Modern Library, 1937), p. 86.

52 Bernard Shaw, *John Bull's Other Island* (New York, Harper & Brothers, 1942), p. 209.

53 Jack London, *People of the Abyss* (New York, Harcourt, Brace, 1946), p. 213.

54 Ralph Waldo Emerson, "Thoreau," *Lectures and Biographies* (Boston, Houghton Mifflin, 1893), p. 362.

59 Henry David Thoreau, *Walden and Other Writings* (New York, The Modern Library, 1937), p. 88.

59 Thomas Henry Huxley, To Charles Kingsley, September 23, 1860, in Leonard Huxley, *Life and Letters of Huxley* (New York, D. Appleton, 1901), I, 235.

60 Michihiko Hachiya, *Hiroshima Diary* (Chapel Hill, University of North Carolina Press, 1955), pp. 11, 91–92.

63 Wallace Stevens, "Adagia," *Opus Posthumous* (New York, Alfred A. Knopf, 1957), p. 179.

66 Stuart Chase, "Writing Nonfiction," *On Writing, by Writers,* edited by William W. West (Boston, Ginn, 1966), p. 327.

70 Dr. Seuss, *Horton Hatches the Egg* (New York, Random House, 1940), n. p.

70 Thomas Paine, "The American Crisis," *The Complete Writings,* edited by Philip S. Foner (New York, The Citadel Press, 1945), p. 55.

70 William Shakespeare, *Macbeth* (New York, New American Library, 1963), IV, iii., p. 105.

73 Lilian Moore, *A Pickle for a Nickel* (New York, The Golden Press, 1961), p. 22.

75 Longchamps advertisement, *New York Times,* May 25, 1966, p. 29.

75 Ralph Waldo Emerson, "The American Scholar," *The Complete Essays and Other Writings,* edited by Brooks Atkinson (New York, The Modern Library, 1950), p. 47.

76 James Baldwin, *The Fire Next Time* (New York, Dell, 1964), pp. 14–15.

76 N. H. and S. K. Mager, editors, *The Pocket Household Encyclopedia* (New York, Pocket Books, 1953), p. 168.

76 Irma S. Rombauer and Marion Rombauer Becker, *The Joy of Cooking* (Indianapolis, Bobbs-Merrill, 1953), p. 313.

Page
77 Samuel Butler, *The Note-Books* (London, Jonathan Cape, 1926), p. 106.

78 Samuel Butler, *The Note-Books* (London, Jonathan Cape, 1926), p. 106.

81 T. S. Eliot interviewed by Donald Hall, *Writers at Work: The Paris Review Interviews*, Second Series (New York, Viking, 1965), p. 96.

83 Marianne Moore interviewed by Donald Hall, *Ibid.*, p. 82.

87 William Wordsworth, "The Prelude," *Complete Poetical Works* (Boston, Houghton Mifflin, 1904), p. 156.

87 Mark Twain, *Huckleberry Finn* (Boston, Houghton Mifflin, 1958), p. 42.

88 J. D. Salinger, *The Catcher in the Rye* (New York, New American Library, 1953), p. 144.

88 May Swenson, *To Mix with Time* (New York, Charles Scribner's Sons, 1963), pp. 86–87.

90 Sidney Cox, *Indirections* (New York, Viking, 1962), p. 6.

96 Truman Capote interviewed by Pati Hill, *Writers at Work: The Paris Review Interviews*, First Series (New York, Viking, 1964), pp. 294–295, 296–297.

98 Anton Chekhov, "My Life," and "In the Ravine," *Ward Six and Other Stories* (New York, New American Library, Signet Books, 1965), pp. 219, 339.

98 Reynolds Price, "The Warrior Princess Ozimba," in "A Story and Why," *Duke Alumni Register* (April, 1963), p. 33.

101 Bernard Shaw, in *Ellen Terry and Bernard Shaw: A Correspondence*, edited by Christopher St John (New York, The Fountain Press, 1931), pp. 113–114.

109 Ralph Waldo Emerson, "Self-Reliance," *The Complete Essays and Other Writings*, edited by Brooks Atkinson (New York, The Modern Library, 1950), p. 165.

111 Kenneth Clark, "The Value of Art in an Expanding World," *Hudson Review* (Spring, 1966), p. 23.

111 Samuel Butler, quoted in Henry Festing Jones, *Samuel Butler* (London, Macmillan, 1920), II, 294–295.

113 Ezra Pound, *ABC of Reading* (New York. New Directions, 1960), p. 62.

115 James Thurber interviewed by George Plimpton and Max Steele, *Writers at Work: The Paris Review Interviews* (New York, Viking, 1959), p. 87.

116 Eudora Welty, "Must the Novelist Crusade?" *Atlantic Monthly* (October, 1965), p. 106.

118 Wallace Stevens, "Adagia," *Opus Posthumous* (New York, Alfred A. Knopf, 1957), p. 170.

119 W. Nelson Francis, "Pressure from Below," *College Composition and Communication* (October, 1964), pp. 147–148.

121 Henry David Thoreau, *Walden and Other Writings* (New York, The Modern Library, 1937), p. 288.

121 William Hazlitt, *The Spirit of the Age* (London, Oxford University Press, 1935), p. 13.

122 Anne Haven Morgan, *The Field Book of Ponds and Streams* (New York, G. P. Putnam's Sons, 1930), p. 388.

122 Sharon Butler, in "The Bicycle Spoke," *The Western Review*, Western Michigan University (January 24, 1966), p. 2.

122 E. E. Cummings, "XIV," *Poems, 1923–1954* (New York, Harcourt, Brace and World, 1954), p. 397.

Page

123 Joseph Conrad, preface to *The Nigger of the "Narcissus"* in *Three Great Tales* (New York, Alfred A. Knopf, Vintage Books, n.d.), p. ix.

124 Lewis Carroll, *Through the Looking Glass* (New York, Random House, 1946), pp. 92–93.

124-125 *Ibid.*, p. 18.

125 Samuel Butler, *The Way of All Flesh* (New York, The Modern Library, 1950), p. 200.

125 Lewis Carroll, *Through the Looking Glass* (New York, Random House, 1946), pp. 64–65.

126 Ring Lardner, source unknown.

127 Henry Vaughan, "The World," *Poetry of the English Renaissance, 1509–1660*, edited by J. William Hebel and Hoyt H. Hudson (New York, F. S. Crofts, 1938), p. 799.

127 William Shakespeare, *Macbeth*, edited by Maynard Mack and Robert W. Boynton (Rochelle Park, New Jersey, Hayden Book Co., Inc., 1973), V, ii.

127 Reynolds Price, *A Long and Happy Life* (New York, Avon Books, 1963), p. 120.

128 William Shakespeare, *Henry IV, Part 1*, edited by Maynard Mack and Robert W. Boynton (Rochelle Park, New Jersey, Hayden Book Co., Inc., 1973), II, ii.

129 *Ibid.*, I, ii.

129 Henry David Thoreau, *Walden and Other Writings* (New York, The Modern Library, 1937), p. 123.

131 Lewis Carroll, *Through the Looking Glass* (New York, Random House, 1946), p. 29.

132 Samuel Butler, *The Note-Books* (London, Jonathan Cape, 1926), p. 102.

147 *The Heart of Emerson's Journals*, edited by Bliss Perry (Boston, Houghton Mifflin, 1926), p. 333.

148 Henry David Thoreau, *Journals* (Boston, Houghton Mifflin, 1906), IX, 158–160.

149 Samuel Butler, *The Note-Books* (London, Jonathan Cape, 1926), p. 97.

150 Dorothy Lambert, "What Is A Journal?" see p. v.

153 Samuel Butler, *The Note-Books* (London, Jonathan Cape, 1926), pp. 231–232.

157 *Benjamin Franklin*, edited by Chester E. Jorgenson and Frank Luther Mott (New York, Hill and Wang, 1962), p. 14.

157 Henry David Thoreau, *A Week on the Concord and Merrimack Rivers*, edited by Walter Harding (New York, Holt, Rinehart and Winston, 1963), p. 106.

157 Henry David Thoreau, "Walking," *Walden and Other Writings* (New York, The Modern Library, 1937), p. 622.

159 Ben Jonson, *Timber, or Discoveries*, in *English Prose, 1600–1660*, edited by Victor Harris and Itrat Husain (New York, Holt, Rinehart and Winston, 1965), p. 330.

159 Anatole Broyard, "The Obstetrics of the Soul" in *The New York Times* (January 25, 1973).

170 A. A. Milne, *The House at Pooh Corner* (New York, E. P. Dutton, 1928), p. 96.

Page

172 Lewis Carroll, *Alice in Wonderland* (New York, Random House, 1946), pp. 140–141.

174 Ray Bradbury, "Seeds of Three Stories," *On Writing, by Writers,* edited by William W. West (Boston, Ginn, 1966), p. 49.

174 Lois Phillips Hudson, "When the Fields Are Fresh and Green," *Reapers of the Dust* (Boston, Little, Brown, 1964), pp. 87–97.

183 Sidney Cox, *Indirections* (New York, Viking, 1962), p. 132.

185 Oscar Wilde, *A Woman of No Importance,* quoted in *The Wit and Humor of Oscar Wilde,* edited by Alvin Redman (New York, Dover, 1952), p. 33.

186 James Agee, *A Death in the Family* (New York, McDowell Obolensky, 1957), p. 3.

187 Karl Shapiro and Robert Beum, *A Prosody Handbook* (New York, Harper & Row, 1965), pp. 14–15.

188 John Donne, "Devotion No. 17," *English Prose, 1600–1660,* edited by Victor Harris and Itrat Husain (New York, Holt, Rinehart and Winston, 1965), p. 274.

189 Ralph Waldo Emerson, "Self-Reliance," *The Complete Essays and Other Writings,* edited by Brooks Atkinson (New York, The Modern Library, 1950), p. 165.

192 Mark Twain, *Huckleberry Finn* (New York, Houghton Mifflin, 1958), p. 4.

193 Sidney Cox, *Indirections* (New York, Viking, 1962), p. 31.

195 Gerhart Wiebe, "Mass Communications," in Eugene and Ruth Hartley, *Fundamentals of Social Psychology* (New York, Alfred A. Knopf, 1952), p. 179.

195 Ernest Hemingway interviewed by George Plimpton, *Writers at Work: The Paris Review Interviews* (New York, Viking, 1965), p. 235.

197 Robert Lipsyte, "Mets Beat Giants 8-6," in *The New York Times,* August 5, 1966.

201 Mike Recht, "Mets Shock Giants," Associated Press story in *The Kalamazoo Gazette,* August 5, 1966.

208 Pete Cooper, "Long Hair Warms the Head," *The Torch,* Rich Township High School Central Campus, Park Forest, Illinois (February 11, 1966), p. 3.

209 Sidney Cox, *Indirections* (New York, Viking, 1962), p. 131.

211 E. M. Forster, "What I Believe," in *Ten Contemporary Thinkers,* edited by Victor Amend and Leo Hendrick (New York, The Free Press, 1964), p. 101.

211 Archibald MacLeish, "The Conquest of America," *Ibid.,* p. 201.

212 Lois Berg, "Old Creepy Death," *Western Review,* Western Michigan University (November 22, 1965), p. 2.

214 Wallace Stevens, "Adagia," *Opus Posthumous* (New York, Alfred A. Knopf, 1957), p. 176.

222 Issa, in *To Walk in Seasons,* edited by W. H. Cohen (Tokyo, Charles E. Tuttle Publishing Co., Inc.), p. 64.

222 Oemaru, in *To Walk in Seasons,* edited by W. H. Cohen (Tokyo, Charles E. Tuttle Publishing Co., Inc.), p. 86.

Page
225 William Carlos Williams, "The Dance," *The Collected Later Poems* (New York, New Directions, 1950), p. 11.

226 William Carlos Williams, "Poem," *The Collected Earlier Poems* (New York, New Directions, 1951), p. 340.

229 Mark Twain, *Huckleberry Finn* (New York, Houghton Mifflin, 1958), pp. 85–88.

234 Kathy Currier, "Triolet," *Aurora 66*, Portage Northern High School, Portage, Michigan, p. 23.

236 Horace, *The Art of Poetry* in *The Complete Works*, edited by Casper J. Kraemer, Jr. (New York, The Modern Library, 1936), p. 401.

237 Henry David Thoreau, *Walden and Other Writings* (New York, The Modern Library, 1937), pp. 84–85.

238 Julie Beach, "Driving's a Dilemma," *The Lakeview Crystal*, Lakeview High School, Battle Creek, Michigan (February 4, 1966), p. 4.

241 Horace, *The Art of Poetry* in *The Complete Works*, edited by Casper J. Kraemer, Jr. (New York, The Modern Library, 1936), p. 398.

242 Gabor Peterdi, *Printmaking* (New York, Macmillan, 1959), p. xxii.

243 J. D. Salinger, *Catcher in the Rye* (New York, New American Library, 1953), p. 157.

245 William Hazlitt, *The Spirit of the Age* (London, Oxford University Press, 1904), pp. 130-131.

248 Archibald MacLeish, "Poetry and the Press," in *Thought and Statement*, edited by William G. Leary and James Steel Smith (New York, Harcourt, Brace, 1960), p. 481.

248 Mark Twain, "The Evidence in the Case," *Ibid.*, p. 373.

248 Walter Lippmann, "Stereotypes," *Ibid.*, p. 221.

248 Ivan Turgenev, "A Fire at Sea," *Ibid.*, p. 25.

248 E. M. Forster, "Anonymity, An Inquiry," *Ibid.*, pp. 440–441.

248 E. B. White, "Walden," *Ibid.*, p. 39.

249 Ezra Pound, *The ABC of Reading* (New York, New Directions, 1960), p. 64.

249 William Hazlitt, *The Spirit of the Age* (London, Oxford University Press, 1904), p. 76.

251 George Eliot, *Middlemarch* (New York. Houghton Mifflin, 1956), p. 52.

252 Reynolds Price, *A Long and Happy Life* (New York, Avon Books, 1960), p. 121.

253 Ben Jonson, *Timber, or Discoveries*, in *English Prose, 1600–1660*, edited by Victor Harris and Itrat Husain (New York, Holt, Rinehart, and Winston, 1965), p. 330.

index